INTRODUCTION TO ESTATE PLANNING

IN A NUTSHELL®

EIGHTH EDITION

ROBERT J. LYNN
Late Professor of Law
Ohio State University, Moritz College of Law

GRAYSON M.P. McCOUCH
Clarence J. TeSelle Professor of Law
University of Florida

WEST ACADEMIC

860 Blue Gentian Road, Suite 350
Eagan, MN 55121
1-877-888-1330

Published in the United States of America

ISBN: 979-8-31770-567-1

PREFACE

This book is a revised edition of a work which first appeared in 1975. It is intended for law students, lawyers, and non-lawyers who are interested in the areas of wills, trusts, future interests, fiduciary administration, insurance, pensions, and federal estate and gift taxation.

Because each chapter stands as much as possible as a separate unit, we have included no internal cross-references, and occasionally a particular topic is discussed more than once. Successive chapters do, however, tend to build on preceding chapters. Therefore, before reading (say) Chapter 8 on trusts, it is helpful to have a working knowledge of the material presented in Chapters 1 through 5.

Citations are few. In a short volume of this sort, it is not feasible to give sufficient citations to satisfy a specialist without distracting and discouraging the non-specialist. Fortunately, there are several excellent treatises directed to the former, and we have therefore chosen to try to assist the latter.

A special word of acknowledgment is due to Professor Robert Lynn, the original author of this book, who passed away in 2008. During a long and distinguished career, he was universally admired and respected for his scholarly erudition and practical wisdom. In addition, he was a beloved teacher renowned for his gentle wit and patient, courteous nature. He is remembered with affection and gratitude by colleagues, friends, and former students.

GRAYSON M.P. MCCOUCH

June 2026

OUTLINE

TABLE OF CASES

References are to Pages

TABLE OF STATUTES

References are to Pages

INTRODUCTION TO ESTATE PLANNING
IN A NUTSHELL®

EIGHTH EDITION

CHAPTER 1
THE ESTATE AND ESTATE PLANNING

§ 1.1 ESTATE PLANNING AND THIS BOOK

"Estate planning" refers to the process of ordering one's property holdings and dispositions, while keeping in mind the possibility of retirement and the certainty of death. Estate planning draws on several distinct substantive fields of law, including property, wills, trusts, future interests, insurance, employee benefits, health care, and taxation. "Estate planning" is sometimes used as a synonym for "tax planning" or "business planning." Although taxation and the existence of business interests are often an important part of an estate plan, the emphasis in this book is on estate planning in the more traditional sense, with allusions to taxation, business interests and other matters to the extent that they are necessary and helpful.

Estate planning in the more traditional sense is of special interest to the middle class, the well-to-do, and the wealthy because it deals with the conservation and transmission of wealth from generation to generation. Nonetheless, this area of the law should not be perceived as the preserve of practitioners who specialize in concocting elaborate tax avoidance schemes for rich clients. Most of estate planning is a part of basic legal literacy. A properly educated lawyer is expected to be acquainted with it. Although only a small portion of the practicing bar regularly engages in probate and trust work, many lawyers draft wills and trusts. Lawyers in general practice represent clients who are beneficiaries (or disappointed putative beneficiaries), executors, administrators, and trustees. They encounter problems in fiduciary administration, including difficult matters of conflict of interest. Lawyers themselves are often fiduciaries.

To the extent that estate planning is a specialty, a student may spend a disproportionate amount of time mastering legal doctrines and devices that seem arcane and removed from the practical concerns of daily life. For example, in drafting trust instruments, lawyers do not "use" the Doctrine of Worthier Title or the Rule Against Perpetuities in the same sense that they use the law on powers of appointment, but some basic knowledge of these doctrines is nevertheless desirable. And with the widespread enactment of statutes authorizing "pour-over" wills, the device called "incorporation by reference" has lost much of its erstwhile significance. But incorporation by reference is still available to lawyers drafting wills, and its limitations should be understood. A competent lawyer does not knowingly supervise the execution of a will by a person lacking testamentary capacity, but if there is a realistic possibility that testamentary capacity will be called in question after the testator's death, the lawyer should take that risk into account in advising the client. In short, the specialist must be an exceptionally well-informed lawyer. The better informed the general practitioner, the more effectively he or she can represent clients with problems in wills, trusts, future interests, fiduciary administration, taxation, and related areas.

The materials in this book are prepared principally for a person who has had an introduction to property law, but who has not yet studied such subjects as trusts and future interests. It does not follow that this book purports to "cover" any subject fully. On the contrary, coverage with respect to most topics is selective, and is intended to acquaint the reader as quickly as possible with some of the key issues that arise in ascertaining a person's existing property arrangements and in determining whether and how those arrangements might be modified to carry out the person's intended disposition more reliably and efficiently. For example, a person might be required as a condition of employment to participate in a contributory pension plan. Although the employee cannot opt out of the forced saving that results from participation in the pension plan, he or she might nonetheless review the available choices under the plan for designating a beneficiary to receive distributions in the form of a lump sum or a survivor annuity upon the employee's death. Here, the employee's property arrangements are not altogether a matter of choice, but even so, to the extent that choice exists, it should be exercised with care.

Materials on estate planning, particularly those prepared for practicing lawyers, often assume familiarity with the vocabulary, the subject matter, and the process of gratuitous transfers (gifts made during life or at death). This chapter and the following one introduce some fundamental aspects of the vocabulary, subject matter, and process of gratuitous transfers that are essential to understanding matters discussed in subsequent chapters.

§ 1.2 LIFETIME GIFTS

If a person makes a gratuitous transfer during lifetime, the gift is called an "inter vivos" gift (as differentiated from a testamentary gift—that is, a gift made by will). If an inter vivos gift is made by way of trust, the trust is called an inter vivos or "living" trust (as differentiated from a testamentary trust—that is, a trust created by will).

Making inter vivos gifts is sometimes recommended as an "estate planning" device. Whether it is wise in a particular case to make lifetime gifts is a matter of informed judgment. In arriving at that judgment, both the prospective donor and the donor's lawyer should remember that in the United States the average lifespan is growing longer and the proportion of older persons in the population is increasing. In times of economic recession, early retirement of employees is often "suggested" or "encouraged" in order to reduce costs for employers. Many people depend heavily on Social Security benefits, augmented by whatever pension benefits and other savings they may have accumulated, to maintain a decent standard of living in retirement. Property is a source of comfort and respect. Many an old person who might otherwise be shunted aside is treated with more consideration because it is known or suspected (perhaps erroneously) that he or she is a person of some wealth. There are exceptions, of course, but generally speaking there is much to be said for holding on to property until death. Refusal to make substantial lifetime gifts may prove frustrating or inconvenient for those who would benefit from such transfers. But a prospective donor may find it easier to put up with the beneficiaries' suppressed resentment while they wait than to endure their open contempt after they have received the bulk of the donor's property.

§ 1.3 "SIMPLE" (NON-TRUST) INTER VIVOS GIFTS

An inter vivos gift of real or personal property requires a subject matter of the intended gift, an intention on the part of the transferor (the "donor") to make a gift, a "delivery" of the subject matter of the gift, and an acceptance of the intended gift by the recipient (the "donee"). Acceptance seldom causes much difficulty. Indeed, there is a presumption of acceptance; unless it is demonstrated that the donee does not accept the gift, the donee is deemed to have accepted it. Intention to give might occasionally be the sole focus of a legal challenge, but more frequently intention is in doubt because of difficulties with the abstraction called "delivery."

What constitutes an adequate delivery depends to some extent on the type of property in question and the circumstances surrounding the making of the gift. If the subject matter of the intended gift is cash or tangible personal property (e.g., a ring, watch, or painting) that can easily be handed over to the donee, delivery ordinarily occurs when the donor transfers physical possession of the property to the donee. Suppose that A owns a ring that she is wearing. She removes the ring, hands it to B, and says, "B, I give you this ring. It is yours." B takes the ring and says, "Thank you." A has made a gift to B because the subject matter of the intended gift, intention to give, acceptance, and delivery are clear. But suppose that A, instead of removing the ring, merely twirls it on her finger, and the words of both A and B are the same as those just described. In these circumstances there is no gift because there is no delivery (relinquishment of "dominion and control") by A. Furthermore, the lack of delivery casts doubt on A's donative intent. A may intend to make a gift, but arguably she does not intend to do so presently—rather, she intends to make a gift at some future time.

Where the subject matter of the intended gift cannot easily be handed over to the donee (e.g., because it is large or heavy or inconveniently located), the donor may nevertheless make a valid gift by a "constructive" or "symbolic" delivery. For example, if A wishes to make a gift to B of the contents of a trunk or a safe, she might make a constructive delivery by giving B a key to the trunk or telling B the combination to the safe. As long as her intent to make a present gift is clear, the gift should be upheld even if B does not immediately take possession of the property. Or A might make a symbolic delivery by executing a written "deed of gift" and handing it over to B. Here the written instrument stands in for the subject matter of the gift, and the donor's delivery of the deed is deemed to be a delivery of the property. Again, the act of delivery must coincide with an intention on the donor's part to make a gift.

If the subject matter of an intended gift consists of intangible personal property such as shares of stock, corporate or government bonds, a savings bank account, or a life insurance policy, making a gift can be more complicated. Although the weight of judicial authority indicates that manual delivery of a stock certificate or a savings account passbook, if made with the required donative intent, results in a valid gift, there should be no need to resort to litigation if the transfer of ownership is properly documented. For many types of intangible personal property, title records are maintained by a registering entity (e.g., a corporation, government agency, bank, or life insurance company) which establishes formal procedures for registering a change of ownership. An owner who wishes to make a gift of such property should observe the prescribed formalities to ensure that the gift is duly recorded on the books of the registering entity. A properly documented gift is far more likely to withstand a challenge, or to avoid litigation altogether, than one which leaves the evidence of delivery and donative intent open to doubt.

A gift of real property is ordinarily accomplished by delivery of a deed in recordable form. Today almost all states have legislation based on the Statute of Frauds which requires that any conveyance of an interest in land must be in the form of a writing signed by the grantor. Merely putting the grantee in possession of the property, without more, creates no legally enforceable interest in the grantee. Furthermore, in every state a recording statute prescribes formalities (typically, signature and acknowledgment) that must be observed if a deed is to be recorded in the local land records. An unrecorded deed may technically be sufficient to convey title from the grantor to the grantee, but it has no binding effect on subsequent good faith purchasers. Thus, as a practical matter, compliance with the recording statute is essential to ensure that the deed is effective to convey marketable title to the grantee.

Occasionally, instead of handing over a deed of real or personal property directly to the intended donee, the donor delivers the deed to a third person. The practice at times is both understandable and defensible—for example, if the intended donee is incapacitated or unreachable, the donor might hand over the deed to an agent or fiduciary for the donee. This method of making a gift is effective where circumstances are such that the intention to give, acceptance, and delivery are clear. (A executes a deed in recordable form conveying Blackacre to B, who is traveling abroad. A delivers the deed to B's spouse and says, "I am giving Blackacre to B. Here is a deed ready to be recorded.") But if the reason for failure to hand over directly to the intended donee is obscure, delivery to a third person may invite litigation. Suppose that A gives the deed to A's lawyer with instructions to hold the deed until A's death and then give it to B. Since A can presumably recall the deed at any time, A has not relinquished dominion or control of Blackacre and there is no completed gift. If the gift does not become complete during A's life, the deed will have no effect at all. A will still own Blackacre at death and the property will pass to A's testate or intestate successors.

Normally an outright gift of personal property must be irrevocable. This is implicit in the concept of delivery, which involves a relinquishment of dominion and control by the donor during life. A revocable gift is permitted, however, in the case of a gift "causa mortis" (in contemplation of approaching death). A gift causa mortis is a revocable gift of personal property which becomes absolute if the donor dies, survived by the donee, without having revoked the gift. A, seriously ill, is about to enter a hospital for treatment. She owns a ring. She hands it to B, saying, "B, this is yours unless I return from the hospital." A enters the hospital and dies survived by B. The gift, not having been revoked by A prior to death, becomes irrevocable at A's death. A gift causa mortis is formally classified as a lifetime transfer which does not have to comply with the wills act. Nevertheless, such a gift is functionally similar to a will and is treated as testamentary for limited purposes. For example, if the donor dies leaving an insolvent estate, property transferred by gift causa mortis generally can be reached by the donor's creditors to satisfy their claims. Because words and other conduct of a donor in apprehension of death are often ambiguous, gifts causa mortis tend to breed litigation.

To facilitate making gifts to minors, every state has enacted some version of the Uniform Transfers to Minors Act (or its predecessor, the Uniform Gifts to Minors Act). Under such statutes, property that is the subject matter of a gift to a minor may be held by a "custodian" for the benefit of the minor. Parents make gifts to children under such statutes with the expectation that as young adults the children will use the gifts wisely. In this connection it is well to remember that such gifts are completed gifts which are irrevocable when made, and that the custodianship normally terminates automatically when the minor reaches age 21.

§ 1.4 THE MEANINGS OF "ESTATE"

Most people acquire numerous items of tangible personal property (an automobile, household furniture, and the like) for their own personal use during life. For many people, the single most valuable asset consists of real property (the family home). In addition, to an increasing extent, personal wealth is accumulated in the form of intangibles. Some of the intangibles are familiar financial assets: shares of corporate stock, corporate or government bonds, mutual fund shares, and bank accounts, for example. Other intangibles are equally important but often overlooked, such as life insurance or pension benefits. Thus, personal wealth consists of an aggregate of tangible personalty, realty, and intangibles. Many of these assets, but by no means all of them, can be consumed during life or passed on to family members or other beneficiaries by gift during life or at death.

The term "estate" can have any of several different meanings depending on the context. In traditional usage, a decedent's estate means the "probate estate," that is, the property owned by a decedent which passes by will or intestacy and is subject to probate administration. This is what lawyers usually have in mind when they refer to the estate in drafting a will, and it is also the sense in which the term is ordinarily used in the statutes concerning intestacy, wills, and estate administration. In a related but different sense, an estate can mean any aggregation of assets administered by a fiduciary for the benefit of creditors or beneficiaries, as in the case of a trust estate or a bankruptcy estate. In speaking of estates in land and future interests, the term estate often denotes a possessory interest classified by its potential duration, as in a "life estate," an "estate for years," or a "fee simple absolute."

For federal estate tax purposes, a decedent's "gross estate" covers a broad range of property interests. The gross estate is not limited to property owned at death (i.e., the probate estate); it also includes various will substitutes such as joint tenancy property, survivor annuities, and life insurance, as well as certain lifetime transfers that are treated for estate tax purposes as testamentary substitutes.

In a broader sense, an estate may realistically be viewed as the aggregate resources available at any given time that allow a person to maintain a standard of living and to make provision during life or at death for family members or other beneficiaries. This is the meaning of the term as it is used in "estate planning." In this sense, a person's estate may include not only accumulations of personal wealth but also benefits provided by governmental programs such as Social Security and Medicare. Although benefits under these governmental programs are not "owned" in the same way as other assets, they represent an important element (sometimes the only significant element) of resources available to meet basic needs of many individuals and their dependent or surviving family members.

Even an expanded view of an "estate" does not include an element that is unquestionably valuable to those benefiting from it, namely, the network of personal, professional, political, and other connections created or cultivated by an individual that can open doors and enhance opportunities for favored family members in their pursuit of a career in public or private life. Benefits of this kind do not readily lend themselves to valuation or accounting and are therefore ignored for purposes of estate planning.

§ 1.5 ADMINISTRATION OF THE ESTATE

Every year people die owning property that is not subject to probate administration. This is not necessarily because decedents have skillfully arranged their affairs to "avoid probate." Rather, non-administration may reflect a lack of assets of substantial value, or absence of assets of the kind that call for administration, or willingness on the part of interested parties to settle the estate informally among themselves. If a decedent owns very little property at death, applicable state law may provide for a simplified estate settlement procedure that minimizes or eliminates the role of the probate court. If the decedent owns no land at death, no automobile, no registered stocks or bonds, and no bank accounts, the surviving family members might simply take over the decedent's assets, which might have substantial value; the survivors might even pay the decedent's debts voluntarily. Even if the decedent is the record owner of land at death, the family might simply continue to occupy it, and to pay the tax bills that continue to arrive in the name of the decedent, although this course of action is likely to create serious problems if the land eventually has to be sold.

In sum, court-supervised administration of a decedent's estate, as it is usually visualized, is not a process that occurs automatically on the death of a decedent. It must be started by someone. And it might not occur at all if the reasons for seeking court-supervised administration are not present in the particular case.

Just as there is no administration unless it is initiated by someone, so too, there is ordinarily no probate (that is, "proving") of the will unless some person brings the will forward. The executor designated in the will or some other interested person might petition the probate court to admit the will to probate and grant "letters testamentary" to the executor. If the decedent died intestate, an heir or next of kin or even a creditor might petition the probate court to grant "letters of administration" to an administrator. Letters testamentary or letters of administration are the personal representative's badge of authority. Bankers, stock transfer agents, and the like, may insist on seeing them before they will turn over control of the decedent's assets to the personal representative. Notice of hearing on the petition is given to interested persons in conformity to statute. If there is a will, admitting it to probate as the last will of the decedent might not be a matter of controversy. But an heir who would benefit if the will were spurious might challenge the validity of the will. If the will is contested, its validity must be determined by the probate court in a special proceeding.

The executor or administrator is commonly called the "personal representative" of the decedent. The personal representative is appointed by the probate court and remains subject to supervision by the probate court throughout the administration of the estate. Unless the will provides otherwise, an individual may be required to furnish bond in order to qualify as personal representative.

The functions of the personal representative fall into three general phases: collecting and preserving the assets of the estate; paying creditors' claims, expenses of administration, and taxes; and distributing the remaining property to the decedent's devisees and legatees (to the extent that the will has dispositive effect) or to intestate successors (to the extent that the decedent died intestate).

In performing these functions, the personal representative must prepare an "inventory" (a list) of assets in the decedent's estate and obtain an "appraisal" (an estimate of their value). In conformity to statute, the personal representative gives notice to known creditors of the decedent to present their claims for payment. If the personal representative rejects a claim, the enforceability of the claim may be determined by a lawsuit. A general creditor who fails to present a claim within the period set by statute may be forever barred from enforcing the claim.

After debts of the decedent, expenses of administration, and taxes have been paid, whatever property is left is distributable to the devisees, legatees, or intestate successors of the decedent, as the case may be. The personal representative submits a final accounting and petitions the probate court to be discharged from further liability. Upon approval by the probate court, the administration of the estate comes to an end.

§ 1.6 RESPONSIBILITY OF THE PERSONAL REPRESENTATIVE

An executor or administrator of an estate (like the trustee of a trust) is a fiduciary—a person who manages property for the benefit of others, subject to duties of loyalty, care, and impartiality. Even if the personal representative is the sole beneficiary of the estate, there might nonetheless be duties to other persons such as creditors or taxing authorities. For example, under the Internal Revenue Code the personal representative is primarily responsible for paying the estate tax if any is due. Although this liability is in a fiduciary capacity, a personal representative who improperly distributes assets to beneficiaries without paying the required estate tax may become personally liable for the unpaid tax.

It is undoubtedly true that appointment as the personal representative of a decedent's estate or as the trustee of a trust can provide great personal and professional satisfaction. Even so, an inexperienced person should not accept fiduciary responsibility lightly. Aside from the challenge of coping with unfamiliar matters, the task might result in altogether unexpected personal liability if a loss of estate or trust property occurs as the result of a failure on the fiduciary's part to comply with applicable standards of fiduciary conduct. In short, a fiduciary appointment should not be viewed as a lucrative sinecure. In a particular case, the result might be just the opposite.

§ 1.7 SETTLING "SMALL" ESTATES

All states have statutes of one kind or another to facilitate the settlement of small estates without a full-fledged, formal administration. For example, under the Uniform Probate Code, if at least 30 days have elapsed since the decedent's death, no administration proceeding is pending, and the net estate does not exceed $25,000, any successor entitled to personal property of the decedent (including debts owed to the decedent) is authorized to collect the property by presenting an affidavit to the person in control of the property, without any probate court proceeding. A person who pays or transfers property to the successor pursuant to the affidavit is protected to the same extent as in dealing with a personal representative. UPC §§ 3–1201 and 3–1202. In some states, the collection-by-affidavit procedure can be used only by the decedent's surviving spouse or children. Also, many states have specialized collection-by-affidavit procedures for particular types of assets such as bank accounts and automobiles. These procedures make it possible to collect assets expeditiously and with minimal expense, but at the same time they provide no protection to other interested parties against a purported successor who fraudulently collects property based on a false affidavit and then absconds.

Because there is no uniformity in statutes dealing with informal settlement of estates, it is necessary to check the applicable state statutes to see which procedures are available in a particular case.

§ 1.8 PROPERTY "OUTSIDE" THE PROBATE ESTATE

Not all of a decedent's property is subject to probate administration. Various "will substitutes" can be used to designate beneficiaries who will receive property at the owner's death outside the probate process.

One familiar will substitute is the joint tenancy with right of survivorship. If A purchases real property (e.g., a house) in the names of "A and B as joint tenants with right of survivorship," A and B are equal co-owners of the property while both are alive. Upon A's death survived by B, A's interest expires and B, the surviving joint tenant, becomes the sole owner of the property by operation of law. No interest in the property passes from A at death. Thus, with respect to the joint tenancy property, A has avoided probate.

Another common will substitute takes the form of life insurance. Suppose that A takes out an insurance policy on her own life and designates a spouse, child, or other beneficiary to receive the proceeds at her death. Upon A's death survived by the designated beneficiary, the insurance company is contractually obligated to pay the proceeds directly to the beneficiary pursuant to the terms of the policy. The proceeds are not a part of A's probate estate.

Similarly, a pension plan sponsored by an employer may allow a covered employee to designate one or more beneficiaries to receive benefits from the plan after the employee's death. A valid beneficiary designation takes effect pursuant to the terms of the pension plan, and the benefits pass to the designated beneficiaries outside the employee's probate estate.

Perhaps the most flexible of all will substitutes is the revocable inter vivos trust. If validly created and funded, such a trust can avoid probate with respect to almost all of a person's assets. For example, if A creates a revocable trust of her investment assets, she can retain control over those assets throughout her lifetime and direct how they are to be disposed of at her death. A's interest in the trust expires at her death, and the trustee is responsible for distributing the remaining trust property or holding it in further trust pursuant to the terms of the trust. Any assets that A put in trust during her lifetime are no longer owned at death and are not part of A's probate estate.

§ 1.9 THE IMPORTANCE OF STATE LAW

Estate planning is largely concerned with the rights and interests of transferors and transferees, which are determined by the applicable law of property, wills, trusts, gifts, and intestate succession. In general, property rights are governed by state law, although in a few areas (e.g., private employee benefit plans, U.S. savings bonds) the effect of state law is preempted by federal law. For purposes of illustration, this book might summarize a reported case or set forth a statute from a particular jurisdiction, or it might demonstrate the application of a property doctrine in a particular state. If the reported case reaches an unexpected or anomalous result, that is stated; and if the statute is unique, that is noted. If the application of a property doctrine is unusual, attention is directed to the deviation from the norm. But even if a reported case is representative of cases from numerous jurisdictions, or a statute is one enacted in some form nearly everywhere, or the application of a property doctrine is exemplary, one should not assume uniformity throughout the United States. There is considerable diversity of doctrine and practice.

A significant number of states seeking to improve the law and to promote uniformity have enacted the Uniform Probate Code, the Uniform Trust Code, and various other uniform laws. Even in states that have not enacted them, some features of the uniform laws have had a significant impact on state statutes relating to trusts, estates, and the probate process.

§ 1.10 THE IMPORTANCE OF FEDERAL LAW

Because the terms "estate planning" and "tax planning" are often used interchangeably, it is reasonable to think that the federal income, estate, gift, and generation-skipping transfer tax provisions of the Internal Revenue Code are the most important parts of federal law affecting the accumulation, management, and disposition of property during life and at death. But the significance of federal law for estate planning goes well beyond the obvious and direct impact of tax statutes.

The functions of federal tax statutes are not limited to raising revenue. For example, the provisions allowing favorable tax treatment for "qualified" plans are deliberately designed to encourage the creation and to regulate the administration of pension plans sponsored by employers or by labor unions (or by both employers and unions acting together). Federal tax statutes are used both to promote and to police gifts to charitable organizations. Under federal law, the expressions "disqualified person," "party in interest," and "prohibited transaction" have become a vital part of the vocabulary of fiduciary administration. A good deal of legislation at the state level represents little more than an attempt by state legislatures to accommodate local property and trust law to the ever-changing requirements of federal tax law. It is not necessary to speculate about an emerging "federal law of property" in order to document the influence of Congress on property and trust law at the state level.

Furthermore, through broad-based programs such as Social Security, the federal government has come to play a pervasive role in areas of daily living that formerly were primarily a matter of private family arrangements (if, indeed, there were any arrangements at all).

Therefore, in planning for retirement, or providing for surviving family members in the event of premature death, it is well to remember that whether a surviving spouse and minor children will have sufficient resources to meet basic requirements may very well turn as much on the availability of (for example) Social Security benefits or life insurance proceeds as on the size of the net probate estate. The law of property is still "local" law, but it is not as local as it used to be.

§ 1.11 MARITAL PROPERTY

There are two basic marital property systems in the United States. A substantial majority of the states have a system of "separate property" derived from the English common law, while several states have a system of "community property" derived from the civil law of France and Spain. The eight traditional community property states are Arizona, California, Idaho, Louisiana, Nevada, New Mexico, Texas, and Washington. Wisconsin's community property act took effect in 1986, and in 1998 Alaska enacted an elective community property system for married couples. In addition, several other states (including Florida, Kentucky, South Dakota, and Tennessee) allow married settlors to designate certain trust property as community property. Together, the community property states account for over one quarter of the nation's total population.

Broadly speaking, in a separate property system, a husband and wife own property as separate individuals and each spouse has considerable freedom to dispose of his or her own property during life and at death. By contrast, in a community property system, any property earned by either spouse during the marriage (as opposed to property acquired by gratuitous transfer during the marriage or by any means before the marriage) automatically belongs to both spouses in equal, undivided shares.

For example, suppose that A and B, a married couple, are domiciled in a community property state. A earns a salary and uses those earnings to purchase a house as the couple's residence. The house is classified as community property in which both spouses have equal, present, vested interests. As long as A and B are both living and married to each other, neither spouse can dispose of the house without the other's consent. (In contrast, if A already owned the house before marrying B, or inherited it from A's parents during the marriage, the house would be classified as separate property belonging exclusively to A.) If A dies survived by B, the community terminates and the community property is severed into two equal shares. A has testamentary power to dispose of one half of the community property (as well as all of A's separate property). The other half of the community property belongs absolutely to B and is not subject to A's testamentary power. The rights of A and B in community property might also become relevant if the marriage terminated by divorce while both spouses were living rather than by the death of one spouse. There are many variations among the community property states in the details of local law concerning the classification of property, management and disposition during the marriage, and the rights of the respective spouses on death or divorce.

§ 1.12 "FOREIGN" ASSETS

Many people move from one state to another during their working years, or seek a retirement home in a better climate when full-time employment ceases because of retirement or failing health. They may move from a separate property state to a community property state (or vice versa). Even a person who remains domiciled in the same state throughout his or her entire lifetime may acquire property in another state. Therefore the estate of a decedent might include assets that are affected by the law of a jurisdiction other than the state where the decedent was domiciled at death, for purposes of testate or intestate succession, estate administration, and estate or inheritance taxation. (An estate might even include assets located in a foreign country.)

Language in some dispositive documents reflects the fact that property arrangements are frequently affected by the laws of more than one jurisdiction. For example, a testator who owns land in more than one state might anticipate probate of the will in more than one state, and the will might explicitly nominate both a "primary" personal representative (a person residing in the state of domicile, to administer the estate in the state of domicile) and an "ancillary" personal representative (a person residing in another state, to administer the estate in that other state to the extent necessary). A will may give the ancillary personal representative an express power to sell land, in order to avoid the need to seek court approval for sale under the law of the state where the land is located and the ancillary personal representative is appointed. Or land might be held in a revocable inter vivos trust in order to avoid probate proceedings altogether.

The matter of "which law governs" with respect to various kinds of property arrangements can become quite complicated. People who move (or have moved) from one state to another, or who own property in more than one state, may find that putting their property affairs in order requires more thought and attention (and entails considerably more expense) than they had anticipated.

CHAPTER 2

THE TRANSFER OF PROPERTY AT DEATH BY WILL OR INTESTACY

§ 2.1 THE PROBATE ESTATE

Estate planning is associated with death. If a person dies owning property that is subject to administration in the probate court, there is a "probate estate." The assets constituting the probate estate are listed in an "inventory" prepared by the personal representative and filed in the probate court. The "net probate estate" consists of the assets, if any, remaining after payment of funeral expenses, administration expenses, creditors' claims, and death taxes.

§ 2.2 TESTACY AND INTESTACY

If a person dies owning property that is subject to administration in the probate court, he or she might die "testate" (leaving a will) or "intestate" (without a will). A person who makes a will is called the "testator," regardless of gender. ("Testatrix," the gender-specific term for a female testator, is no longer widely used.) A person who dies without a will is called "the intestate." Because a will might not purport to dispose of all of the testator's net probate estate, or might not effectively dispose of the entire net probate estate (although it purports to do so), a decedent might die testate with respect to part of the net probate estate and intestate with respect to the balance.

To the extent that a decedent dies intestate, distribution of the net probate estate is governed by statute. Such a statute is called the statute of "descent and distribution." It governs the distribution of all kinds of property—real property and personal property, tangibles and intangibles, present interests and future interests. Statutes of descent and distribution in the United States are not uniform in their provisions. Nonetheless, one aspect of such statutes is noteworthy. Years ago the surviving spouse was not an heir of a decedent (a widow, for example, instead of succeeding to real property as an heir of her deceased husband, might assert "dower" in his land). Today, the surviving spouse of an intestate decedent is generally entitled to a share of the net probate estate under the statute of descent and distribution. Dower in its common law form (and "curtesy," its counterpart for a surviving husband) has been abolished altogether or greatly modified by statute in virtually all states.

§ 2.3 THOSE WHO TAKE THE NET PROBATE ESTATE

The persons who succeed to the property of a decedent under the statute of descent and distribution are called "heirs," "next of kin," or "distributees" of the decedent. (Today the terms are often used interchangeably. In traditional usage, however, the term "heir" referred specifically to a successor to land, while "next of kin" or "distributees" referred to successors to personal property.) The persons who succeed to the property of a decedent by will (by "testamentary" gift) are called "beneficiaries," and those taking "all the rest, residue, and remainder" of a decedent's property by will are the "residuary beneficiaries." A beneficiary taking land (a "devise") under a will is a "devisee," a beneficiary taking money, a "legatee." A testamentary gift of personal property is a "bequest." Today the term "devisee" is often used to refer to the beneficiary of any kind of property under a decedent's will. (Sometimes the foregoing terms are used rather loosely. For example, if A leaves land to B by will, B is a "devisee" under the will, not an "heir," technically speaking. Nonetheless, it is not uncommon to hear B referred to as an "heir under A's will.")

§ 2.4 EXECUTOR AND ADMINISTRATOR

The person who administers a decedent's estate is generally called a "personal representative." "Executor" and "administrator" are simply more precise terms for specific kinds of personal representative.

An "executor" is a person nominated in the decedent's will who is appointed by the probate court to administer the estate. An "administrator" is a personal representative appointed by the probate court without having been nominated in the decedent's will. An administrator may be appointed not only where the decedent died intestate, but also where the decedent left a will but failed to nominate a person to serve as executor, or where the person named in the will was unable or unwilling to serve or failed to complete the administration of the estate after being appointed by the probate court. ("Executrix" and "administratrix," the gender-specific terms for a female executor or administrator, respectively, are no longer widely used.)

§ 2.5 INTESTACY: ESTATE PLANNING "BY OPERATION OF LAW"

The provisions of statutes of descent and distribution, or "intestacy laws," vary from one state to another, but in general the net probate estate of an intestate decedent passes under such statutes to persons related to the decedent by "consanguinity" (blood) rather than "affinity" (marriage), and preference under the statutes is given to those blood relatives most closely related to the intestate, who take to the exclusion of more distant relatives. Blood relatives in a direct line of descent from the decedent ("lineal descendants" or "issue") are preferred over "ancestors" or "collateral" relatives. (A collateral relative is any blood relative other than an ancestor or a lineal descendant.) For example, suppose that A, a widow, dies intestate, leaving no children but survived by one grandchild; A is also survived by her brother. The grandchild, a lineal descendant of A, inherits to the exclusion of A's brother, a collateral relative. (Where the intestate has neither spouse nor descendants, but leaves one or both parents surviving, the parents as ancestors tend to be preferred over collateral relatives.)

A very important exception to the general preference given to blood relationships applies in the case of the decedent's surviving spouse, who occupies a special position under modern intestacy laws. If an intestate decedent leaves a surviving spouse, the spouse is consistently recognized as an heir with first priority, although the size of the spouse's intestate share depends on whether the decedent also left close blood relatives. Under the Uniform Probate Code, for example, the surviving spouse takes the entire intestate estate if the decedent left no surviving descendants or parents. Even if the decedent left surviving descendants, the spouse takes the entire intestate estate if all of those descendants are also descendants of the surviving spouse (and the spouse has no other descendants). If the decedent left no surviving descendants but did leave a surviving parent, the surviving spouse takes the first $300,000 plus three-quarters of any balance of the intestate estate. If all of the decedent's surviving descendants are also descendants of the surviving spouse, but the spouse has descendants of her own (e.g., the decedent's step-children), the spouse takes the first $225,000 plus one-half of any balance of the intestate estate. And if the decedent left surviving descendants who are not descendants of the surviving spouse (e.g., the spouse's step-children), the spouse takes the first $150,000 plus one-half of any balance of the intestate estate. UPC § 2–102. Thus, the Uniform Probate Code requires that a surviving spouse share with the decedent's parents or (in some cases) the decedent's descendants, but not with more remote blood relatives.

It is sometimes said that a statute of descent and distribution creates an "estate plan by operation of law," that is, that to the extent the net probate estate is not effectively disposed of by will, it passes according to statute. In this connection, one should note that the statutory scheme of intestate succession is extremely rigid; the heirs and their respective shares of the estate are determined based solely on status and family relationship, with little or no regard for other circumstances in a particular case. Suppose that A dies intestate at age 60, survived by his wife B and his only child C, leaving a net probate estate of $500,000. Under the Uniform Probate Code, B takes either all or part of the estate, depending on whether C is B's child or her step-child. B's intestate share is based on her status as A's surviving spouse, regardless of whether B is old or young, rich or poor, or whether her marriage to A lasted for one month or several decades. C's intestate share is based on his status as A's surviving child, regardless of whether C is a minor or a middle-aged adult, whether he is independently wealthy or destitute, or whether he is "deserving" in some other sense. In short, a "spouse" means any person who was married to the decedent at death, and a "child" means the immediate offspring of the decedent.

In many states, if a decedent dies intestate with no surviving spouse and no close blood relatives, the estate passes to the "next of kin" pursuant to the intestacy laws. The next of kin might well be remote relatives who had little contact with the decedent and who never expected to share in the estate—hence the expression "laughing heir." To mitigate the administrative problems of tracking down distant relatives (and avoid the unseemly spectacle of laughing heirs), the Uniform Probate Code cuts off all inheritance rights if a decedent dies intestate and unmarried, with no surviving descendants, no parents or their descendants, and no grandparents or their descendants (and no descendants of a predeceased spouse). UPC §§ 2–103 and 2–105. To illustrate, suppose that A dies intestate and unmarried, leaving a great-aunt as her closest surviving blood relative. In a jurisdiction that allows unlimited inheritance, the great-aunt would take the entire estate as A's next of kin, but in a jurisdiction that follows the Uniform Probate Code, the entire estate would escheat to the state.

§ 2.6 REQUIRED SURVIVAL

In order to take property of a decedent, either as an heir under the intestacy laws or as a beneficiary under a will (as the case may be), the heir or beneficiary must survive the decedent. (For this purpose, a person who was conceived during the decedent's lifetime and is born alive after the decedent's death is deemed to be in existence at the time of the decedent's death.) It is not necessary that the heir or beneficiary survive to the time that the net probate estate is actually distributed. Administration of an estate often takes up to a year and in some cases may last for several years.

Generally speaking, a decedent's heirs or beneficiaries are identified as of the time of death. But in this connection (as in so many others), a special rule may be imposed by statute. Under the Uniform Probate Code, a person who fails to survive a decedent by 120 hours is deemed to have predeceased the decedent for purposes of intestate succession and, unless otherwise provided in the governing instrument, for purposes of wills, trusts, and other governing instruments. UPC §§ 2–104 and 2–702. These "five-day statutes" prevent property from passing at death to a person who cannot enjoy it in the ordinary sense of the word because the intended beneficiary dies shortly after the decedent. (In the absence of such a statute, the same property passes through two estates, instead of just one, within a short period of time.) Suppose that A, a widow domiciled in a jurisdiction that follows the Uniform Probate Code, dies with a will leaving her entire estate to her sister B. B is living at A's death, but dies two days later. Under Uniform Probate Code §§ 2–104 and 2–702, A's net probate estate is distributed under the intestacy laws as if B had predeceased A. No part of A's probate estate becomes a part of B's estate.

Further, it should be remembered that the interest a person acquires at the death of a decedent might be a future interest which does not entitle the taker to immediate possession even if the estate is fully administered and "closed" promptly after the decedent's death. For example, A dies survived by B and C, and devises Blackacre in her will "to B for life, remainder to C." Under the will, C acquires a remainder interest in Blackacre at A's death, but he is not entitled to possession of Blackacre until B dies. (Because B's life estate is a transferable interest, C might acquire it during B's lifetime by gift or sale, and thus become entitled to possession of Blackacre before B dies.) Under the traditional law of future interests, C's remainder interest is indefeasibly vested, meaning that if C dies before B the remainder interest will not fail but will pass to C's successors by will or intestacy.

§ 2.7 REPRESENTATION

Often, under the intestacy laws or the terms of a will or trust, property is required to be distributed among the descendants of a decedent "by right of representation." Representation means simply that the property is divided among the nearest living descendants in each line of descent from the decedent. There are several different methods of representation. To illustrate, suppose that a decedent died, unmarried and intestate, survived by six grandchildren. Two of the grandchildren are the children of the decedent's predeceased child A, and the other four grandchildren are the children of the decedent's predeceased child B. The six grandchildren succeed to the decedent's net probate estate under the intestacy laws. Whether they take "per capita" ("by heads") or "per stirpes" ("by roots" or "by stocks") is a matter of local law. If they take per capita, each grandchild takes an equal one-sixth share of the estate. If they take per stirpes, A's children collectively "represent" A and take the share that their deceased parent would have taken had A survived the decedent, and B's children take the share that B would have taken had B survived the decedent. Thus, under a per stirpes distribution, each of A's children takes one-fourth of the estate (one-half of one-half), and each of B's children takes one-eighth of the estate (one-fourth of one-half).

If all of the takers are related to the decedent in the same degree of consanguinity, the intestacy laws in some states provide for a per capita distribution, to ensure that each taker receives an equal share of the estate. Under these intestacy laws, a per stirpes distribution applies only in those cases where there are living takers in more than one generation. For example, suppose that the decedent, a widow, had only two children, A and B. A predeceased the decedent and left two children who survive the decedent. B, the decedent's surviving child, has four children who also survive the decedent. Because there are living takers in more than one generation, a per stirpes distribution gives one-fourth of the estate (one-half of one-half) to each of A's children, and one-half of the estate to B. B's children take nothing because their parent survived the decedent. Children do not represent their living parent.

Many intestacy laws follow the hybrid system of representation set forth in § 2–106 of the Uniform Probate Code as originally promulgated in 1969. Under this system, often referred to as "per capita with representation,"

> the estate is divided into as many shares as there are surviving heirs in the nearest degree of kinship and deceased persons in the same degree who left issue who survive the decedent, each surviving heir in the nearest degree receiving one share and the share of each

deceased person in the same degree being divided among his issue in the same manner.

Some states follow the more elaborate system of representation set forth in the revised version of § 2–106 promulgated in 1990. The revised provision modifies the original approach by requiring that in each generation the shares of any deceased members who left living descendants must be recombined and then divided "in the same manner" among their living descendants. This system, often referred to as "per capita at each generation," ensures that in each generation the living takers who are related to the decedent in equal degree receive equal intestate shares.

In drafting a will or a trust instrument that includes a class gift to the "descendants" or "issue" of a named person, it is advisable to specify how the shares of the takers are to be determined. Because phrases such as "per capita" and "per stirpes" have no uniform, fixed meaning that is universally understood and accepted, they should generally be avoided. Instead, it is preferable to describe the intended method of distribution, or to refer specifically to a method set forth in the local intestacy laws. To avoid confusion and potential litigation, the drafting attorney should make sure that the terms of the will or the trust instrument clearly and accurately set forth the transferor's intended disposition.

§ 2.8 FROM WHOM PROPERTY IS ACQUIRED

It is worth emphasizing the manner in which property passes. Suppose that a decedent had only two children, A and B, both of whom predeceased the decedent. Because A and B did not survive the decedent, they themselves cannot inherit from the decedent under the intestacy laws, nor can they take as beneficiaries under the decedent's will if the decedent died testate. If both A and B left children of their own who survive the decedent, and these grandchildren succeed to the decedent's net probate estate under the intestacy laws, they inherit directly from the decedent, not from their parents, and this is true regardless of whether they take "per capita" or "per stirpes."

Similarly, a beneficiary who takes a gift by substitution under an anti-lapse statute, takes directly from the testator. If A dies leaving her entire estate by will to B, and B predeceases A, the testamentary gift intended for B lapses. If an applicable anti-lapse statute creates a gift by substitution in B's children who survive A, the children of B who take under the anti-lapse statute take directly from A, not from their parent B.

Suppose that A, the absolute owner of Blackacre, transfers it (by deed or will, as the case may be) "to B for life, remainder to C if C survives B, but if C fails to survive B, then to D." B is married to C, and D is their child. B as "life tenant" enters into possession of Blackacre. C dies survived by B (the life tenant) and by D. Then B dies, survived by D. D is now the absolute owner of Blackacre, and her title is derived directly from A. B's life estate ceased at B's death, and D takes nothing from B. C's interest failed when C died during B's lifetime, so D takes nothing from C.

How property interests pass is important not only to potential takers themselves, but also to interested third parties, such as creditors and tax collectors. Tracing interests can be, and often is, a matter of considerable complexity.

§ 2.9 ADVANCEMENTS

If a person who dies intestate made a lifetime gift of property to a donee who turns out to be an heir of the deceased donor, the gift may be treated under some circumstances as an "advancement"—a transfer before death of part or all of the donee's intestate share. If there is an advancement, the donee must bring the property into "hotchpot" if the donee wishes to claim an intestate share of the donor's net probate estate. That is, in calculating the donee's intestate share, the estate is notionally increased by the value of the advancement, and then the donee's share of the grossed-up estate is reduced dollar for dollar by the value of the advancement. In effect, the value of the advancement is offset against the intestate share that the donee would have received had the decedent made no lifetime gift, but in no event is the donee obliged to return any property received from the decedent during life by way of advancement.

Whether a particular gift is treated as an advancement depends on the transferor's intent.

Many states, following the Uniform Probate Code, limit the doctrine of advancements to cases where there is a written declaration or acknowledgment indicating an intention to invoke the doctrine. UPC § 2–109.

§ 2.10 ADOPTION

Statutes regulating adoption are not uniform, but generally speaking a person who has been legally adopted is treated as a member of the family of the adopting parents. Furthermore, the adopted person's legal relationship with his or her natural parents is ordinarily terminated, but this general rule may be subject to exceptions either by the express terms of the adoption statute or by judicial interpretation. For example, if a child is adopted by the spouse of one of the natural parents (a step-parent), the adoption statute commonly preserves that parent's legal relationship with the adopted child. In the absence of legal adoption proceedings, the relationship between a step-parent and step-child, or between a foster parent and foster child, generally does not give rise to any inheritance rights. The consequences of adoption for property purposes are still very much a matter of state law, and that law must be consulted in connection with a particular problem involving such matters as intestate succession, wills, and trusts.

The provisions of the intestacy laws relating to adopted children vary considerably from one state to another. As divorce, remarriage, and the related phenomenon of "blended" families become more common, estate planners should be alert to questions involving the status of adopted children under the law of intestate succession, wills, and trusts. In drafting a will or a trust instrument involving class gifts to "children" or "descendants" of a transferor or beneficiary, it is advisable to specify whether those terms include children brought into the family by adoption (and, conversely, whether children given up for adoption to other family members or third persons are excluded).

§ 2.11 NONMARITAL CHILDREN

In general, the intestacy laws recognize reciprocal rights of inheritance between a child born out of wedlock and its mother (and the mother's relatives), but the situation is more complicated with respect to the father (and the father's relatives). In many states the intestacy laws permit a child born out of wedlock to inherit from its father, but impose restrictions on the child's ability to prove paternity after the father's death. Thus, if the parents never married and paternity was not adjudicated before the father's death (for example, in a child support proceeding), the child may have difficulty obtaining a share of the deceased father's intestate estate. As a practical matter, this is likely to be a problem in cases where the father voluntarily provided support and informally acknowledged the child as his own, but made no formal declaration of paternity during life. As a matter of constitutional law, the Supreme Court, in Trimble v. Gordon, 430 U.S. 762 (1977), struck down a state intestacy law which required marriage on the part of the parents as a condition for inheritance by an out-of-wedlock child from the deceased father. One year later, however, in Lalli v. Lalli, 439 U.S. 259 (1978), the Court upheld another state intestacy law which required a judicial determination of paternity during the father's life, noting that this "evidentiary" requirement was substantially related to the state's interest in providing for the "just and orderly disposition of property at death."

§ 2.12 POSTHUMOUS CONCEPTION

Advances in the technology of "assisted reproduction" have made it possible for a child to be conceived after the death of one or both parents. For example, a husband contemplating a hazardous medical procedure or military deployment might deposit sperm with a sperm bank for the purpose of allowing his wife to conceive a child in the event of his death or disability. If the husband dies and his wife subsequently uses the banked sperm to conceive a child, a question may arise concerning the child's eligibility to inherit from the decedent under the intestacy laws. (Even if the decedent left a will, the intestacy laws may be relevant in determining whether the child is entitled to receive Social Security benefits based on the decedent's lifetime earnings record.) Because the marriage was terminated by the husband's death, the child is technically born out of wedlock. A further complicating factor is that the intestacy laws traditionally made no provision for inheritance by a child conceived after a parent's death. Nevertheless, some states have enacted statutes which allow the child to inherit if the deceased parent consented to the posthumous conception and the child was either in utero or born within a specified time after the parent's death.

§ 2.13 FREEDOM OF TESTATION

Throughout the United States, persons who make gifts of property during life or at death enjoy a high degree of "testamentary freedom." That is, within very broad limits, they are free to select (and, by implication, to exclude) the beneficiaries of their bounty and to impose conditions and restrictions on the use and enjoyment of the property. Occasionally the terms of a gift may raise questions about the transferor's motives or judgment, but courts rarely override conditions or restrictions unless they violate some rule of law or public policy. For example, in Shapira v. Union National Bank, 315 N.E.2d 825 (Ohio Com.Pl. 1974), the testator made a bequest to his son on condition that the son marry "a Jewish girl whose both parents were Jewish." The condition was found to be only a partial restraint upon marriage which was reasonable, not contrary to public policy, and therefore valid and enforceable.

The kind of testamentary disposition that is much more likely to meet with judicial disapproval is exemplified by a bequest to a private, nonprofit hospital to provide housing for "white patients who need physical rehabilitation," with a gift over to another hospital if the terms of the primary bequest are "not acceptable" to the intended beneficiary. In Home for Incurables v. University of Maryland, 797

A.2d 746 (Md. 2002), the court held that the racial restriction was illegal and contrary to public policy. The court allowed the primary beneficiary to take the bequest free of the restriction, and refused to enforce the condition in favor of the alternative taker.

A common limitation on testamentary freedom is embodied in the statutory right of a decedent's surviving spouse to "elect against the will." In addition to the body of law that has developed in connection with the surviving spouse's right of election, courts have imposed limitations on testamentary freedom in cases involving matters such as capricious or illegal conditions, unreasonable restraints on alienation, long-term accumulations of income, and remote vesting of future interests. A lawyer who is asked to draft a testamentary gift that is anything other than an outright, immediate devise or bequest to an identified (or readily ascertainable) person or group of persons should be aware of the limitations on testamentary freedom, and should keep in mind that the effect of a carelessly drafted condition or restriction can often be established only through a lawsuit.

§ 2.14 PROVIDING FOR THE SURVIVING SPOUSE

Everyone has his or her own mental picture of the surviving spouse, and all pictures reflect different facets of reality. The traditional picture of a surviving spouse is of a widow—perhaps old with grown children, or young with minor children, or without any children at all, but in any event largely dependent upon her husband, the deceased breadwinner. It is possible that these views of the surviving spouse, when taken together, do indeed correspond to some hypothetical "average" case (as a statistical matter, wives tend to outlive their husbands), but in a particular case they may miss the mark altogether. The surviving spouse may not be a widow at all. He may be a young man without children who will marry again before the year is out. Or if the surviving spouse is indeed a widow, she may be fully self-sufficient (she may even have supported the decedent), or she may be independently wealthy (the decedent may have made an "advantageous" marriage). In short, the surviving spouse is a person whose marriage (or most recent marriage, as the case may be) has been dissolved by death rather than by divorce or annulment. Making provision for the surviving spouse often means trying to maximize annual income over a period of years when the surviving spouse cannot be gainfully employed. But in some cases, a person might make such provision merely by taking account of the possibility that he or she might be married at death and leave a surviving spouse. Under the circumstances, it might be unnecessary or inappropriate to make "provision" in the usual sense of a substantial beneficial disposition for the surviving spouse.

§ 2.15 THE SURVIVING SPOUSE'S RIGHT OF ELECTION

If a decedent's surviving spouse is dissatisfied with the provision, if any, made for him or her in the decedent's will, the spouse may have a statutory "right of election" to take against the will—that is, to take some part of the decedent's property regardless of the terms of the will. The share available to the electing spouse is called an "elective share" or a "forced share." Elective share statutes have been enacted in all but one of the separate property states, as part of the trend to abolish (or greatly modify) traditional dower and curtesy as means of providing for a surviving spouse. In many states, the elective share is calculated by reference to an "augmented estate" which includes not only the decedent's net probate estate but also other property owned or transferred by the decedent (and in some cases by the surviving spouse).

Elective share statutes are not found in community property states. In a community property system, each spouse has a present, equal, vested interest in community property from the moment of acquisition. When one spouse dies, one half of the community property is subject to the deceased spouse's power of testamentary disposition, and the surviving spouse automatically becomes the owner of the other half by operation of law. The surviving spouse has no right of election with respect to the decedent's half of the community property or to any portion of the decedent's separate property.

The prevalence of divorce and remarriage has given rise to widespread use of prenuptial (antenuptial) agreements. An enforceable prenuptial agreement can affect the distribution of a decedent's net probate estate and the surviving spouse's right of election in particular. When the marriage occurs late in life, one or both spouses may be far more concerned about providing for children from an earlier marriage (or other beneficiaries) than about leaving a windfall to a surviving spouse.

§ 2.16 PRETERMITTED HEIRS

A testator is not obliged to make even a token provision for surviving children or other descendants; unlike a surviving spouse, they have no right to elect against the will. Nevertheless, in many states a "pretermitted" (omitted) heir enjoys a measure of statutory protection against inadvertent disinheritance. In their scope and operation, pretermitted heir statutes vary considerably from one state to another. Under the Uniform Probate Code, a child who was born or adopted after the execution of the will and was not provided for in the will may be entitled to a share of the decedent's net probate estate, unless it appears from the will that the omission was intentional. UPC § 2–302. This provision offers no protection to children who were already in existence when the will was executed or to descendants of a deceased child. In some states, the pretermitted heir statute applies more broadly to children and descendants of deceased children, whether born before or after the execution of the will, who are not named or provided for in the will. A testator can readily prevent the unintended application of a pretermitted heir statute by an appropriate declaration in the will. For example, the will might provide as follows:

> Except as otherwise provided in this will, I intentionally make no provision for any child or other descendant of mine, whether born before or after the execution of this will.

§ 2.17 REVOCATION

A will is said to be "ambulatory" because it has no operative effect during the testator's life. A transfer of property by will takes effect only at the testator's death, and the testator can revoke a will at any time after its execution and before the testator's death. There are two principal methods of revocation: revocation by subsequent testamentary instrument, and revocation by physical act. An existing will is revoked if the testator executes a new will which contains an express clause of revocation (e.g., "I make this my last will, hereby revoking all prior wills and codicils. . . .") or which disposes of property in a manner inconsistent with the earlier will. A will can also be revoked if it is burned, torn, canceled, obliterated, or destroyed by the testator with the intention of revoking it. UPC § 2–507.

Revocation can also occur "by operation of law" (as differentiated from revocation by an act of the testator), but one must check the law of a particular jurisdiction to see whether a testator's will is automatically revoked in whole or in part by a change in family circumstances (such as marriage, divorce, or the birth of a child). For example, under the Uniform Probate Code, a divorce or annulment automatically revokes any provisions of an existing will in favor of the testator's former spouse, unless the will expressly provides to the contrary; apart from the revoked provisions for the former spouse, the rest of the will remains effective. UPC § 2–804.

§ 2.18 ADEMPTION

Because there is often an interval of time between the execution of the will and the death of the testator, specific property that is the subject matter of a devise or bequest contained in the will may be disposed of (or used up, or accidentally destroyed, as the case may be) before the testator's death. For example, suppose that A executes a will devising Blackacre to B. Later, A sells Blackacre to a third person for cash. A then dies, survived by B. Because A no longer owns the specific property devised to B, the devise fails—it is said to be "adeemed."

A testator can anticipate the possibility of ademption and make appropriate provision in the will. For example, A's will might provide as follows: "I give Blackacre to B, but if I no longer own Blackacre at my death, I give the sum of $50,000 to B."

§ 2.19 LAPSE

A gift of property by will does not occur until the testator dies. The will, it is said, "speaks" at the testator's death. If an intended beneficiary under a will dies before the testator, the gift is said to "lapse." In general, lapsed gifts become part of the residuary estate, unless the will directs a different disposition.

Where an intended beneficiary fails to survive the testator, most states have an "anti-lapse" statute which provides an implied gift by substitution, usually to the predeceased beneficiary's descendants (if any) who survive the testator. The anti-lapse statute typically applies only if the predeceased beneficiary was closely related to the testator by blood; it does not operate if the predeceased beneficiary was a spouse or an unrelated person. For example, suppose that A executes a will devising Blackacre to her son B and the rest of the estate to C. B predeceases A, survived by several children. A then dies, survived by B's children. Under an anti-lapse statute such as Uniform Probate Code § 2–603, B's descendants who survive A take the property that B would have received had he survived A, namely Blackacre.

The anti-lapse statute is a rule of construction which yields to an expression of contrary intent in the will. A testator can anticipate the problem of lapse by providing an express gift to an alternative beneficiary in the event the intended beneficiary predeceases the testator. For example, A's will might provide as follows: "I give Blackacre to B if B survives me, but if B does not survive me I give Blackacre to C." There is considerable variation in the provisions of anti-lapse statutes in different jurisdictions, and in drafting a will it is advisable to provide expressly for an alternative disposition of lapsed or failed gifts instead of relying on statutory default rules.

§ 2.20 CODICIL

Aside from changes in a testamentary disposition brought about by ademption or lapse, the testator may expressly modify or amend the terms of an existing will by executing a "codicil." A codicil is a testamentary instrument executed with the same formalities as a will, which relates to an earlier will and modifies its terms. For example, if A originally executed a will devising Blackacre to her child B, she might subsequently execute a codicil revoking the devise to B and leaving Blackacre instead to C. When a testator dies leaving a will and one or more codicils, all of the documents constitute the testator's "last will" and are read together as a single testamentary instrument for purposes of estate administration and distribution.

§ 2.21 SATISFACTION

Just as an advancement made to an heir affects the distribution of an intestate decedent's estate, so too "satisfaction" affects payment of legacies under the will of a deceased testator. Suppose that A's will leaves a bequest of $10,000 to B. After the execution of the will and before her death, A makes a gift of $4,000 to B. A dies, survived by B. If the lifetime transfer to B is in partial "satisfaction" of the legacy, B takes only $6,000 under A's will.

To avoid controversy over satisfaction, a testator might expressly negate the application of the doctrine by an appropriate clause in the will (e.g., "No gift of any kind that I make under this will shall be considered either fully or partially satisfied by any inter vivos gift made by me after the execution of this will."). A number of states, following the Uniform Probate Code, limit the doctrine of satisfaction to cases where there is a written declaration or acknowledgment indicating an intention to invoke the doctrine. UPC § 2–609.

§ 2.22 ABATEMENT

Where the assets of the testator's estate are insufficient to satisfy all of the gifts provided in the will, the testamentary gifts are subject to "abatement"—that is, reduction. Assets may prove to be insufficient because the decedent depleted the estate before death through consumption or prior transfers, or because the debts, administration expenses and death taxes payable from the estate are unexpectedly large, or because a surviving spouse claims an elective share, or because a pretermitted heir claims a share of the estate. Testamentary gifts generally abate in the following order: first, residuary gifts, then "general" gifts, and finally "specific" gifts. UPC § 3–902. (Specific gifts are favored in abatement, but are vulnerable to ademption.)

A specific gift refers to specific, identifiable property (for example, "I give my diamond brooch to A"). A general gift is a gift of a certain amount or quantity of property, usually money (for example, "I give $10,000 to B"). A residuary gift is a gift of the remaining property in the estate after all other gifts have been satisfied (for example, "I give the rest, residue, and remainder of my estate to C").

A testator can include a provision in the will directing that the intended gifts abate in an order different from the usual statutory order. In short, the testator can prefer one beneficiary or class of beneficiaries over another where the net probate estate turns out to be insufficient to satisfy the testator's intention in all respects.

§ 2.23 DISCLAIMER

A person who becomes entitled to receive property by intestate succession, by will, or by inter vivos gift might refuse to accept the property by making a "disclaimer" or "renunciation." (One cannot be forced to accept a gift from the donor.) A person who makes a disclaimer of property passing from a decedent by intestate succession or by will is treated as having predeceased the decedent, and the property is distributed accordingly. The disclaimer generally "relates back" to the time of the transfer, meaning that the disclaimed property is treated as passing directly from the original transferor to the ultimate taker; the property is not treated as passing through the hands of the person making the disclaimer.

CHAPTER 3
SURVIVORSHIP INTERESTS

§ 3.1 WHY CREATE SURVIVORSHIP INTERESTS?

In trying to "avoid probate" or escape death taxes or disinherit a spouse, people often resort to property arrangements that include an incident of survivorship. For example, A and B, husband and wife, purchase a house from a third party, taking title in the form "A and B as joint tenants with right of survivorship." Thereafter A dies, survived by B. If the arrangement works as intended by A and B, B becomes the sole owner of the property at A's death by operation of law. The property does not pass under A's will and is not included in his probate estate for purposes of administration.

Putting property in survivorship form does not always achieve the objectives of those tempted to take advantage of its availability. Furthermore, the survivorship form of ownership has some disadvantages. We will consider both of these matters in some detail after first considering briefly how the incident of survivorship is created.

§ 3.2 CREATING THE INCIDENT OF SURVIVORSHIP

Not all forms of co-ownership have the incident of survivorship. For example, if A, owning land in fee simple absolute, grants or devises "to B and his heirs and C and his heirs," B and C are tenants in common.

Each owns an undivided one-half interest in fee simple absolute in the land, and that undivided one-half interest is alienable, devisable, and descendible. If B dies survived by C, B's undivided one-half interest passes to the devisee under B's will or, alternatively, to B's heirs under the intestacy laws. Of course, C might be the devisee of B's interest in the land under B's will or B's heir under the intestacy laws, but in either case C takes by devise or descent, not by virtue of an incident of survivorship. The incident of survivorship is not a characteristic of the tenancy in common.

The incident of survivorship was a characteristic of both the joint tenancy and the tenancy by the entirety as those tenancies existed at common law. The tenancy by the entirety existed only between husband and wife. Both the joint tenancy and the tenancy by the entirety as they existed at common law have been affected by statutory and judicial modification. Therefore, to determine both the method of creating the incident of survivorship and the kinds of property to which the incident attaches, one must consult applicable state or federal law. With respect to land, savings accounts, checking accounts, certificates of deposit, stock certificates, mutual funds and safe-deposit boxes, one looks to state law. With respect to U.S. savings bonds, one looks to federal law. One should not assume that a method of creating the incident that is effective in one state will necessarily be effective in another, nor should one assume that a method effective with respect to one kind of property will necessarily be effective with respect to another. There is considerable variation in these matters (with consequential risk of misunderstanding and frustration).

For example, A with his separate funds purchases a U.S. savings bond and has it registered in the form "A or B." Either A or B, in possession of the bond, may effectively seek payment. On the other hand, were A to agree with C to purchase land from C, it would be unwise as a matter of state law for A to attempt to take title in the form "A or B" because questions might arise as to the validity and effect of the instrument of transfer. If A wishes to take title to land in a way that creates a present possessory interest in B, or a future interest in B, or an incident of survivorship ultimately advantageous to B, there are generally acceptable means of doing so. In most states, a deed from C, owner in fee simple absolute, to "A and B as joint tenants with right of survivorship and not as tenants in common" is sufficient to create equal present possessory interests in A and B, and on the death of either A or B, the survivor has a fee simple absolute in the entire parcel. There is room for "innovation" in property matters, but, generally speaking, one should not innovate unless conventional methods are inadequate to the task at hand.

§ 3.3 SEVERABILITY

If A and B are tenants in common of a fee simple absolute in land (each owning an undivided one-half interest), the interest of each person is alienable, devisable, and descendible. Because a prospective purchaser of the entire parcel must negotiate with two persons rather than one, the existence of the tenancy in common may impair the marketability of the land. But such a prospective purchaser is no more likely to be discouraged by the necessity of dealing with several tenants in common than would be the case if a tract of like size consisted of several parcels each of which was wholly owned by one of a number of different persons. (In either case, the purchaser must acquire the interests of all of the owners in order to obtain all of the desired acreage.) Where property is held by joint tenants or tenants by the entirety, transferability is more complex. For example, if A and B were joint tenants in fee simple of land at common law, either could sever the joint tenancy by conveying his or her interest to a third person. If A conveyed all of her interest in the land to C, B and C would thereupon become tenants in common (the incident of survivorship having been destroyed).

If, rather than convey to C, A were to devise all of her interest in the land to C, C would take nothing if A died survived by B, because at A's death B would become sole owner by right of survivorship. (The incident of survivorship is not destroyed by a devise, as opposed to an inter vivos conveyance.) Because joint tenancy has been affected by both statutory and judicial developments, one should not assume that what is frequently called "joint tenancy" today necessarily has all of the same characteristics as a joint tenancy at common law. In many states, for example, if D owns land in fee simple absolute and conveys it to A and B under survivorship language such as "to A and B for their joint lives, and then in fee simple to the survivor of them," and A thereafter conveys all of her interest in the land to C, the survivorship interest is not destroyed by the transfer, whereas it would have been if A and B were joint tenants at common law. If A dies survived by B, B has a fee simple absolute by virtue of D's deed. B's title is based not on a right of survivorship incident to a joint tenancy, but rather on the operative words of the deed.

Tenancy by the entirety exists only between spouses who are married to each other. Unlike the joint tenancy at common law, the tenancy by the entirety could not be severed by an attempted conveyance by one of the spouses to a third person. Like the joint tenancy, the tenancy by the entirety as it existed at common law has been affected by statutory and judicial modification. In some jurisdictions, the tenancy by the entirety has been abolished altogether; in some others, what is called a "tenancy by the entirety" is essentially indistinguishable from a joint tenancy between spouses. In those jurisdictions that still recognize the tenancy by the entirety as a distinctive form of co-ownership, as a general rule neither spouse acting alone can sever the tenancy or destroy the incident of survivorship. Accordingly, the tenancy by the entirety can be terminated only by the consent of both spouses during the marriage or by the termination of the marriage on divorce or death.

§ 3.4 JOINT BANK ACCOUNTS

An account in a bank or other financial institution (e.g., a savings and loan association or credit union) can also be held in joint-and-survivorship form. Traditional joint tenancy concepts have been modified in the case of "joint" accounts, in recognition of the reality that the balance in the account may fluctuate from day to day as amounts are deposited and withdrawn. Parties who open a joint account may intend that all amounts on deposit are to be owned equally by the parties while both are alive, and that at the death of either party the survivor will become entitled to the remaining balance. This sort of pooling arrangement is probably most commonly found among married couples.

The parties may have something quite different in mind, however. Suppose that A opens a joint account in the names of herself and her child B. A contributes all of the funds in the account, but B occasionally withdraws funds to be used for A's benefit. Here the reason for creating the joint account may not be to give B any beneficial interest or survivorship right at all, but merely to enable B to withdraw funds on A's behalf during A's lifetime as a matter of convenience. If the terms of the account do not clearly provide for a right of survivorship, A's personal representative may argue that B has no beneficial interest in the account at A's death and that the remaining balance passes instead to the beneficiaries under A's will or to her heirs by intestate succession.

Some banks routinely recommend joint accounts to their customers as a sort of all-purpose vehicle, without inquiring whether a particular account is intended to serve as a true joint-and-survivorship arrangement. In large part, this practice persists because a bank is generally protected by statute in paying amounts from a joint account to any living party, without regard to the beneficial interests of the parties between themselves. A party who withdraws amounts in excess of his or her beneficial interest in the account may be liable to account to the other party, but this is a matter for the parties to settle between themselves; the bank is not involved.

In many states the treatment of joint accounts has been clarified by statutes modeled on the Uniform Probate Code. In general, a joint account belongs to the parties during their joint lifetime in proportion to their respective net contributions (measured by amounts deposited, plus a proportional share of interest received, less amounts withdrawn). At the death of one party, the amounts remaining on deposit are presumed to belong to the surviving party, and this presumption can be rebutted only by clear and convincing evidence of a different intent at the time the account was created. (In some states, the presumption of survivorship rights is conclusive, except in cases of fraud or undue influence.) In effect, these provisions treat each party's net contributions to a joint account as revocable transfers which become complete upon the contributing party's death (or upon earlier withdrawal by the other party with the consent of the contributing party).

§ 3.5 "PAY-ON-DEATH" ACCOUNTS AND "TOTTEN TRUSTS"

A "pay-on-death" account, as the name suggests, is one which by its terms is payable at the death of the owner to a named beneficiary. In jurisdictions where it is recognized, the pay-on-death account operates as a convenient probate avoidance device and avoids most of the ambiguities of a joint account. In many states the validity and effect of pay-on-death accounts are governed by statutes modeled on the Uniform Probate Code. Under these statutes, if A with her own funds opens a bank account in the name of "A, pay on death to B," the account belongs exclusively to A during her lifetime, and at A's death the remaining balance belongs to B if B survives A. UPC §§ 6–211 and 6–212. B's rights as beneficiary accrue only at A's death; having contributed none of the funds on deposit, B has no beneficial interest in the account during A's lifetime. Moreover, A is free to revoke or change the beneficiary designation at any time before her death, but the beneficiary designation cannot be altered by will. UPC § 6–213. Although the arrangement functions as a pure will substitute, it is expressly declared to be "nontestamentary" and hence not subject to the formal requirements applicable to a will. UPC § 6–214. In substance, a pay-on-death account closely resembles a joint account that is funded and controlled exclusively by one person during life and then passes to another person by right of survivorship at the first party's death. The main difference is that the pay-on-death account leaves no doubt concerning the respective beneficial interests of the owner and the designated beneficiary.

A Totten trust is the common law equivalent of a pay-on-death account. Long before the enactment of statutes authorizing pay-on-death accounts, the courts held that substantially the same result could be achieved, in the case of a savings bank account, by means of a "tentative trust." In re Totten, 71 N.E. 748 (N.Y. 1904). In most states, A can create a tentative trust simply by opening a savings bank account in the form "A in trust for B." During A's life the account belongs exclusively to A, and at A's death the remaining balance belongs to B if B survives A. The purported trust is a legal fiction which serves only to avoid probate; no fiduciary relationship arises during A's lifetime, and B has no beneficial interest in the account until A's death. Like a pay-on-death account, a Totten trust is freely revocable by the owner during life. Moreover, in some jurisdictions, the owner may also be empowered to revoke or change the beneficiary designation by will. In this respect, a Totten trust differs from a pay-on-death account. (Under the Uniform Probate Code, however, a Totten trust is subject to the same rules as a pay-on-death account. In both cases, the beneficiary designation cannot be altered by will. UPC § 6–213(b).)

§ 3.6 U.S. SAVINGS BONDS

A person who purchases (or who advises another to purchase) U.S. savings bonds should keep in mind that the issue, reissue, and payment of such bonds are matters of federal law. It is true that the consequence of payment under federal law may be affected by a remedial device such as a constructive trust, but in ordering one's family affairs one ought not to rely on a lawsuit to carry out an intended disposition. If A with her separate funds opens a savings bank account in the names of herself and B in survivorship form, it is likely as a matter of state law and banking practice that A, in possession of the passbook, can close the survivorship account and open a new one solely in her own name. Suppose that A with her separate funds purchases a U.S. savings bond in "coownership form," registered in the name "A or B." May A thereafter, in possession of the bond, have the bond reissued solely in her own name, irrespective of B's consent? This is a matter of federal law, not state law, and one should not assume that the reissue of a U.S. savings bond will proceed in the same fashion as closing a savings bank account and opening a new one. The characteristics of U.S. savings bonds have been developed through administrative regulations and judicial decisions, and constitute a distinct body of substantive law. The regulations state that "[a] request for reissue of bonds in coownership form during the lifetime of the coowners must be signed by both coowners. . . ." 31 C.F.R. § 315.51. However, the regulations also state that "[a] savings bond registered in coownership form will be paid to either coowner upon surrender with an appropriate request, and, upon payment . . ., the other coowner will cease to have any interest in the bond." 31 C.F.R. § 315.37.

A U.S. savings bond may be registered in "beneficiary form" rather than coownership form.

Suppose that A with her separate funds purchases a bond in the form "A, payable on death to B." The regulations state that "[a] savings bond registered in beneficiary form will be paid to the registered owner during his or her lifetime upon surrender with an appropriate request. Upon payment . . ., the beneficiary will cease to have any interest in the bond." 31 C.F.R. § 315.38. Furthermore, "[i]f the owner of a bond registered in beneficiary form has died and is survived by the beneficiary, upon proof of death of the owner, the beneficiary will be recognized as the sole and absolute owner of the bond." 31 C.F.R. § 315.70(c)(1).

A bond registered in beneficiary form serves substantially the same purpose as one registered in coownership form, because the survivor is entitled to payment or reissue. But the two forms are not identical. If A purchases a bond in the form "A, payable on death to B," there is nothing in the regulations suggesting that B is entitled to payment or reissue during A's lifetime.

§ 3.7 SIMULTANEOUS DEATH

If the parties to a joint tenancy die in circumstances that make it impossible to determine which of them survived the other, it becomes necessary to resort to some arbitrary presumption concerning the order of deaths. Many states have enacted statutes modeled on § 3 of the original Uniform Simultaneous Death Act, which provides, in relevant part, that "[w]here there is no sufficient evidence that two joint tenants or tenants by the entirety have died otherwise than simultaneously the property so held shall be distributed one-half as if one had survived and one-half as if the other had survived. . . . The term 'joint tenants' includes owners of property held under circumstances which entitled one . . . to the whole of the property on the death of the other. . . ."

The statute applies only where there is "no sufficient evidence" of survivorship. If it can be shown that one of the joint tenants survived the other for even an instant, the statute has no application. (In contrast, § 2–702(c) of the Uniform Probate Code calls for an equal distribution unless there is "clear and convincing evidence" that one of the joint tenants survived the other by at least 120 hours.)

If the same person or persons are the successors of both joint tenants by will or intestacy, the ultimate disposition of the joint tenancy property is the same regardless of whether the simultaneous death statute applies. For example, suppose that A and B, husband and wife, own property as joint tenants with right of survivorship. A's will leaves his entire estate to B if she survives him, and if she does not, to their only child C. B's will leaves her entire estate to A if he survives her, and if he does not, to C. If A and B die in an airplane crash and the order of their deaths cannot be determined, the joint tenancy property passes to C (one-half from A and one-half from B under their respective wills). If A survives B but dies shortly afterward, so that the simultaneous death statute does not apply, A takes the property as surviving joint tenant, and it then passes to C at A's death under A's will.

By way of contrast, suppose that A and B are siblings who own property as joint tenants with right of survivorship. A's will leaves his entire estate to C. B's will leaves her entire estate to D. A and B die simultaneously, and the simultaneous death statute applies. C takes one-half of the property under A's will, and D takes one-half of the property under B's will. But if A and B die under such circumstances that the statute does not apply, the survivor takes all of the property by virtue of the right of survivorship, and the property then passes to the beneficiary named in the survivor's will.

§ 3.8 RIGHTS OF THE SURVIVING SPOUSE AND THE DIVORCED SPOUSE

A disaffected spouse may use a joint tenancy with right of survivorship or some other kind of will substitute in an effort to disinherit his or her spouse. Whether the effort is successful is a matter of state law. In most separate property states, the surviving spouse's elective share extends not only to the decedent's net probate estate but also to property disposed of by various will substitutes, including joint tenancy with right of survivorship. For example, the Uniform Probate Code allows the surviving spouse to claim an elective share of an "augmented estate" which includes the decedent's net probate estate and the decedent's "nonprobate transfers" as well as certain property owned or transferred by the surviving spouse. UPC §§ 2–204 to 2–207. For this purpose, the decedent's nonprobate transfers include, inter alia, the decedent's fractional interest in property held in joint tenancy with right of survivorship, the decedent's ownership interest in joint accounts and pay-on-death accounts, and property over which the decedent held a presently exercisable general power of appointment immediately before death. UPC § 2–205(1). The elective share provisions of the Uniform Probate Code offer the surviving spouse a substantial measure of protection against disinheritance, with respect to nonprobate assets as well as probate assets. It bears emphasis that the position of the surviving spouse is not so advantageous in this respect in all states.

If a married person executes a will making provision for a spouse, and the marriage thereafter ends in divorce, the provision in the testator's will for the divorced spouse is commonly revoked by statute. There are numerous property arrangements, including survivorship interests, that serve as will substitutes. A statute that on divorce revokes provisions for a spouse in an existing will might be extended to cover will substitutes of which a divorced spouse is beneficiary. But there is no assurance that a statute will be interpreted so broadly. Section 2–804 of the Uniform Probate Code, enacted in some states, revokes provisions for a divorced spouse in various kinds of will substitutes, including a joint tenancy with right of survivorship, a revocable trust, and life insurance. The lesson is clear: On divorce, all property arrangements should be reexamined to determine whether they still reflect the desires of the owner of the property.

§ 3.9 TAXATION—IN GENERAL

Just as one must consult applicable state or federal law with respect to the creation of joint ownership with the incident of survivorship, so too one should be aware of the gift and estate tax consequences of joint-and-survivor arrangements. The Internal Revenue Code includes both gift and estate taxes. Only one state currently imposes a gift tax on lifetime transfers, but a considerably larger number of states impose an estate tax or an inheritance tax on transfers at death. (Estate and inheritance taxes are commonly called "death taxes.") In determining whether either a gift tax or a death tax applies to a transaction involving the incident of survivorship, one should pay particular attention to the kind of property to which the incident attaches. Interests in bank accounts may be treated differently from interests in land or other property. Thus, for example, if A using her own funds opens a joint-and-survivor bank account in the names of herself and her child B, there is no completed gift for gift tax purposes as long as A can freely withdraw the funds without B's consent; but if she allows B to withdraw funds for B's benefit, with no obligation to account to A, there is a completed gift. In contrast, if A uses her own funds to purchase land from a third person and takes title in the names of A and B as joint tenants with right of survivorship, A has made a gift of one half of the value of the land for gift tax purposes.

Putting property in survivorship form does not necessarily result in a tax advantage, and it may result in an unnecessary tax liability. For example, suppose that A purchases a residence with her own funds and takes title in the names of herself and her child B as joint tenants with right of survivorship. A dies survived by B. Under I.R.C. § 2040(a), the entire value of the residence at A's death is includible in her gross estate. Any gift tax paid by A in connection with the creation of the joint tenancy is allowable as an offset against the estate tax imposed at her death, but the joint-and-survivor arrangement produces no tax saving compared to an outright devise of the residence under A's will. (In contrast, if B unexpectedly died before A, none of the value of the residence would be includible in B's estate, since B contributed none of the purchase price. But A would merely end up owning the same property that she originally purchased, having incurred an unnecessary gift tax upon the creation of the joint tenancy.) It is often impossible to predict with certainty who will be the survivor of two or more persons, and therefore in a particular case, viewed solely from the standpoint of the tax law, it might be better for A to take title to the residence solely in her own name.

§ 3.10 CONCLUSION

When one has little property, joint ownership with the incident of survivorship is justifiable both as a matter of convenience and as a means of avoiding probate. But as a couple accumulates more substantial amounts of property, use of joint-and-survivor arrangements should be confined to kinds of property and amounts of property which make sense both as part of an overall property disposition and from the standpoint of tax planning. The tax advantage of joint ownership with the incident of survivorship is often illusory, and unscrambling interests held in survivorship form can be troublesome, especially in the event of a disagreement between the parties or an unexpected early death. Generally speaking, from a tax planning perspective, couples of considerable means may find it desirable to equalize their respective individual holdings of property. Joint-and-survivor arrangements serve limited purposes. They do not defeat the tax collector. They might not defeat a surviving spouse seeking an elective share of the decedent's estate. And the savings achieved in avoiding probate may not be worth the potential trouble caused by putting property in survivorship form.

CHAPTER 4
COMMUNITY PROPERTY

§ 4.1 THE NATURE OF COMMUNITY PROPERTY

If A, married to B in a community property state, acquires property through (say) employment (as opposed to inheritance, devise, bequest, or gift), A and B each hold equal, undivided interests in the acquired property as "community property." Property that A owned before marriage, and brought to the marriage, along with any property that A acquires during the marriage by inheritance, devise, bequest, or gift, is A's "separate property." Generally speaking, if A dies survived by B, A has testamentary power of disposition over both the separate property and an undivided one-half share of the community property. By way of contrast, if A, married to B in a common law state, acquires $100,000 through (say) employment, A has power of disposition over the entire $100,000 during lifetime. If A dies survived by B, A has testamentary power of disposition over the $100,000 at death, subject only to any statutory right in B to elect to "take against the will"—that is, to claim some part of A's property regardless of the terms of the will. The principle underlying the system of community property is that whatever property is acquired during the marriage by the efforts of either one of the spouses belongs equally to both of them—to the "community" of which each is a member. Because each member of the community during the marriage owns an equal, present, vested interest in such acquired property, on the death of one spouse survived by the other, the survivor already owns one half of the community property and does not "take" that half from the decedent. Whether the survivor takes part or all of the decedent's one-half share of the community property turns on the provisions of the decedent's will, or on the law of intestacy (to the extent that the decedent dies intestate).

§ 4.2 WHERE THE COMMUNITY PROPERTY SYSTEM EXISTS IN THE UNITED STATES

The eight traditional community property states are Arizona, California, Idaho, Louisiana, Nevada, New Mexico, Texas, and Washington. Wisconsin's community property act took effect in 1986, and in 1998 Alaska enacted an elective community property system for married couples. In addition, several other states (including Florida, Kentucky, South Dakota and Tennessee) allow married settlors to designate certain trust property as community property. All the rest of the states and the District of Columbia are common law jurisdictions. (A handful of common law states briefly adopted the community property system in the 1940s to gain federal tax advantages. However, those states abandoned their short-lived experiment with community property after Congress enacted legislation to reduce the disparities in treatment of married couples in common law states and community property states for federal tax purposes.)

Although it is conventional for purposes of considering marital property to classify states as "community property" or "separate property" states, even the community property states generally recognize common law forms of property ownership between spouses insofar as the common law forms are consistent with the community property system. For example, A, married to B in a community property state, might hold real estate as community property with B, and at the same time maintain separate property in A's own name or in a tenancy in common or a joint tenancy with B. In community property states, as in common law states, it is essential to be familiar with the details of property law and practice in a particular jurisdiction in order to determine ownership and avoid or resolve disputes over property.

§ 4.3 COMMUNITY PROPERTY DISTINGUISHED FROM SEPARATE PROPERTY

Separate property consists of property that a spouse owned before marriage and brought to the marriage, as well as any property that a spouse acquires during the marriage by inheritance, devise, bequest, or gift. In general, property purchased or acquired with separate funds, or otherwise traceable to a separate property source, retains the separate character of the original property. However, income generated by separate property may be classified as separate property or as community property, depending on the jurisdiction. Property acquired during the marriage by the efforts of either spouse—

property acquired by "onerous" title—is community property. Rents, issues, profits, and fruits of community property are community property.

It bears emphasis that all property in the possession of either spouse during marriage or on dissolution of marriage in a community property state is presumed to be community property, and all property acquired by either spouse during marriage is presumed to be community property. The burden of proving that property is separate property is on the party asserting separate ownership. The quantum of proof required to overcome the presumption of community ownership has been described as "clear and convincing," and although as a practical matter this might amount to little more than a preponderance of the evidence, it may be difficult to overcome the presumption of community ownership in a particular case. If A, married to B, dies in a community property state, survived by B, knowledge possessed by A regarding evidence of ownership may be irretrievably lost. Where there is no evidence of the time or means of acquisition of property, or where the evidence is scanty or closely balanced, both the presumption and the allocation of the burden of proof are important.

By "transmutation," community property may be changed to separate property, or vice versa. There are variations among the community property states with respect to both the permissibility of transmutation and the means of effecting change. In some states, a transmutation of community property to separate property, or vice versa, requires an express declaration or an agreement in writing. In other states, transmutation may be accomplished relatively easily. For example, in Schmanski v. Schmanski, 984 P.2d 752 (Nev. 1999), a husband sold stock which he had received as a gift from his father and deposited the proceeds in a brokerage account titled in the names of himself and his wife as joint tenants with right of survivorship. The court found that the husband's act of placing his separate property in joint tenancy with his wife raised a presumption of a gift to the community, and affirmed an equal division of the property between the spouses when the marriage terminated in divorce.

§ 4.4 LIFE INSURANCE

Difficulties in classifying property as separate property or community property, and differences in classification among community property states, are illustrated by the treatment of life insurance policies and life insurance proceeds.

A policy of life insurance is a form of intangible property. Questions on life insurance are complicated by whether the insurance is on the life of the decedent or the life of another; whether the policy was procured before marriage or during marriage; the original beneficiary designation, attempts to change the beneficiary designation, and whether the decedent retained the right to change the beneficiary designation; the source of funds used to pay premiums; how one makes gifts to a spouse or to a third person in a community property state; and when rights "vest" with respect to an insurance policy or its proceeds.

Suppose that A before marriage purchases a policy of ordinary or straight life insurance on his own life and designates his mother M as beneficiary. The policy is kept in force by periodic premium payments, and the policy has customary "incidents of ownership," such as the right to change the beneficiary designation, the right to terminate the policy and receive its cash surrender value (if any), the right to use the policy as collateral for a loan, the right to assign the policy, and the right to select a method of payment under a settlement option.

While the policy is in force, A marries B. Thereafter A pays premiums on the policy with community funds. A dies survived by both his mother M and his wife B. A has never changed the beneficiary designation on the policy. What are B's rights, if any, in the proceeds of the policy?

Because A procured the policy before marriage and brought it to the marriage, the policy was initially A's separate property. Under the "inception of title" rule followed in some states, the proceeds at A's death are separate property, and the community is entitled to reimbursement for any community funds that were used to pay premiums. (The use of community funds to pay premiums on life insurance is treated like the use of community funds to improve land that is the separate property of a spouse—the improvements follow the property.) Under the "apportionment" rule followed in other states, the proceeds are allocated in accordance with the amount of premiums paid with separate funds and the amount paid with community funds. (This allocation accords with the community property principle that the increase in value of separate property should be shared by the community to the extent the increased value is attributable to community funds or to the efforts of either spouse during the marriage.) Another possible view is that B has no rights in the proceeds because A had the power to make "reasonable" gifts from community property during his lifetime (and did so when paying premiums from community funds), or because the proceeds did not "vest" until A died, when the community had ended.

Suppose that A, married to B, purchases a policy of ordinary life insurance on his own life and designates his mother M as beneficiary. The policy has the customary incidents of ownership, including the right to change the beneficiary designation. A keeps the policy in force by the payment of premiums with community funds. A dies survived by both his mother M and his wife B. What are B's rights, if any, in the proceeds of the policy?

In Washington, neither spouse can make a gift of community property without the express or implied consent of the other, but each spouse has the right to devise or bequeath one half of the community property. Wash. Rev. Code § 26.16.030. The policy, having been acquired during the marriage with community funds, is classified as community property, and the designation of M as beneficiary is voidable as to half of the proceeds at A's death. Accordingly, M and B are each entitled to half of the proceeds. Francis v. Francis, 573 P.2d 369 (Wash. 1978). By way of contrast, in Louisiana it has been held that A had the right to purchase insurance on his own life in favor of any designated beneficiary, that under the circumstances outlined above A had made no gift either inter vivos or causa mortis, that M acquired no vested rights until after A's death (when the community had ended), and that B has no effective claim to the proceeds. Pearce v. National Life & Accident Ins. Co., 125 So. 776 (La.App. 1930).

§ 4.5 MANAGEMENT AND DISPOSITION OF COMMUNITY PROPERTY

Because of the emphasis in modern law on equal treatment of men and women, community property states, generally speaking, give both spouses equal powers of management and disposition of community property. Contemporary law should be differentiated from the traditional view which gave the husband a dominant role in management of community assets.

Joinder of spouses is commonly required to buy, sell, encumber, or dispose of community real property. Either spouse, acting alone, frequently has full power to manage, encumber, or dispose of community personal property. But in this connection, gratuitous transfers (gifts) should be differentiated from commercial transactions. For example, in a community property state, a spouse who has full power, acting alone, to encumber community personal property might be disabled from making gifts (other than nominal gifts) of such property without the other spouse's consent. Furthermore, the law of management and disposition of community property continues to be complicated by the origin of the community property in question, and the way in which title to the property is held.

§ 4.6 COMMUNITY PROPERTY AND FEDERAL ESTATE TAXATION

In a common law state, if A, married to B, by her earnings amasses property valued at $20 million and dies survived by B, all of the property is a part of A's gross estate for federal estate tax purposes. In a community property state, if A, married to B, by her earnings amasses property valued at $20 million and dies survived by B, only one half of the property, being community property, is included in A's gross estate for federal estate tax purposes. The other half of the community property already belonged to B from the time of acquisition during the marriage, and it does not "pass" from A to B at A's death.

Because of this and other disparities in the federal tax treatment of married persons in common law and community property states, Congress in 1948 made the marital deduction a part of the federal gift and estate taxes, "gift splitting" a part of the federal gift tax, and "income splitting" a part of the federal income tax. These devices were intended to put married couples in common law states on a rough parity with those in community property states for federal tax purposes. Therefore, they are primarily of interest to taxpayers in common law states.

Nonetheless, a married couple in a community property state may also make use of the marital deduction. For example, suppose that A, married to B in a community property state, by her earnings amasses property valued at $20 million. A has no separate property. A dies survived by B. A's gross estate of $10 million consists solely of A's one-half share of the community property. In her will, A leaves all of her property to B. The community property qualifies for the marital deduction, to the extent it is included in the decedent's gross estate and passes to the surviving spouse absolutely (or by another qualifying form of disposition). Because there is no limit on the amount of the marital deduction, all of the property passing from A to B escapes estate tax at A's death.

Furthermore, community property is eligible for one significant federal tax advantage that is not available for separate property. For federal income tax purposes, property acquired from a decedent generally takes a "fresh start" basis in the recipient's hands equal to the value of the property at the decedent's death. I.R.C. § 1014(a). For this purpose, property is generally treated as acquired from the decedent if it is includible in the decedent's gross estate for estate tax purposes. I.R.C. § 1014(b). For example, suppose that A and her husband B, domiciled in a common law state, hold Blackacre as tenants in common, each spouse having contributed $500,000 toward the purchase price many years ago. A dies survived by B, when Blackacre is worth $2 million. In her will, A devises her one-half interest in Blackacre (worth $1 million) to B. B retains his original cost basis of $500,000 in his half of the property, but he receives a fresh start basis of $1 million in the one-half share devised to him under A's will. Thus, if B subsequently sells Blackacre for $2.5 million, he will realize a gain of $1 million for federal income tax purposes. In contrast, under a special rule, the entire value of community property at the death of one spouse—not just the one-half interest included in the decedent's gross estate—qualifies for a fresh start basis in the recipient's hands. I.R.C. § 1014(b)(6). Thus, if A and B are domiciled in a community property state and hold Blackacre as community property, B takes a fresh start basis of $2 million at A's death (even though only one half of the property is included in A's gross estate for federal estate tax purposes), and on a subsequent sale for $2.5 million, B will realize a gain of only $500,000 for federal income tax purposes.

§ 4.7 "ELECTION" BY A SURVIVING SPOUSE IN A COMMUNITY PROPERTY STATE

In common law states, such protection as is afforded against disinheritance of a spouse is achieved through forced heirship such as a statutory "elective share." Forced heirship is not a part of the community property system of ownership. In a community property state, at the death of one spouse, the surviving spouse already owns an undivided one-half interest in the community property. Accordingly, the survivor does not take his or her one-half interest from the decedent, and the decedent has no power of testamentary disposition over the survivor's share of the community property.

Nonetheless, the will of a deceased spouse in a community property state may affect the devolution of the surviving spouse's share of the community property. For example, suppose that A, domiciled in a community property state, dies testate survived by his wife B and owning community property. A's will purports to put A's separate property and all of the community property (including B's undivided one-half interest) in a testamentary trust from which B is to receive the income for life, with remainder at B's death to other beneficiaries. B must elect whether to take under the will (thereby assenting to A's disposition of both halves of the community property) or to assert her right to outright ownership of one half of the community property (thereby foregoing the provision made for her in A's will).

§ 4.8 COMMUNITY PROPERTY, CONFLICT OF LAWS, AND PROTECTION OF THE SURVIVING SPOUSE

Difficult questions concerning the classification of property frequently arise when a married couple moves from a common law state to a community property state, or vice versa. In either a common law state or a community property state, purchasers, creditors, tax collectors, or the spouses themselves may be vitally interested in how property is treated for a particular purpose. For example, suppose that A, married to B in a common law state, by his earnings amasses personal property valued at $10 million. If A were to die survived by B, an "elective share" statute in the common law state would afford B some protection against a testamentary attempt by

A to disinherit B. A and B move to a community property state, A taking his personal property with him. A dies in the community property state, still owning that personal property, survived by B. A's will leaves his entire net probate estate to C, A's child by a prior marriage, who also survives A. The community property state has no elective share statute. Have A's change of domicile and change of situs of A's personal property permitted A to disinherit B?

Classification of property interests of married persons who move from one state to another is determined in part by applying principles of conflict of laws. A generally recognized principle is that the character of property is determined at the time of acquisition, and it is not changed by moving the property to another state. If this principle is applied to the case where A, married to B, moves and takes his personal property from a common law state to a community property state, then A can effectively disinherit B with respect to that personal property. Even though A acquired the property during marriage by his earnings, it is "his" in a common law state and is, therefore, separate property on his removal to a community property state. Even so, some community property states, including California, by statute preclude disinheritance in this situation. Had A acquired his property in California while married to B, it would have been classified as community property. Accordingly, it is classified as "quasi-community property" in California and is treated in much the same way as community property for purposes of devolution at death. At A's death, one half of the quasi-community property belongs to B. The other half is subject to unrestricted testamentary disposition by A. Cal.Prob.Code §§ 101(a) and 6101(c).

Succession to real property on the death of the owner, testate or intestate, is governed by the law of the situs. If A, married to B in a common law state, by his earnings acquires real property in the common law state, and A and B thereafter move to a community property state, a testamentary attempt by A to disinherit B can be thwarted with respect to the real property by applying the law of the situs. For example, the law of the situs might give B the right to claim an elective share of the real property regardless of the terms of A's will.

The problem is somewhat different in the case where a married couple moves from a community property state to a separate property state. Applying the principle that the character of property is determined at the time of acquisition, the courts have held that the couple's accumulated community property retains its character, despite the change of domicile, and each spouse retains his or her present, equal, vested interest in the property, unless the spouses agree to convert it to separate property. In several common law states, by statute, at the death of one spouse, the decedent has testamentary power over one half of the community property and the other half belongs to the surviving spouse. The decedent's one-half share of the community property is not subject to the surviving spouse's elective share.

Uniform Community Property Disposition at Death Act § 6.

CHAPTER 5
"SIMPLE" WILLS

§ 5.1 THE LIMITED FUNCTION OF THE WILL

It bears emphasis at the outset that the will, like the statute of descent and distribution, affects only the net probate estate of the decedent—property distributable at death under the supervision of the probate court. Inter vivos or lifetime dispositions of property are ordinarily beyond the purview of the probate court. The decedent may have purchased U.S. savings bonds payable at death to a surviving beneficiary. The decedent and his or her spouse may have held the family residence as joint tenants with right of survivorship. The decedent's spouse or child may be designated as the beneficiary to receive insurance proceeds on the decedent's life or pension benefits at the decedent's death. The decedent may have put property in a revocable inter vivos trust to be distributed at death to named beneficiaries. In all of these cases, beneficiaries who survive the decedent receive possession or enjoyment of interests in property originating with the decedent, but all of these transfers occur outside the probate system and accordingly are not governed by the decedent's will. For purposes of taxation, or election by a surviving spouse, a lifetime transaction may be viewed as essentially testamentary in nature, and treated accordingly, but we are not immediately concerned with those matters here. In any event, a testator should be informed that a will has a limited sphere of application and that lifetime arrangements for the disposition of property may operate without regard for the terms of the will. That information in itself may motivate the client to review the entire range of his or her existing property arrangements, and to make any necessary modifications.

§ 5.2 THE CASE AGAINST INTESTACY

For many people the will is an important dispositive document. For a person of modest or moderate means the will may well be the most important dispositive document in the estate plan. It certainly should not be assumed that if a person has little property, it is of little consequence whether or not he or she executes a will.

If a wealthy person dies intestate survived by a spouse and children, distribution of the estate among the surviving spouse and the children under the intestacy laws may cause no hardship because there is ample property to meet the needs of the surviving family members. But suppose the intestate decedent was a person of modest means. Requiring the surviving spouse to share a small estate with children may effectively deprive the spouse of property needed for the spouse's support. Furthermore, if one or more of the children are minors, property passing to them under the intestacy laws may require a cumbersome and expensive guardianship, resulting in unnecessary depletion of a child's estate. When a couple has little property, it is ordinarily preferable that the decedent's entire estate pass to the surviving spouse on the reasonable assumption that the survivor will provide for others to the extent that he or she can.

Even a person who is generally indifferent to the devolution of property at death might be understandably concerned about the care of minor or incompetent children. Executing a will affords a parent an opportunity to state preferences regarding custody of a child or children when circumstances at death require guardianship. Just as devolution of an estate under the intestacy laws may work out satisfactorily, so too guardianship of minors or incompetents might proceed smoothly without any direction by the decedent. But there is little to be said for leaving so important a matter to chance. Young parents with little property frequently overlook this important function of a properly prepared will, and for them, appointment of an appropriate guardian for the person of a minor child may be the most important function of the will.

In this connection, it is important that both spouses should execute wills. When one spouse dies, the surviving spouse is ordinarily the guardian of the person of any minor children of their marriage. Thus, for example, a husband's designating a guardian of the person of a minor child in his will in the event his wife predeceases him avails nothing if she in fact survives him. Both spouses in their respective wills should anticipate possible guardianship of the person and of the estate of a minor child. (If prospective estates are more than nominal, trusteeship of the estate of a minor as an alternative to guardianship should be considered.)

If a married couple have no children or descendants, each spouse may assume that on his or her death intestate, the surviving spouse will take the entire probate estate. That notion may be erroneous. The Uniform Probate Code § 2–102(2) provides that the intestate share of the surviving spouse is "the first [$300,000], plus three-fourths of any balance of the intestate estate, if no descendant of the decedent survives the decedent, but a parent of the decedent survives the decedent. . . ." (The surviving parent or parents take the remaining one-fourth of the intestate estate not passing to the surviving spouse.) If a couple are in their mid-fifties, each having an aged parent or parents, it is possible that each spouse would prefer that on death, his or her estate be shared by the surviving spouse and an aged parent or parents. If so, that should be a matter of informed choice, not chance. One must know the terms of the applicable statute. Although statutes regulating intestate succession are broadly similar from state to state, they differ in important details. Even if a person is familiar with the intestacy laws of his or her present state of domicile, the devolution of the intestate estate at death may follow a different course if the legislature changes the existing laws or if the person moves to another state.

Viewed solely from the standpoint of the devolution of the probate estate, the intestacy laws may in a particular case direct distribution in accordance with the preferences of the decedent. But a statutory distribution that is satisfactory to the prospective decedent at a particular time may become unsatisfactory a moment later if a beneficiary dies unexpectedly. For example, suppose that A, married to B, has no living parents or descendants. A has no will. If A were to die survived by B, all of A's estate would pass to B under the applicable intestacy laws. But if A were to survive B and then die intestate, all of A's estate (including property received from B) might pass to distant cousins for whom A cares nothing. Although it is possible that A might execute a will after B's death for the purpose of leaving the estate to beneficiaries other than the cousins, it is better for A immediately to execute a will setting out an alternative disposition of the estate in case B predeceases A.

The will affords an opportunity to nominate an executor of the decedent's choice to administer the estate. The person considered by the decedent to be suitable for the task of administering the estate may be someone other than the person entitled under state law to preference in appointment as administrator if the decedent were to die intestate. A will may also give the personal representative powers to administer the estate that are more extensive than those provided by statute, and the will may exempt the executor from the requirement (and expense) of furnishing bond.

Execution of a will by no means solves all of the problems connected with the orderly disposition of property, but a will is an appropriate and useful device for making gratuitous transfers at death. And it serves purposes beyond directing the devolution of the estate. In sum, there is usually little to be said for dying intestate.

§ 5.3 INTERVIEW WITH THE TESTATOR

Before drafting the will, the lawyer should interview the prospective testator to determine the nature and extent of the property involved and to identify the intended beneficiaries. The client should be encouraged to bring relevant personal papers (deeds, insurance policies, bank and brokerage account statements, and the like) to the initial interview. The client's perception and memory of existing property arrangements may be unreliable. Examination of documents reveals how assets are titled—under what name, and in what form. The client should be encouraged before the initial interview to consider alternative dispositions of the estate should there be births or deaths in the interval between execution of the will and death of the testator. The interview also offers the lawyer an opportunity to assess the client's state of mind and to take appropriate steps to guard against a possible will contest on grounds of undue influence or lack of testamentary capacity. Generally speaking, a lawyer should avoid drafting a will for a person not personally interviewed.

§ 5.4 DRAFTING THE "SIMPLE" WILL

It is customary for the testator to identify himself or herself in the introductory clause or the opening paragraph of the will. In this connection it may prove helpful for the will to list the names used by the testator or by which the testator is known to others. For example, the will might begin "I, William J. Smith, also known as William John Smith, William

Smith, and Will Smith. . . ." The testator may have acquired title to real or personal property, tangible or intangible, in a variation of his or her name that is different from the one commonly used. To facilitate working with deeds, stock certificates, certificates of title, bonds, bank accounts, mutual funds, and insurance policies after the testator's death, it is essential that the letters of appointment issued to the personal representative reveal the names under which the testator held property at death.

Next, the will should recite the testator's place of permanent residence, for example, " . . . of the City of Columbus, County of Franklin, State of Ohio. . . ." The domicile of the testator affects such matters as jurisdiction of courts and choice of governing law. The will may also include a declaration of testamentary capacity: " . . . being of full age, sound mind and disposing memory, and knowing the nature and extent of my property and the objects of my bounty. . . ." On disputed issues of domicile or testamentary capacity, the declarations of the testator are of course not conclusive, but they are evidence. The declaration of testamentary capacity is frequently omitted altogether. The will should include a clear statement of the testator's purpose in executing the document: " . . . do make, publish, and declare this to be my last will. . . ."

A principal purpose of the introductory part of the will is to revoke prior wills and codicils: " . . . and I hereby revoke all wills and codicils heretofore made by me." In the absence of express revocation, the new will revokes prior wills and codicils only insofar as its provisions are inconsistent with those of the prior instruments. Unless circumstances are such that preparation of an entirely new will is impracticable—because, for example, the testator is very old or seriously ill—it is not usually desirable to draft a codicil to make changes in the testamentary plan. Applying a single instrument at the testator's death is sometimes difficult; constructing the "last will" of the testator from multiple instruments executed at different times tends to compound problems.

The introductory clause ("exordium") in its entirety is:

> I, William J. Smith, also known as William John Smith, William Smith, and Will Smith, of the City of Columbus, County of Franklin, and State of Ohio, being of full age, sound mind and disposing memory, and knowing the nature and extent of my property and the objects of my bounty, do make, publish, and declare this to be my last will, and I hereby revoke all wills and codicils heretofore made by me.

Or, more simply (omitting the declaration of mental capacity):

> I, William J. Smith, also known as William John Smith, William Smith, and Will Smith, of the City of Columbus, County of Franklin, and State of Ohio, do make, publish and declare this to be my last will, and I hereby revoke all wills and codicils heretofore made by me.

§ 5.5 DISPOSITIVE CLAUSE

Following the introductory clause, the will may set forth any gifts of specific property and legacies of money, followed by a residuary clause disposing of the rest of the testator's net probate estate. These provisions may include alternative gifts to take effect in case the primary intended beneficiary dies before the testator.

[specific bequest]

I give the gold watch which was left to me by my father to my son John, if he survives me. If my son John does not survive me, I give the gold watch to my son James.

[cash legacy]

I give the sum of five thousand dollars ($5,000) to my sister Elizabeth Johnson, if she survives me. If my sister does not survive me, this gift shall lapse and pass as part of my residuary estate.

[residuary clause]

I give my residuary estate, comprising all the rest, residue, and remainder of my estate, of whatever kind and wherever situated, including gifts that fail through lapse or otherwise, as follows:

(1) to my wife Mary A. Smith, if she survives me;

(2) if my wife Mary A. Smith predeceases me, my residuary estate shall be divided

into as many shares as there are surviving descendants of mine in the nearest degree of kinship and deceased descendants in the same degree who left descendants who survive me, and each surviving descendant in the nearest degree shall receive one share and the share of each deceased descendant in the same degree who left descendants who survive me shall be divided in the same manner among such descendants;

(3) if my wife Mary A. Smith and all of my descendants predecease me, one-half to my parents, William M. and Anne R. Smith, or the survivor of them if only one of my parents survives me, and one-half to the parents of my wife, Thomas E. and Eleanor C. Rundell, or the survivor of them if only one of my wife's parents survives me.

"Pretermitted heir" statutes are common. Under such a statute a child omitted from the will of his or her deceased parent may nonetheless in some cases be eligible to share in the parent's estate. A testator desiring to leave all of his or her estate to a surviving spouse should anticipate the possible application of a pretermitted heir statute and avoid it by appropriate language:

> Except as otherwise provided in this will, I intentionally make no provision for any child or other descendant of mine, whether born before or after the execution of this will.

Section (3) of the above residuary clause assumes that the married couple view their property as resulting from common effort, and that in the absence of a surviving spouse or descendants, it should be split between the families of the respective spouses. Property in an estate that is not disposed of by will passes in accordance with the applicable intestacy laws. Generally speaking, the intestacy laws direct the devolution of property to blood relatives of the decedent, not to relatives of a spouse who predeceased the decedent. If rather than naming persons specifically, the testator prefers generality at this point, an alternative to the language of Section (3) above is as follows:

> (3) if my wife and all of my descendants predecease me, one-half to my heirs and one-half to those persons who would have been the heirs of my wife had she died immediately after my death.

§ 5.6 CAVEATS

Do not direct that the debts (or the "just" debts) of the decedent, funeral expenses, taxes, and expenses of administration be paid. Payment of debts, taxes, and expenses is required by statute. A direction that "just" debts be paid may unnecessarily raise questions about payment of debts discharged in bankruptcy or debts barred by the statute of limitation. Specific directions to the executor concerning the procurement of a marker for the testator's grave, or the disposition of the testator's body, are appropriate parts of a will, although with respect to what are now called "anatomical gifts," sole reliance should not be put on the will.

Avoid expressions such as "per capita" or "per stirpes." These words are unfamiliar to laymen, and may be incomprehensible to the testator. Instead of "equally to my surviving children and the issue of any deceased child, per stirpes," specify the method of representation to be used in dividing property among the testator's descendants. Section (2) of the above residuary clause follows the "per capita with representation" method set forth in § 2–106 of the original Uniform Probate Code. If a strict per stirpes division is desired, the testator might direct that the residuary estate "be divided into as many shares as there are surviving children of mine and deceased children who left descendants who survive me, and each surviving child shall receive one share and the share of each deceased child who left descendants who survive me shall be divided in the same manner among such descendants."

Do not use precatory language in connection with a gift. "I give $1,000 to my brother John in the hope that he will use it for his family" may at least cause ill feeling should John disregard the testator's hope. Worse, it may provoke litigation.

Do not accept without further inquiry the testator's description of his or her property. A testator who says she wants her "new Cadillac" to go to her nephew John may mean "any automobile that I own at my death." The interval between execution of the will and the death of the testator (and changes in persons and property) should be considered in choosing language to describe the gift. Although at times it is undoubtedly wise to be quite specific, a more general description of property may afford the flexibility necessary to carry out the testator's intent reliably and accurately.

Avoid expressions such as "if my wife Mary and I die as a result of a common disaster. . . ." Persons may reasonably disagree on whether or not a particular event is a "common disaster." "If my wife Mary and I die at about the same time" is subject to a similar objection. If the testator desires that beneficiaries take only if they survive the testator by some specified period of time, a clause of this kind might be used:

> Any beneficiary under this will who dies within sixty (60) days after the date of my death shall be treated for the purposes of this will as having predeceased me.

Remember that given names are frequently common within a family. To avoid difficulties in identification, it may be necessary to identify a beneficiary by describing in full a blood relationship or using a street address. As opposed to writing "to my nephew James W. Smith," it may be essential to write "to my nephew James W. Smith, son of my brother John" if, for example, the testator has two nephews named James W. Smith.

Do not forget that if the intended beneficiary of a gift predeceases the testator, a gift by substitution may arise under an anti-lapse statute. The beneficiary of the gift arising under the anti-lapse statute may be a person to whom the testator prefers to leave nothing. Application of the anti-lapse statute can be anticipated and avoided. The will might read:

> I leave my two-carat diamond ring to my niece Alice Kendall; if my niece Alice Kendall predeceases me, I leave my two-carat diamond ring to my niece Amy Kendall. If both Alice Kendall and Amy Kendall predecease me, my two-carat diamond ring shall be disposed of as part of my residuary estate.

Be hesitant to create a legal life estate, or a legal life estate with a power to consume. Frequently the probate estate is so small that a legal life estate is altogether inadequate to achieve its intended purpose, quite aside from its other disagreeable characteristics. A power to consume provokes litigation. A testator with wealth sufficient to justify the creation of a life estate might consider creating a trust. (Nevertheless, if the testator insists on express provision in the will for successive enjoyment of an heirloom, the legal life estate with remainder may be appropriate.)

Do not disinherit a child of the testator or any other person by leaving a nominal bequest of one dollar. Simply write "I leave nothing to my daughter Margaret." The probate procedure ordinarily requires receipts from the beneficiaries. A beneficiary of one dollar is still a beneficiary. Leaving a beneficiary one dollar may amuse the testator, but it may cause unnecessary trouble for the personal representative in administering the estate.

Do not insert derogatory statements about beneficiaries or non-beneficiaries. The will is principally a dispositive document. It is not an appropriate device for airing grievances. However, it may be appropriate to indicate that the testator has thought of a particular person:

> Having made occasional gifts to my son John during my lifetime, I make no provision for him in this will.

§ 5.7 GUARDIANSHIP

Because the testator may die survived by one or more minor children (irrespective of whether the children's other parent survives the testator or dies first), the testator should consider the possible need for guardianship of the person and the estate of minor children. The law of guardianship, like the law of intestacy, wills, and administration of decedents' estates, varies from one state to another. But generally speaking, a court may be reluctant to appoint a non-resident of the state as guardian of the estate of a minor. On the other hand, a court may be quite willing to appoint as guardian of the person of a minor a non-resident nominated by the testator, especially if the nominee is a relative. The "guardian of the person" of a minor is responsible for the care of the minor. The "guardian of the estate" of a minor is responsible for managing the minor's property. Although the same person may (and on occasion should) act as guardian in both capacities, it is often preferable to designate different persons as guardian of the person and guardian of the estate. A person who is acceptable as guardian of the person may not be suitable to manage property. In any event, the testator should carefully consider the selection of guardians prior to the drafting of the will, and should confirm that the nominees are willing to serve in the capacities designated in the will. And here (as in the nomination of the executor), the testator should provide for an alternative or successor guardian. If we assume that the testator has left his entire estate to his spouse if she survives him, the guardianship clause might read as follows:

> If my wife Mary A. Smith predeceases me, and I am survived by a minor child or children, I nominate my sister Helen E. Smith to be guardian of the person and estate of such minor child or children. If my sister Helen E. Smith predeceases me, or is unable or unwilling to accept such appointment, or, having undertaken her duties, is unable or unwilling to continue to serve, then I nominate my sister Georgia R. Kendall to be guardian of the person and estate of such minor child or children. I direct that any guardian nominated by me be exempted from the requirement of furnishing bond.

Exemption from the requirement of furnishing bond should be a matter of thought, not form. The usual justifications for the exemption are that the nominated guardian is honest, and exemption from furnishing bond saves the cost of the bond. But even an honest person may err, and here (as elsewhere), the protection afforded by insurance may well be worth the price.

Where the prospective estate is more than nominal, a trusteeship should be considered as an alternative to guardianship of the estate. The usual (but not the only) argument for preferring trusteeship over guardianship is that trusteeship permits greater flexibility.

If the testator has a minor child who is already well beyond infancy at the time the will is executed, the testator might nominate as guardian of the person an individual selected by the minor child himself or herself from a group listed by the testator:

> If my wife Mary A. Smith predeceases me, and I am survived by my son Lawrence, still a minor at my death, then I nominate as guardian of the person of my son Lawrence that person selected by Lawrence from among the following: my sister Helen E. Smith, my sister Georgia R. Kendall, my brother Raymond S. Smith.

The matter of compatibility aside, consulting the minor child with respect to guardianship may reveal facets of the matter (geographical location of the nominee) that may be important to the minor but overlooked by the testator, or unknown (and unknowable) to the testator at the time the will is executed.

§ 5.8 NOMINATING THE EXECUTOR

If we assume that the testator has only a moderate amount of property (a residence, an automobile, and some bank accounts), and, in particular, that the testator is not operating a business that will require active and continuing management after death, it may be appropriate to nominate the surviving spouse as executor of the estate. As in nominating the guardian, so too in nominating the executor, the testator should anticipate an alternate or a successor. The clause might be drafted as follows:

> I nominate my wife Mary A. Smith to be executor of my last will. If my wife Mary A. Smith predeceases me, or is unable or unwilling to accept such appointment, or, having undertaken her duties, is unable or unwilling to continue to serve, then I nominate my sister Georgia R. Kendall to be executor of my last will. I direct that any executor nominated by me be exempted from the requirement of furnishing bond.

§ 5.9 POWERS OF THE EXECUTOR

An executor, like a guardian or a trustee, is a fiduciary charged with the responsibility of managing property for the benefit of others. Under the statutory or judge-made law on fiduciary administration, the executor often has limited powers to manage assets of the estate, and may be obliged to seek court approval before engaging in certain transactions.

Generally speaking, a testator may enlarge the scope of the executor's authority or grant the executor additional powers beyond those provided under applicable statutory or judge-made law. When the nominated fiduciary is a person of sound judgment in whom the testator has trust and confidence, it may be appropriate to provide freedom of action by enumerating broad powers in the will. Even if the executor has general authority under local law to perform routine acts of administration, third parties dealing with the executor may be more willing to proceed without explicit court approval if the executor's powers are expressly set out in the will itself. When the testator is a person of modest means, the clause on powers might be correspondingly brief:

> Without the necessity of obtaining leave of any court, my executor shall have full power: (1) to sell (at public or private sale), exchange, or otherwise dispose of any real or personal property in my estate, on such terms, for cash or credit, secured or unsecured, and in such manner as may seem advisable; (2) to borrow money, if deemed necessary or advisable, and to secure any such loan by mortgage or pledge of any property in my estate; (3) to settle, adjust, compromise, or pay claims asserted in favor of or against my estate, and to agree to any rescission or modification of any contract or agreement made by me; and (4) to make any required division or distribution wholly or partly in cash or in kind, whether or not the same type of property is distributed to others, and the valuation of any such distribution in kind determined by my executor shall be final and conclusive as to the distributee or distributees.

§ 5.10 THE CLOSING RECITATION

The effort of drafting a will is wasted if the will is not properly executed. The "testimonium" clause affords an opportunity to describe the format of the will (" . . . consisting of this page and the two preceding typewritten pages . . ."), the means used to identify pages not signed by the testator (" . . . initialed by me at the left margin thereof . . ."), and the circumstances, date, and place of execution:

> In witness whereof I have hereunto set my hand to this my last will, consisting of this page and the two preceding typewritten pages initialed by me at the left margin thereof, in the presence of the two persons who have at my request and in my presence and in the presence of each other acted as witnesses this _______ day of _______, 20__, at Columbus, Ohio.

Even if there is no statutory requirement that the date and place of execution appear in the will, the closing recitation should note both. The date of execution assists in determining whether or not the document offered for probate is the last will of the decedent. The place of execution is an index to compliance with the requirements for execution. Most jurisdictions accept as valid a will executed according to the law of the place of execution.

The usual place for the testator's signature is below the closing recitation and above the attestation clause. Typing the testator's name below the signature line assists in execution of the will. The testator should sign his or her name in the same form as it appears in the heading of the will and in the introductory clause. Only a single copy of the will should be executed. Executing a will in duplicate or triplicate should be avoided because failure to produce all executed copies at death may raise a presumption that the testator destroyed an executed copy with intent to revoke the will.

§ 5.11 THE ATTESTATION CLAUSE

The attestation clause affords an opportunity to state that the execution of the will complies with all requirements prescribed by law. Even though modern wills statutes generally require only two attesting witnesses, a cautious lawyer may prefer to use three, in case one of them dies or is unavailable for some other reason to testify in a probate proceeding. If the names and addresses of the witnesses are known in advance of execution, it is sensible to type each name and address immediately below the line on which each signs as an attesting witness. Locating a witness may be important for purposes of probating (proving) the will. A will may be proved if all of the witnesses are dead, but one starts by trying to get the witnesses themselves. Furthermore, typing in the names minimizes confusion at the time of signing. If names and addresses are not known in advance of execution, they should be typed thereafter on a carbon copy or photocopy of the will for record purposes. The attestation clause might read as follows:

> The foregoing instrument of three typewritten pages, including this page, was signed at the end

by William J. Smith and acknowledged by him to be his last will before us and in our presence, and subscribed by us as attesting witnesses in his presence, at his request, and in the presence of each other on the day and year last above written. And we and each of us declare that we believe William J. Smith to be of sound mind and memory.

§ 5.12 EXECUTION

Witnesses to the will should be younger than the testator, in good health, and likely to be available at probate of the will. Although all witnesses should be acquainted with the testator, none should be a beneficiary under the will (or married to a beneficiary). The lawyer drafting the will is a permissible (some say desirable) witness. In advance of execution the lawyer should explain to the testator that although the witnesses need not know the contents of the will, they must be told that they are being asked to attest to execution of the testator's will (as opposed to some other kind of document).

The lawyer, the testator, and all witnesses being assembled, the testator should state to the witnesses that the document to be signed is his or her will and request that they act as witnesses. In the presence of the witnesses, the testator then initials the pages of the will preceding the last page and signs the will at the end. The witnesses should have a clear and unobstructed view of the testator's execution of the will. The witnesses then read the attestation clause (or one witness reads the clause aloud, the others listening) and sign their respective names (and write their addresses, if not previously provided) following the attestation clause.

If the lawyer drafting the will believes that the testamentary capacity of the testator (ability to execute a will) might be questioned, the lawyer might sensibly arrange to have the entire execution ceremony videotaped. A carefully prepared videotape may be more compelling as evidence of testamentary capacity than the recollections of attesting witnesses offered long after the time of execution.

§ 5.13 THE "SELF-PROVED" WILL

By statute in many states, a will may be "self-proved" by means of an affidavit which may be an integral part of the will or a separate instrument attached to a previously executed will. The affidavit preserves the sworn testimony of the witnesses, taken at the time of execution, which raises a presumption of due execution and makes it possible to dispense with live witness testimony in the probate proceeding following the testator's death. For example, § 2–504(a) of the Uniform Probate Code provides in part as follows:

> A will . . . may be simultaneously executed, attested, and made self-proved, by acknowledgment thereof by the testator and affidavits of the witnesses, each made before an officer authorized to administer oaths under the laws of the state in which execution occurs and evidenced by the officer's certificate, under official seal. . . .

The affidavits are required to take "substantially" the following form:

> I, ______, the testator, sign my name to this instrument this ______ day of ______, and being first duly sworn, do hereby declare to the undersigned authority that I sign and execute this instrument as my will and that I sign it willingly (or willingly direct another to sign for me), that I execute it as my free and voluntary act for the purposes therein expressed, and that I am [18] years of age or older, of sound mind, and under no constraint or undue influence.
>
> ______________________
> Testator
>
> We, ______, ______, the witnesses, sign our names to this instrument, being first duly sworn, and do hereby declare to the undersigned authority that the testator signs and executes this instrument as (his) (her) will and that (he) (she) signs it willingly (or willingly directs another to sign for (him) (her)), and that each of us, in the presence and hearing of the testator, hereby signs this will as witness to the testator's signing, and that to the best of our knowledge the testator is [18] years of age or older, of sound mind, and under no constraint or undue influence.

____
Witness

____
Witness

STATE of ______

COUNTY of ______

Subscribed, sworn to and acknowledged before me by ______, the testator, and subscribed and sworn to before me by ______, and ______, witnesses, this ______ day of ______.

(Seal)

(Signed) ____________________

____
(Official capacity of officer)

Alternatively, § 2–504(b) of the Uniform Probate Code permits a previously executed will to be made self-proved by attaching to it an affidavit in "substantially" the following form:

STATE of ______

COUNTY of ______

We, ______, ______, and ______, the testator and the witnesses, respectively, whose names are signed to the attached or foregoing instrument, being first duly sworn, do hereby declare to the undersigned authority that the testator signed and executed the instrument as the testator's will and that (he) (she) had signed willingly (or willingly directed another to sign for (him) (her)), and that (he) (she) executed it as (his) (her) free and voluntary act for the purposes therein expressed, and that each of the witnesses, in the presence and hearing of the testator, signed the will as witness and that to the best of (his) (her) knowledge the testator was at that time [18] years of age or older, of sound mind, and under no constraint or undue influence.

____
Testator

____
Witness

____
Witness

Subscribed, sworn to and acknowledged before me by ______, the testator, and subscribed and sworn to before me by ______, and ______, witnesses, this ______ day of ______.

(Seal)

(Signed) ____________________

____
(Official capacity of officer)

§ 5.14 STATUTORY WILLS

A few states have enacted statutes which set forth simple will forms for use by the general public. The statutory forms include standard introductory and concluding language (exordium, testimonium, and attestation clauses) as well as generic dispositive and administrative provisions, with blank spaces for specific details concerning the testator, executor, and beneficiaries. Although these forms make it easy for a testator to prepare and execute a will without the assistance of an attorney, they are suitable only for a limited range of situations and should be used with caution.

§ 5.15 SAFEGUARDING THE WILL

Two additional copies or photocopies of the unexecuted will should be made. These copies can be "conformed" to the executed will by inserting the typewritten names of the testator and the witnesses over the signature lines, and similarly completing any other handwritten information (e.g., the date of execution and the addresses of the witnesses) from the original will. The conformed copies accurately reflect the contents of the will but they cannot be confused with the original, executed will. One such copy should be kept by the lawyer who drafted the will and one should be kept by the testator. The original, executed will should be kept by the testator in a secure location such as a safe deposit box, or deposited with the probate court (if permitted by applicable state law).

A conformed copy of any prior will or wills should also be made and deposited with the lawyer who drafted the last will, and thereafter any extant original prior will or wills should be destroyed by the testator, or at the testator's direction in his or her presence. (If two different original "wills" are found after the testator's death, both might be offered for probate, creating unnecessary problems and possibly defeating the testator's wishes.)

§ 5.16 LISTS OF PROPERTY AND BENEFITS

Because the testator may own a great variety of both real and personal property at death, and because surviving beneficiaries may become entitled at the testator's death to joint-and-survivor accounts, life insurance proceeds, pension benefits, Social Security benefits, and the like (many of which are unaffected by the provisions of the will), the testator should be encouraged to prepare lists of owned assets (and their locations) and lists of other benefits available to surviving beneficiaries. In addition, the testator should prepare a separate list of "digital assets," including e-mail accounts, on-line financial accounts, weblogs and social media accounts, with user names and passwords, to preserve access to important personal and financial information upon disability or death. These lists should be reviewed periodically to ensure that they are up to date. They should be as complete as possible, so that essential information known to the testator about his or her property (but neither known nor easily ascertained by others) is readily available to the family and the personal representative at the testator's death. (A properly prepared list, for example, facilitates giving notice to insurance companies of the death of the insured and collecting insurance proceeds expeditiously.) These periodically reviewed lists might be accompanied by such written suggestions as the testator might think appropriate with respect to the enumerated items. A testator may have sensible suggestions to make that are not appropriate parts of a will, but that are nonetheless worth committing to paper. Because of the great variety of rights in property that can exist today, even in persons of moderate means, it is conceivable that a list of property and benefits, properly prepared and updated, with accompanying suggestions, may be almost as important to a decedent's family as the will itself.

§ 5.17 A "SIMPLE WILL" IN ITS ENTIRETY, WITH SELF-PROVING AFFIDAVIT

WILL OF WILLIAM J. SMITH

I, William J. Smith, also known as William John Smith, William Smith, and Will Smith, of the City of Columbus, County of Franklin, and State of Ohio, do make, publish, and declare this to be my last will, and I hereby revoke all wills and codicils heretofore made by me.

I give all of my property, of whatever kind and wherever situated, as follows:

(1) to my wife Mary A. Smith, if she survives me;

(2) if my wife Mary A. Smith predeceases me, my property shall be divided into as many shares as there are surviving descendants of mine in the nearest degree of kinship and deceased descendants in the same degree who left descendants who survive me, and each surviving descendant in the nearest

degree shall receive one share and the share of each deceased descendant in the same degree who left descendants who survive me shall be divided in the same manner among such descendants;

(3) if my wife Mary A. Smith and all of my descendants predecease me, one-half to my parents, William M. and Anne R. Smith, or the survivor of them if only one of my parents survives me, and one-half to the parents of my wife, Thomas E. and Eleanor C. Rundell, or the survivor of them if only one of my wife's parents survives me.

Except as otherwise provided in this will, I intentionally make no provision for any child or other descendant of mine, whether born before or after the execution of this will.

If my wife Mary A. Smith predeceases me, and I am survived by a minor child or children, I nominate my sister Helen E. Smith to be guardian of the person and estate of such minor child or children. If my sister Helen E. Smith predeceases me, or is unable or unwilling to accept such appointment, or, having undertaken her duties, is unable or unwilling to continue to serve, then I nominate my sister Georgia R. Kendall to be guardian of the person and estate of such minor child or children. I direct that any guardian nominated by me be exempted from the requirement of furnishing bond.

I nominate my wife Mary A. Smith to be executor of my last will. If my wife Mary A. Smith predeceases me, or is unable or unwilling to accept such appointment, or, having undertaken her duties, is unable or unwilling to continue to serve, then I nominate my sister Georgia R. Kendall to be executor of my last will. I direct that any executor nominated by me be exempted from the requirement of furnishing bond.

Without the necessity of obtaining leave of any court, my executor shall have full power: (1) to sell (at public or private sale), exchange, or otherwise dispose of any real or personal property in my estate, on such terms, for cash or credit, secured or unsecured, and in such manner as may seem advisable; (2) to borrow money, if deemed necessary or advisable, and to secure any such loan by mortgage or pledge of any property in my estate; (3) to settle, adjust, compromise, or pay claims asserted in favor of or against my estate, and to agree to any rescission or modification of any contract or agreement made by me; and (4) to make any required division or distribution wholly or partly in cash or in kind, whether or not the same type of property is distributed to others, and the valuation of any such distribution in kind determined by my executor shall be final and conclusive as to the distributee or distributees.

In witness whereof I have hereunto set my hand to this my last will, consisting of this page and the two preceding typewritten pages initialed by me at the left margin thereof, in the presence of the two persons who have at my request and in my presence and in the presence of each other acted as witnesses this ______ day of ______, 20__, at Columbus, Ohio.

____
WILLIAM J. SMITH

The foregoing instrument of three typewritten pages, including this page, was signed at the end by William J. Smith and by him acknowledged to be his last will before us and in our presence, and by us subscribed as attesting witnesses in his presence, at his request, and in the presence of each other on the day and year last above written. And we and each of us declare that we believe William J. Smith to be of sound mind and memory.

________________ residing at ________________

________________ residing at ________________

STATE of ______

COUNTY of ______

We, ______, ______, and ______, the testator and the witnesses, respectively, whose names are signed to the attached or foregoing instrument, being first duly sworn, do hereby declare to the undersigned authority that the testator signed and executed the instrument as the testator's will and that (he) (she) had signed willingly (or willingly directed another to sign for (him) (her)), and that (he) (she) executed it as (his) (her) free and voluntary act for the purposes therein expressed, and that each of the witnesses, in the presence and hearing of the testator, signed the will as witness and that to the best of (his) (her) knowledge the testator was at that time [18] years of age or older, of sound mind, and under no constraint or undue influence.

____

Testator

____

Witness

____

Witness

Subscribed, sworn to and acknowledged before me by _______, the testator, and subscribed and sworn to before me by _______, and _______, witnesses, this _______ day of 20__.

(Seal)

(Signed) __________________________

____

(Official capacity of officer)

CHAPTER 6
INSURANCE

§ 6.1 INSURANCE AND ESTATE PLANNING

For a prospective decedent, insurance on his or her own life is important because it augments or creates an estate, using the word "estate" in the largest sense. Because the proceeds of a life insurance contract (the "policy") are commonly payable under the policy directly to the surviving spouse of the insured decedent (the "life insured" or the "insured"), or to some other designated beneficiary (as differentiated from the estate of the insured), the proceeds ordinarily are not subject to administration as part of the decedent's probate estate.

Various kinds of insurance commonly lumped together and referred to by lawyers as "property and liability" insurance (including, for example, homeowner's or renter's insurance, automobile insurance, and casualty insurance) are also important in ordering one's affairs because they protect against losses that might deplete or exhaust altogether the assets that the prospective decedent is accumulating to leave to his or her family. The owner whose property is protected against loss under a property or liability insurance policy is also commonly called the "insured."

A homeowner's insurance policy commonly covers loss or damage to real and personal property caused by fire, theft, or vandalism. It might also cover loss or damage caused by natural disasters such as windstorm, flood, earthquake, or landslide. A person who does not own his or her own home may obtain similar coverage for loss or damage to personal property under a renter's policy. Casualty insurance includes the liability insurance that is a characteristic feature of automobile insurance and of some homeowner's insurance policies.

Traditionally, an insurance policy has been viewed as a contract of indemnity—the insurer agrees to pay because of a loss suffered. (A "bond" issued by a surety company is not usually considered to be a contract of insurance. The law on insurance and the law on suretyship overlap to some extent, but each has its own history.) Because a contract of insurance even today is basically a contract to indemnify for a loss, a person buying insurance should be informed about the "coverage" under a policy—that is, what losses are insured against. In this connection, the most reliable source of information is the insurance policy itself. It is undeniably true that (say) a homeowner's policy is replete with "exclusions," "deductibles," "conditions," and "endorsements," and that often only a person experienced in insurance matters can determine the scope of coverage in a particular case. Nonetheless, any policy of insurance should be examined when received. For example, a buyer should be able to determine by reading a policy whether the dollar amount of coverage is sufficient to provide the desired level of protection.

Because a person's circumstances change as time passes, it is desirable to review (that is, to think systematically about) one's insurance periodically. For example, as the insured under a homeowner's policy acquires additional possessions (or as inflation runs its course), he or she might consider increasing the dollar amount of coverage under the policy. Upon marriage or the birth of a child, a person who previously had no dependents might consider taking out a life insurance policy. Because ours is an increasingly litigious society, a person who once might reasonably have thought of liability insurance in connection with high-risk medical practice, today might seriously consider purchasing such insurance to protect ordinary assets from depletion through litigation.

§ 6.2 WHY LIFE INSURANCE?

There are various kinds of life insurance, and innumerable life insurance "plans." Regardless of the kind of insurance on a person's life, if the insured dies while the policy remains in force (and there is no effective "defense" available to the insurer), the proceeds are payable to the designated beneficiary. This result follows even though the proceeds payable under the policy (the "face amount") may be $100,000 and the total premiums paid may be only $5,000 when death occurs. The ability to create what is sometimes called an "instant estate" through life insurance is of particular interest to the prospective decedent who has little or no accumulated property. Such a person might be young, never having had an opportunity to pursue a systematic saving strategy, or middle-aged and unable to accumulate much property. In either case, by maintaining an insurance policy on his or her own life, a person of modest means can provide some financial protection for dependents or other beneficiaries in the event of early death.

Even if there is no need to create an instant estate, a person might sensibly consider buying life insurance to provide ready cash to meet obligations incident to death—for example, funeral costs, debts, family living expenses, and death taxes. Having cash available from insurance proceeds to make such payments may avoid a forced sale of estate assets under unfavorable market conditions.

Because of the way payments for insurance ("premiums") are calculated, life insurance other than "term" insurance includes a forced savings feature. During the early years of the contract, the premium paid is greater than the sum required for "pure" insurance protection, and the savings accumulate in the hands of the insurer. Consequently, the insurance policy has a "cash surrender" value. The owner of a policy (the "policyholder") who decides to terminate the insurance can surrender the policy to the issuing company (the "insurer") and receive its then cash surrender value. More importantly, because the insurance includes a savings feature, the policy can be pledged to an individual or a commercial lender as security for a loan. The policy by its terms may allow the policyholder to pledge it as security for a loan from the insurance company, often at a favorable rate. Although on (say) an "ordinary life" policy, premiums are payable during the lifetime of the insured, if the policyholder "drops" the insurance, that is, fails or ceases to pay premiums, the policyholder may be able to avoid a "lapse" of the policy by using the accumulated value to convert to "paid up" life insurance with a reduced face amount. If the policyholder lives to retirement age, the policy by its terms may enable the policyholder to draw retirement benefits payable over a period of years from the accumulated savings. (While accumulating, the savings are not includible in the policyholder's gross income for federal income tax purposes.)

Life insurance may play an important role in planning for the orderly succession of a closely held business. The owners of the business—shareholders in the case of a corporation, or partners in the case of a partnership—may wish to ensure that when one of them dies, the business will continue in the hands of the surviving owner or owners. To this end, they may enter into a "buy-sell" agreement which provides for the sale of a deceased owner's interest in the business on specified terms. Under a "cross-purchase" agreement, the surviving owners would have the right (or perhaps the obligation) to purchase the decedent's interest for a specified price; alternatively, under a "redemption" agreement, the business entity itself would be the purchaser. In either case, a policy of insurance on the life of each owner, with proceeds payable at death to the other owners (in the case of a cross-purchase agreement) or to the entity (in the case of a redemption agreement), provides a timely, reliable, and convenient source of funds to purchase the decedent's interest.

Even a person of modest means might procure life insurance to fund a trust for the benefit of the decedent's family. Instead of directing that the proceeds be paid out to the beneficiaries immediately at the death of the insured in a "lump sum," or paid out over time under a "settlement option," the proceeds might be paid to a trustee with discretion to make distributions from time to time to the trust beneficiaries in accordance with their respective needs and requirements.

Finally, a person may automatically receive life insurance coverage in connection with his or her employment. Many employers provide life insurance for their employees as a mandatory fringe benefit, which the employees cannot elect to forego. This protection is commonly provided through "group" life insurance, usually in the form of an annually renewable group term policy.

§ 6.3 LIFE INSURANCE PROCEEDS UNDER STATE LAW AND UNDER THE FEDERAL ESTATE TAX

Because the life insurance industry is well established and influential, a policy of life insurance or its proceeds may be eligible for preferential treatment compared to other types of property under state law. If a decedent leaves assets at death that are subject to administration as part of the probate estate, any debts of the decedent that are allowed as claims against the estate (as well as expenses incurred in administering the estate) are payable from estate assets. (As a consequence, the probate assets may be exhausted, leaving none for distribution to the decedent's testate or intestate successors.) By way of contrast, suppose a decedent dies owning an insurance policy on his own life, payable to his surviving spouse. Because the proceeds are payable directly to the beneficiary under the terms of the insurance policy, they are not subject to administration as part of the probate estate. By statute in most states, life insurance proceeds payable to or for the benefit of a decedent's surviving spouse, children or certain other relatives are wholly or partially exempt from claims of the decedent's creditors. Furthermore, if life insurance proceeds are held by the insurer or by a trustee after the insured's death, the undistributed proceeds may be protected from claims of the beneficiaries' creditors if the insurance policy or the trust agreement contains a valid "spendthrift" clause.

The federal estate tax treatment of insurance proceeds on a decedent's life is governed by § 2042 of the Internal Revenue Code. That provision applies the "incidents of ownership" test to determine whether life insurance proceeds payable to a beneficiary (other than the estate) are includible in the decedent's "gross estate"—that is, the estate for federal estate tax purposes. (The gross estate may include, and commonly does include, property in addition to that included in the decedent's probate estate.) The term "incidents of ownership" generally refers to the economic benefits of the policy, including the right to change the beneficiary of the policy, the right to surrender or cancel the policy, the right to assign the policy, the right to pledge the policy as security for a loan, and the right to obtain a loan from the insurer against the cash surrender value of the policy. If a decedent held any one or more incidents of ownership at death, the proceeds of the policy on his or her life are includible in the gross estate for federal estate tax purposes. Inclusion may also occur if the decedent transferred or relinquished incidents of ownership within three years before death. However, if the decedent irrevocably assigned all rights in the policy to another person at least three years before death, no part of the proceeds is includible in the gross estate. As a result, a decedent may pass proceeds of insurance on his or her own life to beneficiaries free from the federal estate tax, even though the decedent personally procured the policy and paid the premiums on the policy from the time of procurement until death, as long as the decedent divested himself or herself of all incidents of ownership in the policy at least three years before death.

§ 6.4 WHY PROPERTY AND LIABILITY INSURANCE?

Property insurance protects the insured against loss or damage to real or personal property arising from various kinds of perils or hazards. Liability insurance protects the insured against loss arising from legal liability.

If a person owns property outright, such as a house or an automobile, ordinary experience suggests that it may be prudent to procure property insurance to guard against the risk of loss or damage to the property. Experience also suggests that ownership of property may expose the owner to a risk of legal liability. For example, a house guest might be injured on the premises and bring suit against the property owner alleging negligence in failing to maintain the premises. The property owner may carry liability insurance to guard against the depletion of assets as a result of being held legally liable for loss or injury to another.

A trustee of a private express trust or a charitable trust (irrespective of whether the trustee is an individual or a corporation) is not the beneficial owner of the property held in trust—the beneficial ownership is in one or more individual beneficiaries (of whom the trustee might be one) in the case of the private trust, and in the public in the case of the charitable trust. Nonetheless, the trustee, like the executor or administrator of an estate, is under a fiduciary obligation to preserve and protect the property that is the subject matter of the trust. Fulfilling that duty may require, and ordinarily does require, procuring property and liability insurance to protect the trust property against loss or damage.

§ 6.5 INSURABLE INTEREST

An insurance policy is essentially a contract for indemnity, that is, reimbursement for loss or damage. The indemnity principle underlies a doctrine called "insurable interest"—a contract of insurance is valid only if the policyholder has an insurable interest in the subject matter of the contract, irrespective of whether it is life or property.

As to life insurance, an insurable interest must exist at the time the contract is made. It need not exist at the death of the life insured. As to property insurance, an insurable interest must exist at the time of loss. It often exists both at the time a property insurance contract is made and when loss occurs. For example, suppose that A, the owner and occupier of a single-family residence, procures fire insurance covering the house. Thereafter, while A is in possession and the policy is in force, a fortuitous fire damages the house. A had an insurable interest both at the time she procured the fire policy and at the time the loss occurred.

It is said that everyone has an insurable interest in his or her own life. All this means is that a person who is legally competent may validly contract for insurance on his or her own life, designating anyone as beneficiary. A more useful statement is that a person generally may procure insurance on his or her own life without regard to insurable interest. However, if one seeks to procure a contract of insurance on the life of another person, one must have an insurable interest in the other person's life.

Some kinds of family relationships give rise to generally recognized insurable interests. In the case of a married couple, each spouse has an insurable interest in the life of the other spouse. A parent has an insurable interest in the life of his or her minor child, and the minor child has an insurable interest in the life of the parent. Beyond these close family relationships, however, generalization on family relationship as a basis for insurable interest is difficult.

Outside the family relationships that give rise to an insurable interest, some kinds of business relationships suffice. A creditor has an insurable interest in the life of a debtor, a partner in the life of another partner, and a business entity in the life of a key employee.

There are three bases of insurable interest in property that deserve mention: property right, contract right, and legal liability.

A person who owns a valuable commercial building outright has a property right that may be destroyed altogether or diminished if the building is destroyed or damaged by fire. The owner therefore has an insurable interest in the building. Even if the building were mortgaged as security for a debt, the owner of the building has a property right, and therefore an insurable interest, and the creditor has a property right, and therefore an insurable interest. Either can lawfully procure insurance against loss by fire or similar hazard. (Commonly, only the owner procures insurance, with proceeds in the event of loss being payable to both mortgagor and mortgagee as their interests appear.)

Even a person who is not the outright owner of property may nonetheless have a relation to the property, based on a legal right or duty, such that he or she will derive a benefit from its continuing existence or suffer a loss or liability because of its destruction or damage. A merchant who contracts to buy goods at a distance on condition that the goods arrive safely at his or her place of business has an insurable interest in the goods because the merchant will suffer a loss of expected profit if the goods do not arrive safely. Here, a contract right is the basis for the merchant's insurable interest in goods. Similarly, a building contractor who contracts to build a structure on the land of another has an insurable interest in the building as construction progresses because the contractor is obligated to rebuild the structure if it is fortuitously damaged or destroyed before acceptance by the owner. Here, a contract duty is the basis for the contractor's insurable interest in the building.

A person may have a property right with respect to property, and also a duty with respect to the property, resulting in an insurable interest in the property based on more than one ground. A trustee of a private express trust ordinarily has legal title to the property held in trust. The trustee is under a fiduciary duty to preserve and protect the trust property, and in the event of a breach of that duty the trustee may be liable in damages to the beneficiaries of the trust. The trustee has an insurable interest in the trust property, based both on his or her property right as holder of legal title to the trust property and on his or her potential liability for breach of the duty to preserve and protect the trust property.

In virtually every instance in which a person seeks insurance for a sensible purpose, he or she will be found to have an insurable interest, and therefore the doctrine is usually not a bar to advantageous arrangement of one's personal and business affairs. But lack of insurable interest is a defense occasionally raised by an insurer in an action on a policy. A lawyer or an insurance advisor should be aware of it.

§ 6.6 KINDS OF LIFE INSURANCE

There are many variations in the terms and conditions that make up a life insurance plan. Below are some terms commonly employed to identify various types of life insurance.

"Whole life" insurance provides coverage during the entire lifetime of the insured and the proceeds become payable only at death. Whole life insurance can be differentiated further. In the case of "ordinary" or "straight" life insurance, premiums are payable either throughout the lifetime of the insured or until attainment of a specified advanced age (say, 100 years). In the case of "limited payment" life insurance, premiums are payable over a specified period of time (say, 20 years) or until the occurrence of a specified event (such as attaining age 60). Under a limited payment plan, the premiums are higher, and at the end of the payment period the policy is "paid up"; no further premium payments are required to maintain insurance coverage, and the face amount of the policy is payable at the death of the insured, whenever that may occur. "Single premium" life insurance is what the words imply. Instead of paying periodic premiums over time, the purchaser pays only one premium at the outset to procure the policy. "Joint life" insurance covers more than one life (commonly, a married couple or business partners). The face amount is payable on the death of the first of the insured lives. Under a "survivorship" policy, a variation of joint life insurance, the proceeds become payable at the death of the last of the insured lives.

"Endowment" life insurance provides for payment of a specified sum if the insured dies within a specified endowment period (usually a fixed number of years, or the attainment of a fixed age), or for payment at the end of the endowment period if the insured survives the endowment period. An endowment policy functions essentially as a savings plan, providing a guaranteed source of funds at a definite future time (e.g., retirement) along with insurance protection against the insured's death during the endowment period.

Both whole life and endowment policies include a forced savings feature. Although the risk of death increases with the age of the insured, the premiums remain fixed at the same amount ("level") throughout the time that they are payable. Consequently, the policyholder pays more than is required for pure insurance protection during the early years, and the excess payments generate an accumulation of cash value which is used to subsidize the increased cost of pure insurance protection during the later years.

Both "universal" and "variable" life insurance policies include a cash value component. A universal policy allows the policyholder to adjust the premium payments and the amount of insurance coverage, within limits. Premium payments are credited (after deductions for the cost of pure insurance protection and expenses) to a cash value account, which earns interest at a guaranteed minimum rate, plus any additional amount declared by the insurer from investment earnings. A variable policy generally requires fixed premium payments and provides a guaranteed minimum amount of insurance. The cash value of the policy is allocated to one or more mutual funds or other investment vehicles selected by the policyholder, and the investment performance of the cash value account determines the amount, if any, of additional insurance coverage provided by the policy.

"Term" life insurance is sometimes referred to as pure insurance—it has no savings feature. If the insured dies while the contract is in force, that is, during the term of the policy—commonly one year or five years—a stated sum is payable to the designated beneficiary. Because term insurance has no savings feature, it has no cash surrender value. And once the current term expires, the insurance policy is no longer in force unless it is renewed. Nonetheless, term insurance often plays an important role in estate planning. The lack of a savings feature means that a term policy can be purchased for considerably less than a whole life policy with a comparable face amount. Term insurance is often sold as "mortgage" insurance, for the purpose of providing a guaranteed source of payment for a mortgage on the family home in the event that the insured dies while the mortgage is still outstanding. The term insurance contract might by its terms give the policyholder an option to renew insurance coverage for an additional term without regard to the insured's state of health at the time of renewal. The policy might also allow the policyholder to convert the policy from term insurance to a more permanent type of life insurance, without regard to the insured's state of health at the time of conversion.

A life insurance policy, whether of whole life or term insurance, is said to be a "participating" policy if the policyholder is entitled to "dividends." (If the policy does not pay dividends, it is a "non-participating" policy.) Insurance dividends should not be confused with dividends paid to shareholders of a corporation. An insurance dividend is an annual payment made to the policyholders by the insurance company in its discretion, and represents a refund of excess premiums previously paid. Accordingly, the policyholder's actual cost for a policy in a given year is determined by subtracting the dividends received (if any) from the total premiums paid.

§ 6.7 SETTLEMENT OPTIONS

"Settlement options" are provisions of a life insurance policy that permit flexibility in the manner in which the proceeds are paid to the beneficiary following the death of the insured. Instead of paying all of the proceeds to the beneficiary in a lump sum immediately upon the death of the insured, the insurer may agree to retain the proceeds and pay them out over time in accordance with the terms of a settlement option. If the policyholder is the same person as the life insured (as is often the case), the policyholder might personally select a settlement option before death. (Some courts have held that the right to select the method of payment under a settlement option is an "incident of ownership" that could cause the proceeds to be included in the decedent's gross estate for federal estate tax purposes.) Alternatively, it might be left to the beneficiary to select the method of payment under a settlement option.

The insurer who pays in accordance with the terms of a settlement option does not hold the proceeds of the policy in trust. Insurance is a contractual device. Payment of the proceeds of a life insurance policy is the fulfillment of a contractual obligation, whether payment is in a lump sum or under a settlement option. In a particular case, payment under a settlement option to the beneficiary over a period of time might well be preferable to payment of the proceeds in a lump sum, but it might be possible to achieve even greater flexibility in payment by designating a trustee to receive the entire proceeds and using a separate trust instrument to govern the manner of distribution by the trustee to the person or persons intended by the policyholder to benefit ultimately from the proceeds. Payment of the proceeds to a trustee in the way just described gives rise to a private express trust, with the proceeds of the policy constituting the trust property. Both life insurers and trustees are ordinarily investors of funds, but a trustee holding life insurance proceeds in trust can be given investment powers that are tailored to the circumstances of the individual trust beneficiaries, and the trustee can be given a discretionary power to make distributions to the beneficiaries from time to time in accordance with their respective needs. In sum, settlement options provide some flexibility in paying out the proceeds of a policy, but they do not achieve the full measure of flexibility available through a private express trust.

§ 6.8 KINDS OF SETTLEMENT OPTIONS

Under an "interest" or "deposit" settlement option, the proceeds of a life insurance policy are left with the insurer, and only periodic payments of interest are made to the beneficiary. At a predetermined time, the proceeds themselves are payable to the beneficiary. Usually interest is payable at a guaranteed minimum rate, but the minimum rate is low. (By way of contrast, an ordinary income interest payable from a trust is not guaranteed, and depending on investment experience, the income forthcoming in a particular case may be negligible.)

An "installment" option is either for a fixed amount or for a fixed period of time. Under a "fixed amount" or "installment amount" option, periodic payments of both policy proceeds and income are made to the beneficiary until policy proceeds and income are exhausted. Under a "fixed period" or "installment time" option, periodic payments of both policy proceeds and income are made to the beneficiary for a predetermined period of time, the amount of each payment being dependent upon both the total amount available for distribution and the length of time over which periodic payments are to be made. Under a fixed amount option, if the first or "primary" beneficiary dies before the funds are exhausted, the balance is payable to one or more "secondary" beneficiaries. Under a fixed time option, if the primary beneficiary dies before the predetermined period of time has elapsed, the periodic payment is payable to the secondary beneficiary for the rest of the predetermined period.

Because neither the amount payable nor the number of payments is contingent upon the survival of the primary beneficiary, the options described above do not involve "life contingencies." Other options commonly available do involve life contingencies. The "straight" life annuity, the "joint and survivor" annuity, and some combination of the installment option and life annuity all make the amount or duration of payments dependent in whole or in part on the longevity of one or more beneficiaries.

Under a straight life annuity option, the proceeds of the policy are in substance used to pay level periodic payments to the primary beneficiary for life. Nothing is payable to the secondary beneficiary, even if the primary beneficiary dies shortly after the payments commence. By the same token, a straight life annuity option ensures that the primary beneficiary will continue to receive payments until his or her death. Unless the proceeds of the policy are unusually large, or the primary beneficiary is advanced in age, the periodic payments from a straight life annuity tend to be low in amount.

A "joint and survivor" annuity provides for periodic payments during the joint lifetime of two beneficiaries, with reduced payments (often half of the original amount) during the survivor's lifetime.

A combination of an installment option and a life annuity might take this form: The primary beneficiary receives a fixed amount per month for ten years or for life, whichever is the longer. If the primary beneficiary dies before the expiration of the ten-year "term certain," the fixed monthly payments become payable to the secondary beneficiary for the rest of the ten-year period, when the payments terminate.

§ 6.9 CHANGE OF LIFE INSURANCE BENEFICIARY

When a person procures a policy of life insurance on his or her own life, or on the life of another person (assuming the insurable interest requirement is met), the policyholder ordinarily retains the right to change the designation of the beneficiary of the proceeds of the policy without obtaining the beneficiary's consent. Under such circumstances, the beneficiary has no vested rights under the policy, but has a mere "expectancy." (The beneficiary's situation is comparable to that of a person who has been named as a devisee or legatee under the will of a living testator.) If the policyholder changes the beneficiary designation in accordance with the formalities prescribed in the policy, the change is effective even though the original beneficiary did not consent, or even though the original beneficiary had no knowledge of the change.

Indeed, if the policyholder clearly expresses in writing an intention to designate a new beneficiary and takes all reasonable steps within his or her power to accomplish that purpose, but dies before the change of beneficiary is made by the insurer in its records, the attempted change may be given effect under the doctrine of "substantial compliance," with the result that the new beneficiary (rather than the original beneficiary) will be entitled to the proceeds. For example, in Connecticut General Life Ins. Co. v. Gulley, 668 F.2d 325 (7th Cir. 1982), the insured designated his wife as the original beneficiary of a group life insurance policy maintained by his employer. Under the terms of the policy, the insured could change the beneficiary by filing a written request with the issuing company. The insured executed a proper form to change the beneficiary from his wife to his daughter and left the completed form with the daughter, telling her that he would retrieve the form and deliver it to his employer. One week later, before taking any further action, the insured suffered a fatal heart attack. Two days after his death, the daughter mailed the form to the employer. The insurer, faced with conflicting claims by the widow and the daughter, filed a bill of interpleader, paid the proceeds of the policy into court, and submitted the matter of who was entitled to payment to the court for decision. The court found that there was substantial compliance with the terms of the policy and held that the daughter, not the widow, was entitled to the proceeds.

Despite the existence of litigated cases demonstrating that a change of beneficiary can be made by substantial compliance with the policy provisions governing change, the policy provisions should be complied with in every respect whenever that is possible. A lawsuit is an expensive way to determine whether an attempted change of beneficiary will be given effect.

In particular, the policyholder should not attempt to change the beneficiary designation by will. The terms of the policy seldom authorize a change of beneficiary by will, and the courts generally hold that a policyholder's attempt to name a new beneficiary by will cannot be given effect under the doctrine of substantial compliance. In Stone v. Stephens, 99 N.E.2d 766 (Ohio 1951), for example, the insured had designated his wife Jeannette as beneficiary of his life insurance policy. Jeannette thereafter divorced the insured, and although the insured was aware of the divorce, he made no attempt to change the beneficiary of his insurance policy in accordance with its provisions. But in a subsequently executed will, the insured provided that if he died unmarried, all of his property, including his life insurance, should go to his grandmother. Both Jeannette and the grandmother survived the insured. The insurers paid the proceeds of the policies into court and submitted the matter of who was entitled to payment to the court for decision. It was held that the right to change the beneficiary was a personal right of the insured, exercisable only during his lifetime. The attempted change by will was ineffective, and Jeannette was therefore entitled to the proceeds as the designated beneficiary of the policy at the death of the insured.

Frequently a married policyholder names his or her spouse as the primary beneficiary to receive the proceeds of the policy at the death of the insured spouse. Upon separation or divorce, all beneficiary designations should be reviewed in light of the change in family circumstances, and any desired changes should be made in accordance with the terms of the policy. If the owner-insured spouse dies without having taken any action, the other spouse—who is still designated as the beneficiary in the policy—may be entitled to receive the proceeds, even if this result was not contemplated by the parties. Under § 2–804 of the Uniform Probate Code, a divorce or annulment automatically revokes a designation of the former spouse as the beneficiary, but this provision has not been enacted in all states, and in any event it does not apply if the couple remained legally married, even if they obtained a decree of separation.

Designation of the beneficiary may be irrevocable, and an irrevocable designation frequently occurs as an incident to the separation or divorce of a married couple. Irrevocable designation should ordinarily be avoided. If the policyholder has made an irrevocable designation of the beneficiary with the knowledge of the insurance company issuing the policy, the policyholder can no longer act effectively as sole owner of the policy. For example, if the policyholder wishes to surrender the policy and receive its cash value, it may be necessary to procure the consent of the designated beneficiary.

§ 6.10 ASSIGNMENT

"Assignment of insurance" is an expression that has more than one meaning. The meaning of "assignment," if determinable at all, depends on the context. "Assignment of insurance" might mean transfer of a right to money under an insurance policy after loss has occurred; it might mean transfer of all rights or some rights under a policy before loss has occurred; or it might mean transfer of "coverage" under a policy to a substituted "insured."

Some kinds of rights existing or arising under insurance policies are unquestionably transferable or "assignable" as it is usually said. For example, if proceeds have become payable under a life policy on the death of the insured, the beneficiary's right to the proceeds is a right to money that is assignable. Similarly, if loss has occurred under a policy of property insurance, the insured's right to payment is a right to money that is assignable. Of course, an assignment under the circumstances just suggested is subject to the general limitation that the assignor can transfer no greater rights than he or she had before the assignment. Therefore, any defenses available to the insurer before the assignment remain available to the insurer after assignment.

It is not assignment of insurance proceeds after loss that is of primary interest to a person arranging his or her personal and business affairs in the expectation of retirement or death. Rather, with respect to insurance of various kinds, such a person is concerned mainly with what can be transferred before loss has occurred. In this connection it is desirable to differentiate among life insurance, property insurance, and liability insurance. It is also desirable to know whether the transfer is made with the consent of the insurer. And for property and liability insurance purposes, it is essential to differentiate between an assignment of rights and a transfer of "coverage"—that is, substitution of another person as the "insured" under the policy. (The owner of a life insurance policy can transfer ownership to another person, but it is not possible to substitute another person as the insured under a life insurance policy.)

§ 6.11 ASSIGNMENT OF LIFE INSURANCE

The owner of a policy of (say) whole life insurance generally has the right to change the designated beneficiary, the right to surrender the policy for cash, and the right to pledge the policy for a loan. The policyholder may also have the right to receive any dividends paid by the insurer, and the right to designate a method of payment under a settlement option.

The owner of such a life insurance policy might transfer all of his or her rights irrevocably to another by way of gift or sale (thus making an "absolute" assignment), or might assign certain rights for the limited purpose (say) of providing security or collateral for a loan (thus making a "collateral" assignment). The insurance policy itself usually contains provisions concerning assignment, and the procedures set forth in the terms of the policy should be followed scrupulously to minimize controversy and litigation. Under modern policies of life insurance, prior to the death of the insured, the designated beneficiary has no enforceable rights in the policy or the proceeds of the policy merely by virtue of a revocable beneficiary designation. The policyholder generally retains the right to change the beneficiary designation, and the designated beneficiary has a mere expectancy in the proceeds. Therefore, if an assignment of rights in a policy is made in conformity with the provisions in the policy concerning assignment, the assignee has rights in the policy superior to those of the designated beneficiary. Although an assignment of rights is not a change of beneficiary, the assignee under an absolute assignment may be entitled to the proceeds of the policy on the death of the insured to the complete exclusion of the designated beneficiary. In the case of a collateral assignment to secure a debt, the assignee is entitled to priority in the proceeds only to the extent of the unpaid debt.

If assignment of rights in a life insurance policy is not made in conformity with the provisions in the policy concerning assignment, and the position of the insurer is not prejudiced by the failure to conform to the policy provisions, the assignee should have (and usually does have) rights in the policy superior to those of the designated beneficiary. But to determine priority at the cost of a lawsuit is to pay a high price for the failure of the assignor to follow the procedures for assignment set forth in the policy.

Although an absolute assignment of all rights in a life insurance policy may result from a sale to another, it is more likely to arise as a result of a gift. Here it is well to remember that a completed gift is not subject to revocation. Suppose that A, a widow, owns a policy of insurance on her own life. Wishing to exclude the proceeds of the policy from her gross estate for federal estate tax purposes, she gratuitously assigns all of her rights in the policy to her daughter B. B is married to C, and they have no children. B dies survived by A and by C. B's will leaves her entire estate to her husband C. B's estate includes the insurance policy on A's life, and it is irrelevant that in assigning all rights in the policy A intended to benefit only B, not C.

§ 6.12 ASSIGNMENT OF PROPERTY INSURANCE

A policy of property insurance is said to be a "personal" contract—the insurer is entitled to choose the person with whom he or she contracts in order to decrease the moral hazard. The property insurer assumes the risk of the insured's carelessness, but does not assume the risk of intentional destruction of the property by the insured in order to collect the proceeds of the policy.

Because a policy of property insurance is a personal contract, coverage under an existing policy is not extended automatically on transfer of the "insured" property to a new owner. For example, if A carries homeowner's insurance on her residence, and then sells the residence to B during the term of the policy and moves out, B is not covered by A's homeowner's policy. By way of contrast, if unspecified personal property in A's residence (for example, household furnishings and the like) is covered by a homeowner's policy, and A acquires additional furniture, the new acquisitions are covered by the existing insurance policy. But in this connection it bears emphasis that property insurance, like other kinds of insurance, has a dollar limitation on coverage. A dollar limitation on coverage that was adequate at one time may become inadequate with the passage of time.

Of course, if on sale of A's residence to B, A, A's insurer, and B all agree that on B's assuming ownership of the residence, B is to be substituted for A as the insured under the existing homeowner's policy, then B is covered. This arrangement is called a "novation" as a matter of contract law.

§ 6.13 ASSIGNMENT OF LIABILITY INSURANCE

Although automobile insurance is written with relation to a particular vehicle, a sale of the vehicle during the term of the policy does not carry insurance coverage with it. Tying the validity of a liability policy to vehicle ownership is illustrated in Bendall v. Home Indemnity Co., 238 So.2d 177 (Ala. 1970), where Susie, the named insured of an automobile liability policy had, together with her husband, signed a promissory note and a chattel mortgage to enable Wanda (Susie's sister) to purchase, and to become the registered owner of, an automobile. A person who was involved in an accident while the automobile was being driven by Wanda was joined as a defendant with Wanda, Susie, and Susie's husband, in a declaratory judgment suit brought by the insurer to determine its obligations. The court found that

Susie had no insurable interest to support liability coverage under the policy, that the liability insurance was therefore void, that the insurer was not obligated to defend Susie, her husband, or Wanda, and that the insurer was not obligated to pay any judgment against them in an action arising out of the accident.

CHAPTER 7

SOCIAL SECURITY, PRIVATE PENSION PLANS, AND OTHER ARRANGEMENTS BASED ON STATUS

§ 7.1 PROVIDING FOR DEPENDENTS THROUGH STATUS

Many people die each year in the United States without leaving much in the way of probate assets, yet their surviving family members may nonetheless be eligible to receive benefits based on their status or employment history. Such benefits do not originate in property arrangements with a survivorship feature intended to avoid probate, or in life insurance, or in something as sophisticated as a revocable trust. Rather, they originate in various plans or programs based on the status of the decedent as, for example, a worker covered by Social Security, or a participant in some other governmental or private pension plan, or a veteran of military service in the armed forces. To state the matter in another way, governments and other institutions and organizations over the years have created various arrangements to provide retirement benefits to older or disabled persons as well as benefits for their dependents and survivors. These benefits range considerably in amount and are payable under specified circumstances.

It is not feasible to consider (or even to list) all of the sources of benefits of the kind just mentioned.

Rather, what follows is a very brief introduction to: (1) the program of "social insurance" widely known (and often poorly understood) as Social Security, which provides benefits to retired or disabled workers and their dependents and to surviving family members of deceased workers; (2) private pension plans, established by employers to provide benefits to employees during retirement; (3) individual retirement accounts; and (4) governmental arrangements that provide benefits to veterans of the armed services (as differentiated from retired career service personnel). A brief examination of these distinct programs and arrangements gives some notion of both the scope of the benefits they provide and of the complex rules governing eligibility and payment for participants and for their dependents and survivors.

§ 7.2 SOCIAL SECURITY

Of the governmental arrangements, by far the most important is the Social Security system. Both the importance and the effect of Social Security are demonstrated by the following example: Suppose that A, married to B, and having several minor children, dies at age 30, survived by his spouse and children. At his death, A is "covered" and "fully insured" under Social Security. Total benefits payable to A's spouse and children over a period of years under Social Security might easily exceed $1 million.

For many millions of Americans, Social Security, like retirement or death, is a part of the future. Apart from payment of the Social Security tax (which from their standpoint might be simply a matter of another unavoidable payroll deduction), Social Security for these millions may be of little immediate interest. But for many other millions, some kind of Social Security benefit is a present reality.

The Social Security Act has been amended from time to time since its enactment in 1935, and further amendments are likely. That being so, it is more important to learn the basic structure of the benefits available, and to whom and under what conditions benefits are payable, than it is to master the details of the Social Security system, for those details will surely change over time. In its earliest years, Social Security covered only "insured" workers themselves, and provided retirement benefits. In 1939, the law was amended to provide benefits for survivors and dependents. Disability benefits were added in 1954. Medicare was added in 1965 and expanded in the 1970s. Exactly what is available under Social Security, and to whom, is very much a matter of current law, and that should be kept in mind when considering the material that follows.

There are two major programs of social insurance that are administered solely by the federal government. These are the program of old-age, survivors, and disability insurance (commonly known as "Social Security") and the program of health insurance (commonly known as "Medicare"). It is the Social Security program that is of primary interest to those arranging their property affairs.

At the inception of Social Security, "coverage" was confined principally to employees of business and industry. Over the years coverage has been extended to self-employed persons, federal civilian employees, members of the armed forces, farm and household employees, members of the clergy, and some state and local government employees. Today nine out of every ten workers in the United States are covered by Social Security. Covered employees pay a Social Security tax on their employment earnings, up to a specified amount. (And as one might expect, both the maximum amount of an employee's earnings subject to Social Security tax and the rate of the tax have increased from time to time.) This payroll tax, along with a similar tax imposed on employers, finances the old-age, survivors, disability, and health insurance benefits that are paid out each year to current Social Security and Medicare beneficiaries.

One of the most important features of Social Security is the "portability" (transferability) of status. If a person works for wages or salary as an employee covered under the Social Security system, and then changes jobs and goes to work for a different employer, the Social Security credits that the employee earned during the first job are a part of his or her Social Security record and are not lost when the employee takes the new job. (One of the drawbacks of many traditional private pension plans is that status as a covered employee is not transferable on a change of employment. There are exceptions, however. For example, a single pension system may be in effect throughout an industry. If so, employees who move from one employer to another within the industry do not lose their pension coverage.)

For purposes of arranging one's affairs for possible retirement and certain death, it should be emphasized that, under specified circumstances, Social Security provides benefits not only to a covered worker who is retired or disabled, but also to family members during the worker's life and after his or her death. It should also be emphasized that the amount of Social Security benefits, the classes of beneficiaries entitled to receive them, and the conditions for eligibility are specified by law and cannot be altered by any action on the part of a covered worker. In this connection, the planning has been done by Congress.

Although not essential for estate planning purposes, it is interesting to note that the payroll taxes collected each year to finance Social Security and Medicare benefits wind up in the "Federal Old-Age and Survivors Insurance Trust Fund," the "Federal Disability Insurance Trust Fund," and the "Federal Hospital Insurance Trust Fund." To the extent not needed to pay benefits for current beneficiaries, these funds are invested in U.S. Treasury obligations. In effect, the excess payroll taxes collected each year are borrowed from the trust funds and used to pay for other government outlays. According to current projections, as the ratio of retired workers to current workers increases over time, the total amount of promised benefits will exceed total revenues, resulting in the depletion and eventual insolvency of the trust funds. Thus, if the promised benefits are to be paid in full, some adjustments in the Social Security and Medicare systems—increases in payroll taxes, decreases in benefits, or some combination thereof—appear inevitable.

§ 7.3 BECOMING "INSURED" UNDER SOCIAL SECURITY

Just as a specialized vocabulary has developed with respect to traditional property devices such as the trust, a specialized vocabulary exists with respect to the Social Security system. A basic understanding of some of that vocabulary is important for understanding the operation of the Social Security system.

In order to be eligible to receive Social Security benefits, a person must have performed work for wages or salary as an employee, or earned income as a self-employed person, in "covered employment" for a specified number of calendar quarters. A worker who works in covered employment during a calendar year is credited with up to four "quarters of coverage," depending on the amount of his or her reported earnings. The Social Security Administration maintains a lifetime earnings record for each individual worker, reflecting his or her reported annual earnings up to a specified amount.

As a condition of eligibility for most of the benefits available under Social Security, a worker must be "fully insured," that is, the worker must have a specified number of quarters of coverage credited to his or her lifetime earnings record. In general, a worker who has accumulated 40 quarters of coverage is "fully insured" for life and is eligible to receive retirement benefits on attaining retirement age. Thus, for example, if A accumulates 40 quarters of coverage over many years of covered employment, she is fully insured. Even if A decides (voluntarily) to leave her job at age 55 and cease working, she will be entitled to receive retirement benefits on attaining the retirement age specified by law. Under certain circumstances, a worker who has accumulated less than 40 quarters of coverage may be eligible for certain benefits. (For example, a worker who becomes disabled before age 31 may be fully insured and hence eligible for disability benefits with less than 40 quarters of coverage.)

To summarize, a person must be "insured" in order to be eligible to receive any benefits under Social Security. Being insured turns on the number of calendar quarters of coverage credited to a worker during his or her working years. One acquires quarters of coverage by earning at least a specified amount in covered employment over a period of time. Under conditions outlined in detail in the law, an insured worker is entitled to benefits on becoming disabled or on retirement; in addition, the worker's spouse or dependent family members may be eligible for benefits while the worker is alive and after his or her death.

§ 7.4 BENEFITS UNDER SOCIAL SECURITY

There are several different kinds of benefits payable under Social Security: (1) retirement or disability benefits paid to the worker; (2) benefits paid to the worker's spouse or dependent family members; (3) benefits paid to surviving family members of a deceased worker; and (4) lump-sum death benefits. These old-age, disability, and survivors benefits are commonly referred to as "OASDI" (old-age, survivors, disability insurance) benefits.

From its inception, the Social Security system was intended to provide basic support during retirement, supplemented with whatever private pension benefits might be provided through employer-sponsored plans and any additional savings accumulated by workers during their working years. Although the Social Security system has steadily expanded its coverage in subsequent years, the minimum monthly benefits paid today remain modest in amount, in accordance with the original purpose of the system.

On attaining the retirement age specified by law, a fully insured worker ordinarily becomes eligible to receive a monthly retirement benefit. The basic benefit, known as the "primary insurance amount," is calculated under a formula based on the worker's "average indexed monthly earnings." The benefit formula is tilted in favor of workers at the bottom of the wage scale, who receive retirement benefits representing a proportionately higher portion of their reported lifetime earnings than do high-wage workers. Nevertheless, in absolute terms, high earners receive larger benefits than do low earners.

A fully insured worker who waits until "full retirement age" to begin receiving benefits is entitled to monthly payments equal to his or her full primary insurance amount. For this purpose, full retirement age depends on the worker's year of birth. (Under current law, full retirement age increases gradually from age 65 for workers born before 1938 to age 67 for workers born after 1959.) The monthly payments continue for the worker's lifetime, and are subject to annual cost-of-living adjustments.

A fully insured worker may elect to begin receiving retirement benefits as early as age 62, in which case the level of benefits is reduced to reflect the increased duration of the expected stream of payments. Alternatively, if the worker elects to wait beyond full retirement age (up to age 70) to begin receiving retirement benefits, the level of benefits is correspondingly increased.

Social Security retirement benefits are not affected by income from sources such as interest on savings, investment income, or life insurance proceeds. Benefits may be temporarily reduced, however, if a worker elects to receive retirement benefits before reaching full retirement age but continues to earn income from performing personal services. (The earnings test will no longer apply and benefits will be recalculated at an increased level when the worker reaches full retirement age.) The "retirement earnings" test reflects the persistent notion that Social Security benefits are a replacement of earned income rather than a payment of pure insurance proceeds.

A spouse or dependent child of a retired or disabled worker may also be entitled to Social Security benefits, under circumstances specified by law. These benefits are often called "derivative" benefits because they derive from the worker's lifetime earnings record and are based on the worker's primary insurance amount, but they have no effect on the worker's own benefits. For example, suppose that A, a fully insured worker, reaches full retirement age and begins receiving retirement benefits. A is married to B, who has also reached full retirement age. In general, B is entitled to a monthly payment equal to one-half of A's primary insurance amount, even if B has no earnings record of her own. (If B is already entitled to receive benefits based on her own lifetime earnings record, her total benefits are equal to the larger of her own primary insurance amount or one-half of A's primary insurance amount.) Furthermore, if A has an unmarried, dependent child under age 18, the child is eligible for derivative benefits equal to one-half of A's primary insurance amount. (If A has several eligible children, each child is entitled to derivative benefits, but there is a ceiling on the total amount of derivative benefits payable to A's spouse and children.)

If a fully insured worker dies survived by a spouse or by an unmarried, dependent child under age 18, the spouse and child are entitled to survivors benefits. The surviving spouse receives the full amount of the deceased worker's benefits, and the child receives three-quarters of the deceased worker's primary insurance amount. Again, if there are several eligible children, each child is entitled to survivors benefits, but there is a ceiling on the total amount of survivors benefits. In addition to these survivors benefits, Social Security provides a lump-sum death benefit of $255 to the surviving spouse or eligible children of a deceased worker.

Upon the death, disability, or retirement of a parent, many thousands of persons receive monthly Social Security benefits because they have severe disabilities that began in childhood and continue into their adult years. Ordinarily, a child's derivative benefits cease at age 18, but those benefits may continue indefinitely if the child has a severe disability that began before age 22 and prevents substantial gainful work. To qualify for such benefits, it is not necessary for a person disabled since childhood to have worked in covered employment. Such a person's benefits are payable on the basis of his or her parent's coverage. And a parent who might not qualify for Social Security benefits in any other way may do so by caring for the disabled child.

§ 7.5 OTHER GOVERNMENTAL AND PRIVATE PENSION PLANS

Even before the Social Security Act was enacted in 1935, federal, state, and local governments as well as many businesses had already established pension plans for their employees. During World War II, creation of new "private" pension plans (plans sponsored by private corporations, or labor unions, or corporations and labor unions together) was stimulated by the permissibility of extending "fringe" benefits to employees in the form of pension benefits at a time when wages were fixed or "frozen" by law.

A substantial portion of all full-time nongovernmental employees in the United States are covered by private pension plans. Many persons employed by federal and state governments are covered by government pension plans (often referred to as "civil service" pension plans). The accumulated funds of pension plans are enormous. Indeed, at times there seems to be greater public concern with the behavior and impact of pension plans as "institutional investors" in the capital markets than with their ostensible purpose of providing a reliable source of income for retired employees.

Some of the language that has become a part of the standard working vocabulary with respect to pension plans should be noted. In a traditional "defined benefit" plan, the level of pension benefits payable to a retired employee is determined under a formula. For example, under a typical formula, an employee might be entitled upon retirement to receive monthly pension benefits equal to a fixed percentage of his or her average salary multiplied by the number of years of service. An important feature of a defined benefit plan is that the promised pension benefits represent an obligation of the employer. If the amounts contributed to the plan, with any net investment gains, are insufficient to pay the promised pension benefits, the employer is liable to make up the difference. In contrast, a "defined contribution" plan does not specify any level of promised pension benefits. Instead, the plan maintains an individual account for each employee, and amounts contributed by the employer are allocated to the employees' accounts. The amount of an employee's benefits depends on the balance in his or her account at retirement, including any investment gains or losses. Accordingly, a defined contribution plan places the risk of investment gain or loss squarely on the individual employee.

A "qualified" plan is one which qualifies for favorable tax treatment under the Internal Revenue Code. As an example of favorable tax treatment, contributions made by the employer on behalf of a covered employee give rise to an immediate deduction for the employer, but neither the contributions nor the income thereon are taxable to the employee until he or she actually receives distributions from the plan. The tax incentives provided by the Internal Revenue Code for qualified plans are intended to encourage employers to provide comprehensive retirement benefits for employees. Similar (though not identical) tax treatment is available to self-employed persons through so-called "Keogh" plans (named after the Congressional representative who sponsored the legislation).

A qualified plan generally takes the form of a trust fund which is held and administered by a trustee for the benefit of covered employees. The trustee is subject to fiduciary duties based on the traditional law of trusts, and is responsible for receiving contributions, investing the assets held in trust, and making distributions according to the terms of the plan.

There is great variation in the employee benefit plans sponsored by federal, state and local governments, by employers, by unions, and by employers and unions working in concert, but even so, "health" and "welfare" benefits, in addition to pension benefits, are a characteristic feature of many such plans. And so one frequently encounters the expression "pension and welfare" plans. (In this connection, it should be noted that "welfare" does not carry its common connotation of need-based public assistance. Rather, the expression "health and welfare" benefits under a private employee benefit plan usually refers to benefits other than retirement income benefits.)

§ 7.6 "VESTING" AND "PORTABILITY"

Criticism has often been leveled at both governmental and private pension plans that lack "vesting" and "portability" of benefits. The two notions are related, but they are not the same. For example, suppose that A is a state employee. The state has created its own pension plan for state employees (as opposed to electing coverage for them under Social Security). The plan is a "funded" plan that requires continuing contributions by A during the period of her employment, and accumulated contributions are invested in a trust fund. Under the terms of the plan, if A terminates her employment before retirement (but after having been employed for five years), she does not lose her right to a pension because she has acquired "vested" rights. (Here, a typical plan might give the employee a choice: (1) a right to withdraw his or her accumulated contributions on terminating employment, or (2) a right to let the contributions remain a part of the trust fund to provide minimal pension benefits to the former employee upon reaching retirement age.) Nonetheless, A's "vested" rights might not be transferable at all to (say) a retirement system in another state in which A has relocated. In short, "vesting" does not assure "portability." By way of contrast, a worker who is "insured" under Social Security carries his or her quarters of coverage from one covered employment to another.

There are continuing efforts to improve pension plans. But the variations in both the structure and the quality of pension plans are great. The possible causes of loss of pension benefits are many. Therefore, in considering one's own status as a covered employee or in advising another who is covered under such a plan, one should be cautious in making any assumptions about the availability of benefits on retirement or at death. The pension systems that work best tend to be those sponsored by the federal government or by economically successful and financially sound corporations. Some private pension systems have been established by employers or unions (or the two working together) under economic conditions that make it rather improbable that the pension held out by the employer as an inducement to entering employment, or to continuing employment, will in fact be paid.

The Employee Retirement Income Security Act of 1974 (commonly referred to as "ERISA") was enacted to try to assure retirement incomes to those participating in private pension plans. Among the devices used to assure retirement incomes are provisions requiring prompt vesting of pension rights, and the creation of a fund (administered by the Pension Benefit Guaranty Corporation) from which benefits can be paid when a pension plan fails. Enforcement of ERISA is shared by the Department of Labor (which can impose civil penalties) and the Internal Revenue Service (which can impose excise taxes). It bears emphasis that ERISA does not extend to all pension plans, nor does it require the creation of pension plans for those persons who fall under no plan at all.

§ 7.7 FORCED RETIREMENT

Propaganda accompanying the creation of private pension plans stresses the prospect of providing a dependable source of income to employees on reaching retirement age (the "golden years") and leaving the work force. No thoughtful person can seriously quarrel with the desirability of working out an orderly system to provide an income for those no longer employed because of age or disability (or no longer employed full-time for those reasons). But as a realistic matter, an employee who is thinking ahead to retirement should be aware that a pension plan can be used in more than one way. A pension plan is conventionally viewed as an inducement to employees to remain "loyal" to the sponsoring employer in order to build up the highest possible benefit on retirement. (Both length of employment and rate of pay as a "covered" employee may affect the level of benefits under a defined benefit plan.)

This conventional view ignores economic realities. In an increasingly volatile labor market, many willing and able employees find themselves out of work through no fault of their own, due to "downsizing" or "outsourcing." And even employees who remain loyal for years may be "encouraged" by an employer to take "early retirement" (that is, to retire before the customary age of 65 or 70) with a pension far below their current wage or salary while fully employed and significantly less than what they might reasonably expect by way of retirement income were they to continue to work until attaining (say) age 65. Moreover, although the federal Age Discrimination in Employment Act generally prohibits age-specific mandatory retirement rules, it does not prevent the structuring of pension benefits in a manner that encourages employees to accept early retirement.

The point is this: Aside from all other contingencies that might occur, an employee covered by a private pension plan who is attempting to estimate what his or her financial position will be as of the time of normal retirement (for example, at age 65) should take account of the possibility that he or she might be forced or induced to retire at an earlier age. In the event of early retirement, the employee might have to forego relatively high earnings as an employee and be forced to draw down any available savings to make ends meet until he or she becomes eligible for Social Security retirement benefits.

§ 7.8 DISTRIBUTIONS FROM QUALIFIED PLANS

The Internal Revenue Code offers substantial tax benefits for retirement saving through qualified plans. An employer who makes contributions to a qualified plan on behalf of a covered employee is entitled to an immediate income tax deduction, but the employee is not taxable on any of the plan's assets or income until he or she actually receives distributions from the plan. A qualified pension trust itself is exempt from tax, with the result that contributions to the trust fund and investment earnings thereon are sheltered from income tax until they are distributed from the plan.

To ensure that qualified plans fulfill their intended purpose of providing retirement benefits, the statute imposes restrictions (backed up by a 10% penalty tax) on distributions made to an employee before age 59½. Moreover, to prevent a defined contribution plan from serving as an open-ended tax shelter, the employee is generally required to receive at least a specified amount (the "minimum distribution") from the plan each year upon reaching age 73. (In some cases, the required minimum distributions may be deferred until the employee actually retires.) Any balance remaining in the employee's account at death must be distributed to the employee's designated beneficiary or to the employee's estate within a limited period of time. I.R.C. § 401(a)(9). The minimum distribution rules do not prohibit larger or earlier distributions, if permitted by the terms of the plan; their purpose is merely to ensure that the employee's entire interest in the plan will be distributed during the employee's lifetime or within a limited period of time after death.

Under ERISA, a qualified pension plan must prohibit employees from assigning or alienating their benefits under the plan. I.R.C. § 401(a)(13). Accordingly, subject to limited exceptions, an employee's interest in a qualified plan is protected from the claims of creditors in much the same way as the interest of a beneficiary of a traditional "spendthrift" trust.

In general, an employee is free to designate a beneficiary to receive any pension benefits payable at or after the employee's death under a qualified plan and to select a method of payment in accordance with the terms of the plan. As a matter of federal law, however, the options available to a married employee are constrained. Under amendments to ERISA enacted in 1984, pension benefits generally must be paid to the employee and his or her spouse in the form of a "qualified joint and survivor annuity" if the employee reaches retirement age. (If the employee dies before retirement age, survived by a spouse, the spouse is entitled to receive the pension benefits in the form of a "qualified preretirement survivor annuity.") The employee may elect a different form of benefits (including a "qualified optional survivor annuity") with the spouse's written consent, subject to specified formal requirements. In some cases, the surviving spouse may be entitled to receive the entire remaining benefit at the employee's death. I.R.C. § 417. The employee may designate a beneficiary other than the spouse, but only with the spouse's written consent. In effect, the surviving spouse's rights are functionally equivalent to a special elective share in the deceased employee's pension benefits. Note that the spouse must survive the employee in order to qualify for protection under the statute. If the spouse dies first, the employee is free to dispose of post-death pension benefits in any manner permitted by the terms of the plan. Moreover, the Supreme Court has held that the federal statute preempts state community property law, with the result that if the spouse dies before the employee, the spouse has no right to dispose of any interest in undistributed pension benefits. Boggs v. Boggs, 520 U.S. 833 (1997).

§ 7.9 INDIVIDUAL RETIREMENT ACCOUNTS

An individual retirement account ("IRA"), as authorized by ERISA, commonly takes the form of a savings account administered by a qualified "custodian" who invests the IRA funds in any of a broad range of permissible investments selected by the owner. (An IRA can also be established in the form of an annuity administered through an insurance company.) A person who has earned income and meets additional eligibility requirements can make limited annual tax-deductible contributions to an IRA. (Non-deductible contributions are also possible, but the tax benefits are correspondingly reduced.) The investment earnings on funds in an IRA accumulate free of federal income tax until they are withdrawn, resulting in tax benefits comparable to those available under qualified pension plans. The owner of an IRA can withdraw funds without penalty upon reaching age 59½. Upon reaching age 73, he or she must begin to make annual withdrawals at least equal to the required "minimum distributions" specified by statute. Amounts withdrawn from an IRA (other than non-deductible contributions, if any) are taxed as ordinary income for federal income tax purposes. Any amount remaining in the IRA at the owner's death becomes payable to the owner's designated beneficiary, if any, or to the owner's estate. If the owner's surviving spouse is the designated beneficiary, the spouse may "roll over" funds from the decedent's IRA into the spouse's own IRA free of income tax. A beneficiary other than the surviving spouse is generally required to withdraw the entire remaining account balance no later than 10 years after the owner's death (except in the case of an "eligible designated beneficiary," who may "stretch" the required annual distributions over his or her life expectancy). The minimum distribution rules establish an outer limit on the tax benefit of income deferral. The federal income tax treatment of IRAs is governed by § 408 of the Internal Revenue Code and the Regulations thereunder.

In 1997 Congress amended the Internal Revenue Code to authorize the creation of a new type of individual retirement account, known as the "Roth IRA" (named after the Senator who sponsored the legislation). Unlike a traditional IRA, a Roth IRA is funded with "after-tax" contributions—that is, no federal income tax deduction is allowed for contributions when they are made. However, the investment earnings on those contributions accumulate tax-free, and "qualified distributions" are completely exempt from federal income tax. Moreover, although there are restrictions on early withdrawals, the statute does not require any minimum distributions during the owner's life. (After the owner's death, however, the remaining account balance in a Roth IRA is subject to the same mandatory withdrawal rules as a traditional IRA.) As a result, once contributions have been made, the Roth IRA provides potentially unlimited income tax exemption for investment earnings prior to distribution. The federal income tax treatment of Roth IRAs is governed by § 408A of the Internal Revenue Code, which sets forth detailed requirements and restrictions concerning eligibility, contributions, and distributions.

§ 7.10 WORKERS' COMPENSATION

Workers' Compensation laws were enacted by all states during the period between 1911 and 1948, with coverage for federal employees and the District of Columbia being established by the federal government. Although the type of law, extent of coverage, and amount of available benefits vary from state to state, all such laws were designed to eliminate the common law procedure under which an injured worker, in order to recover damages, had to file suit and prove that the employer's negligence was the proximate cause of the worker's injury. Depending upon the jurisdiction, recovery could not be had at common law against an employer who successfully defended on the grounds of assumption of risk, the fellow-servant rule, or contributory negligence.

Under Workers' Compensation, eligibility for benefits is determined on a "no-fault" basis, with the general standard requiring "personal injury by accident arising out of and in the course of employment." Occupational diseases are included in coverage everywhere. Most states provide for payment of unlimited medical benefits on behalf of injured workers. The quid pro quo of the availability to the employee of no-fault benefits is that Workers' Compensation becomes the exclusive remedy of the employee against the employer, and the employee is precluded from seeking a higher tort liability award.

Workers' Compensation laws may be classified as compulsory or elective. Under compulsory laws every employer and employee subject to the law must comply with its provisions. Nearly all Workers' Compensation laws are compulsory.

Under elective laws the employer has the option of either accepting or rejecting the act, but rejection results in the loss of such common law defenses as assumption of risk, the fellow-servant rule, and contributory negligence.

In most states voluntary coverage is available for employments that are exempted from compulsory or elective coverage. Unlike the employer who rejects elective coverage, the employer who does not accept voluntary coverage may still be able to assert the traditional common law defenses.

Whether compulsory or elective, many state Workers' Compensation laws provide for exclusion of coverage for certain categories of employment such as agricultural, domestic service, and "casual" employment. Furthermore, employers may be excluded from coverage if they have fewer than a prescribed number of employees in otherwise covered employment. However, exclusions will become fewer as states broaden coverage.

Benefits payable to an injured worker under Workers' Compensation are intended to replace the worker's earnings while he or she is unable to return to employment. Consequently such benefits usually do not reflect the worker's marital status or the number of children or other dependents in his or her family. The actual amount of benefits payable is determined by the rate set by the law (often two-thirds of the weekly wage), the term or period of payment, the weekly maximum, and the aggregate maximum.

In instances of permanent total disability the trend throughout the states is toward payment for the entire period of disability.

All states provide for (sometimes contingent) burial allowances and for the payment of death benefits to the spouse of a worker whose death results from a covered accident. Although some states provide for continued payments to the spouse for life or until remarriage, other states limit the time period over which payments are to be made, or the aggregate amount of payments. Further allowance for children or other dependents of deceased workers is common.

Although Workers' Compensation benefits can mitigate the financial effects of a disabling injury upon a worker's eventual estate at death, or perhaps even result in an increase in the value of the estate in the case of death from a covered accident, Workers' Compensation laws are of little use in planning the affairs of one not yet injured. Unlike Social Security, which provides somewhat predictable disability and death benefits to and on behalf of fully insured workers, the amount of benefits, if any, receivable under Workers' Compensation depends primarily on the jurisdiction in which the accident occurs, and may be determined by the nature of the accident, the type and extent of injury, the type of employment, the number of employees employed, and numerous other variables which may affect the amount of benefits and the period of time over which they are payable. In short, for estate planning purposes, receipt of any Workers' Compensation benefits can only be classed as a fortuitous event.

§ 7.11 VETERANS' BENEFITS

Suppose that a decedent owned so little property at death that there is no net probate estate. The decedent never had occasion to create survivorship arrangements or other will substitutes intended to avoid probate. The decedent had no coverage under Social Security or under a private pension plan, and carried no conventional life insurance.

Nevertheless, if such a decedent was a veteran who had active service in the military, naval, or air service of the United States, the decedent's surviving spouse may be entitled to modest monthly benefits. Because the United States has been at war intermittently since the beginning of the twentieth century, there are large numbers of veterans eligible for benefits based on their service in World War II, Korea, Vietnam, Iraq, or Afghanistan. Further, if the decedent was covered by service-related life insurance, the decedent's surviving spouse (or other designated beneficiary) may be entitled to life insurance proceeds. A small sum may also be available from the government toward payment of funeral and burial expenses.

Benefits available to a veteran—as veteran—during lifetime will not enable living a life of ease, and benefits available to the veteran's family at death are modest. Nonetheless, the availability of such payments should be noted as an example of the broad range of benefits available today arising out of status—employment covered by Social Security, employment requiring participation in a private pension plan, career service as a member of the armed forces of the United States, and so on. A person who might otherwise accumulate little or no property for dependents and successors may nonetheless leave benefits at death that in cumulative effect are fairly substantial. (A veteran's surviving spouse might receive only a small amount each month, but that stream of monthly payments may continue for many decades.)

Disability benefits that are now a familiar feature of Social Security have their counterpart in veterans benefits. A veteran who has a "service-connected" disability is entitled to a level of benefits that varies according to the seriousness of the disability. A veteran who is permanently and totally disabled from a non-service-connected cause may be entitled to small monthly payments, but only if his or her other sources of income do not exceed a rather low threshold. (These means-tested monthly payments may be slightly larger if the veteran is married or has a child, or if the disability gives rise to a need for regular aid and attendance from another person.) Severely disabled veterans may also be eligible for grants to assist them in acquiring suitable dwellings.

If a member of the armed forces dies while in active service or from a service-connected disability after discharge, the decedent's surviving spouse may be entitled to monthly payments based on the decedent's level of compensation. If the decedent was entitled to benefits based on permanent and total disability from a non-service-connected cause, the decedent's surviving spouse or children may be entitled to small monthly payments, but as with the lifetime payments to the veteran, the amount of the survivors benefits is limited depending on the family's other sources of income.

Under eligibility requirements that vary considerably to allow for such factors as when the veteran served, the duration of service, and the cause of the mental or physical disability, a veteran may receive either out-patient or in-hospital medical and dental care. In some circumstances, eligibility requirements include inability of the veteran to defray expenses from the veteran's own resources. Where hospital care is required, the availability of benefits may be constrained by the limited capacity of Veterans' Administration facilities.

Frequently a member of the armed forces who obtains life insurance under a government plan during military service elects to continue coverage under the same policy after the period of service ends. Government life insurance is similar to insurance procured from commercial life insurers in that, for example, the life insured who is the owner of the policy has the right to designate the beneficiary, a policy of term insurance is convertible into an ordinary life policy, and proceeds of the policy are payable in a lump sum or in installments. Upon payment of an additional premium, the insured may be entitled to monthly benefits in the event of total disability. Government life insurance is commonly regarded as a "good buy" because costs of administering the insurance system are borne by the taxpaying public.

§ 7.12 BENEFITS FROM MORE THAN ONE SOURCE

Because rights based on status have developed on a piecemeal basis, it is not unusual for a beneficiary to qualify for disability benefits, retirement benefits, or survivors benefits from more than one source. For example, suppose that A, married to B, dies survived by B. As A's surviving spouse, B might prima facie be entitled to Social Security benefits, Workers' Compensation benefits, and veterans benefits, as well as survivors benefits under a private pension plan created by A's employer.

The extent to which a beneficiary can lawfully draw benefits from more than one source turns principally on the existence of somewhat crude controls implemented through the various sources of payment. Because ordering rules are often not well coordinated, adjustments in benefits ("offsets") originating in multiple plans or programs are a continuing source of misunderstanding, confusion, and irritation both for administrators and for recipients of benefits.

CHAPTER 8
TRUSTS—AN INTRODUCTION

§ 8.1 THE PRIVATE EXPRESS TRUST

A private express trust is a device whereby a trustee (who may be a natural person or a corporation authorized by law to act as trustee) holds legal title to property and manages the property for the benefit of one or more beneficiaries. The trustee usually has extensive management powers over the trust property, including powers of sale and investment. The trustee also has a fundamental fiduciary duty to administer the trust exclusively for the benefit of the beneficiaries, in accordance with the terms of the trust. In estate planning, the private express trust has long been used to conserve and manage property, and to transfer wealth from one generation to the next within a family. (By way of contrast, the charitable trust is used to provide funds to carry out charitable or public purposes, rather than for the benefit of private beneficiaries.)

Although the beneficiaries have no direct, legally recognized interests in the trust property itself, they do have the right to compel the trustee to carry out the terms of the trust and they can pursue equitable remedies against the trustee (and in some cases against a third party) for any breach of trust. For this reason, the beneficiaries are said to have "equitable" interests in the trust, in contrast to the trustee's legal title to the trust property. If A, the sole owner of securities, transfers them to a trust company in trust to manage and to pay the net income to B for life, and at B's death to pay the principal to C, B's income interest and C's remainder are equitable interests, not legal ones. The private express trust need not include both present and future interests, but it almost always does. Most of the future interests created today are created through trusts, and the law of future interests plays a significant role where the creation or design of a trust is influenced by tax considerations.

In addition to the trustee and the beneficiaries, a trust involves a creator (usually called the settlor, grantor, or trustor) who furnishes the property that is the subject matter of the trust and specifies the terms of the trust, usually in a written instrument. It is permissible, and indeed common, for one person to act in more than one of these capacities. For example, A may create an inter vivos trust to pay income to herself for life with remainder at her death to B. A is both the settlor and the life income beneficiary of the trust. If A also names herself as trustee, she is the trustee as well. However, if A is the sole beneficiary of the trust, she cannot also be the sole trustee. It would make no sense to say that A (as sole trustee) owes fiduciary duties to herself (as sole beneficiary), or that A (as sole beneficiary) can enforce those duties by suing herself (as sole trustee).

The private express trust may be created by the settlor during his or her lifetime (an "inter vivos" or "living" trust), or at death by the terms of the settlor's will (a "testamentary" trust). A trust created by will is a matter of public record because a will is probated ("proved") in a court proceeding. An inter vivos trust is not necessarily a matter of public record, but it may be so either at its creation or thereafter. If A owns real property and transfers it by deed to T as trustee and designates beneficial interests in the deed itself, recording the deed makes the details of the trust public. If A creates an inter vivos trust of real property without revealing the fact of trust on the face of the deed, the trust may nevertheless become public as a result of litigation. (Because instruments of title revealing the fact of trust inhibit the transfer of trust property, many instruments of title to property held in trust do not reveal that fact.) The comparative confidentiality of the terms of the inter vivos trust (along with such factors as avoiding probate and general acceptance of the "pour-over" will) have made inter vivos trusts increasingly popular in the United States.

Property held in trust is referred to as the trust property (or corpus or res). An instrument creating a trust, particularly an inter vivos trust, may provide for additions to the trust property by the settlor or by others. When the corpus of an existing trust is augmented by a transfer of property made by will, the will is frequently called a "pour-over" will. Either real or personal property may be the subject matter of a trust, but commonly today the subject matter consists of personal property, particularly stocks, bonds, mutual funds, or other intangibles. Although the trustee ordinarily has legal title to property that is the subject matter of the trust, the corpus of a trust may consist entirely of equitable interests in property.

Traditionally, a settlor creates an inter vivos trust by transferring property to another person in trust for one or more beneficiaries: A transfers $1,000 to T as trustee, to pay income to B for life with remainder to C; T accepts the trust and agrees to carry out its terms. Functionally, this transaction resembles a contract between A and T (with B and C as third-party beneficiaries), but for historical reasons it is seldom so analyzed. An alternative method of creating an inter vivos trust, which has become widely used in recent years, is a declaration by the settlor that he or she holds property as trustee for one or more beneficiaries: A sets aside $1,000 from her own funds and declares herself trustee of that sum to pay income to B for life with remainder to C. Because A already owns the trust property, there is no need to transfer legal title to herself as trustee. A's declaration by itself operates to create a trust of the property in her hands for the benefit of B and C. In creating an inter vivos trust, whether by transfer to another person or by self-declaration, a settlor should be careful to identify the trustee, the beneficiaries, and the subject matter of the trust, and should also set forth the terms of the trust in full, preferably in a written trust agreement or declaration of trust.

The creation of trusts forms a part of the law of "gratuitous transfers." Within rather broad limits, a settlor may give away property under such conditions and restrictions as he or she sees fit to impose. It follows that the settlor may condition the creation of a trust on the willingness of a particular person to act as trustee, and may make provision for removal or resignation of the trustee and appointment of successor trustees. These matters are flexible and are of considerable interest to lawyers because effective representation of clients includes anticipating events, providing for alternatives, and avoiding controversy and litigation.

§ 8.2 THE STATUTE OF FRAUDS AND THE WILLS ACT

The private express trust is a means of making gifts, and just as intention by the donor to make an outright gift of property is insufficient by itself to create an interest in the intended donee, intention alone does not result in the creation of a private express trust. The intention to create a trust must coincide with the other elements of a valid trust: a trustee, one or more beneficiaries, and existing trust property.

Even if all the foregoing elements of a trust exist, a trust may fail if the trustee refuses to perform his or her duties and the beneficiaries are unable to obtain relief because the trustee successfully interposes the Statute of Frauds or the statute governing the execution of wills as a defense to a suit for enforcement. (In some instances where evidence is not admissible to establish an express trust because one or the other of these defenses is raised, courts have afforded relief against unjust enrichment by way of a "constructive trust.")

When a testator attempts to create a testamentary trust, he or she must comply with the requirements of the jurisdiction's wills act. When a settlor attempts to create an inter vivos trust of land, he or she must comply with the requirements of the jurisdiction's Statute of Frauds, if any. A majority of American jurisdictions have statutes requiring a writing for the creation of an express inter vivos trust of land.

Because most trusts are created with the advice and assistance of lawyers and professional trustees, compliance with the requirements of the Statute of Frauds and the wills act ordinarily presents no problems. A competent drafter will invariably prepare a written document or group of documents identifying the settlor, the trustee, the beneficiaries, the subject matter of the trust, and the nature of the beneficial interests. Where problems arise in connection with such trusts, it is not because of failure to put such important matters in writing. Instead, reported litigation involving noncompliance with the Statute of Frauds or the wills act often originates in informal family transactions that have little to do with making gifts. An owner of land may attempt to insulate it from claims of his or her creditors by conveying bare legal title to a friend or relative. An aged person owning property may orally agree to leave it by will to another person in exchange for the latter's promise to provide continuing care to the property owner. Or a testator may devise or bequeath property outright to a relative on the strength of the relative's oral promise to share the property with other family members. These cases arise with regularity.

The requirements of the Statute of Frauds should be differentiated from the formalities of conveyancing. From the fact that a jurisdiction requires that an express trust of land must be created (or "manifested and proved") by a writing, it does not follow that the existence of the trust and the identity of the beneficiaries must be revealed on the face of the deed when the trust is created by a "transfer out" (as opposed to a self-declaration of trust). If A owns land in fee simple absolute and wishes to make T trustee of the land, A might execute and deliver a deed in which the operative words are "to T and his heirs, in trust, to hold, administer, and manage, and to pay the net income to B for life, and at B's death to convey to B's issue then living." But if A prefers, she may transfer title to T by "absolute deed," that is, by a deed that does not reveal that the grantee holds as a fiduciary. To comply with the requirements of the Statute of Frauds, A contemporaneously prepares a writing, signed by T, in which T agrees to hold the land as trustee for designated beneficiaries. (Because a transfer of land or securities is facilitated if the owner designated in the deed or instrument of title appears to own absolutely, institutional pressures and practices encourage the use of a separate writing to show that T holds as a trustee for the benefit of one or more beneficiaries.)

Traditionally, a testamentary transfer of property to be held in trust is made by a will that reveals the existence of the trust and sets forth the complete terms of the trust. Thus, A might execute a will leaving her residuary estate "to T and his heirs, in trust, to hold, administer, and manage, and to pay the net income to B for life, and at B's death to convey to B's issue then living." Setting forth the complete terms of the trust in the will itself is consistent with the wills act, which generally requires that a gratuitous transfer at death must take the form of a writing signed by the testator and attested by at least two witnesses. In most jurisdictions, the terms of a testamentary trust may be set forth in a separate written instrument if that instrument was in existence at the time the will was executed and is "incorporated by reference" in the will. This practice is consistent with the wills act because the incorporated matter becomes known when the will is offered for probate (and indeed might be filed together with the will as part of the probate proceeding). However, a mere transfer of legal title by will to the intended trustee, with the identities of the beneficiaries and the nature of the beneficial interests set out in a separate letter prepared by the testator, does not satisfy the requirements of the wills act. Although the letter is a writing, it has no testamentary significance unless it is executed in accordance with the wills act or is properly incorporated by reference in the will. More recently, testators seeking to avoid public disclosure of the terms of a trust funded at death have increasingly made use of the "pour-over" will, which adds property at the testator's death to an inter vivos trust established outside the will. Although the property passing by will is subject to probate administration and creditors' claims, the terms of the inter vivos trust generally remain private unless the trust itself becomes the subject of a lawsuit.

If an intended private express trust is unenforceable because of failure to comply with the requirements of the Statute of Frauds or the wills act, and relief is sought by way of constructive trust, there is considerable variation in result. Sometimes property is transferred in reliance on the transferee's promise or agreement to carry out the terms of the intended trust, but the instrument of transfer (a deed of land or a will) fails to reveal the existence or terms of the intended trust. Such a "secret" trust cannot be given effect as an express trust, but courts routinely hold that the transferee can be compelled to hold the property as a constructive trustee for the intended beneficiaries, in order to prevent unjust enrichment.

The doctrine is less well settled in cases involving a "semi-secret" trust, where the instrument of transfer reveals on its face that the transferee takes as a trustee but fails to specify the terms of the trust ("to T, in trust" or "to T, as trustee"). Many courts hold that the beneficial interest is in the transferor (or the transferor's successor in interest) by way of resulting trust. (The instrument of transfer reveals on its face that the transferee is intended to take as trustee, but fails to designate any beneficiary. The transferee has no beneficial interest in the property, but instead holds it for the benefit of the transferor or the transferor's successor in interest.) Nonetheless, there is support for the notion that where a semi-secret trust is attempted by will (as opposed to by deed), a constructive trust for the intended beneficiaries of the express trust (rather than a resulting trust for the testator's successors in interest) should be imposed. Because lawyers must contend with attempted dispositions of property that have gone awry, this part of trust law is relevant; but, again, the lawyer does not "use" it in the ordinary sense. Rather, being aware of it, the lawyer takes account of it in counseling and representing transferors, and in sorting out property interests when an imperfect trust plan has led to controversy.

§ 8.3 THE REVOCABLE TRUST

An inter vivos trust may be either revocable or irrevocable. If revocable, it is commonly revocable by the settlor acting alone. If the instrument of trust is silent with respect to revocability, the law in the United States is not uniform as to the consequence. Under the traditional view, which is still followed in a number of jurisdictions, the trust is presumed to be irrevocable. Recently, however, the trend has shifted in the opposite direction, and many states now have statutes making the trust presumptively revocable. For example, § 602(a) of the Uniform Trust Code provides in part as follows: "Unless the terms of a trust expressly provide that the trust is irrevocable, the settlor may revoke or amend the trust." The lesson for the lawyer is clear: Be explicit regarding revocability or irrevocability. (And if the trust is revocable, be explicit regarding the method of revocation.)

The revocable trust is frequently used as a will substitute, not because it affords any tax advantage (for federal estate tax purposes, the transfer is treated as testamentary), but because using it reduces some expenses incident to administration of probate assets, and permits distributions to beneficiaries during the period when probate assets are being administered. (Assets transferred to the revocable trust during the settlor's life are not part of the probate estate.)

Perhaps more importantly, the revocable trust affords the settlor, while living, an opportunity to observe the results of making property arrangements that frequently remain in effect at his or her death, and that may endure during and after the administration of the probate estate. For example, A, the sole owner of securities, transfers them by a written deed of trust to her son C to manage, and to pay the net income first to A for life, then to B (A's spouse) for life, then to D (the daughter of A and B) for life, and at D's death to pay the trust principal to such one or more of D's surviving issue as D appoints by will, and in default of appointment to pay the principal to D's surviving issue by right of representation. A reserves the power to revoke, amend, modify, or terminate the trust. Apart from the reserved income interest in A, the settlor, the terms of this revocable inter vivos trust are similar to those that A might create by will: There is a life income interest in A's spouse, followed by a life income interest in A's daughter D, who has a special testamentary power to appoint the corpus among her issue, followed by a gift over "in default of appointment" (that is, in absence of an effective appointment) to D's issue by right of representation. In sum, the settlor of an inter vivos trust can create administrative and dispositive powers in a trustee, and beneficial interests in various beneficiaries, that approximate (and in some instances replicate) those that will exist under the trust at the settlor's death. The settlor can observe the administration of the trust by the trustee and the effect of the existence of the trust on the beneficiaries. If the existence of the trust proves to be altogether unsatisfactory, or unsatisfactory in some particular, the settlor can destroy or modify the trust by exercising the reserved power to revoke or amend. Knowledge acquired by watching one's own trust in operation is also available to the settlor of an irrevocable inter vivos trust, of course, but there is little evidence that most persons of means are willing to divest themselves completely of substantial amounts of property, by trust or otherwise, before death. The revocable trust, like the executed will before the death of the testator, may be destroyed or modified by the settlor as long as the power to revoke exists. (A trust is modified by "amendment"; a will is modified by "codicil.") But unlike execution of a will, creation of a funded revocable trust results in the immediate creation of beneficial interests that persist until they end by their own terms, or are destroyed or modified by act of the settlor.

To execute a will, a testator must possess "testamentary capacity." To create an inter vivos trust (revocable or irrevocable), the settlor must be "competent." Nonetheless, there is reason to believe that disappointed putative beneficiaries may have more difficulty in attacking an inter vivos trust on grounds of incompetency than they have in attacking a will on grounds of lack of testamentary capacity. Therefore, a testator who is concerned about the possibility of a contest of his or her will (particularly one executed later in life) might create a revocable trust of substantial assets. Although possible application of a "pretermitted heir" statute to a will can be anticipated (and avoided) by the drafter of a will, it is worth noting that most pretermitted heir statutes do not apply to inter vivos trusts.

In view of the general acceptance of the "pour-over" will, it has become common practice for a settlor to use a revocable trust created during life as a receptacle for probate assets passing by will at death. Because the terms of the revocable inter vivos trust can to a considerable extent be kept confidential, use of a revocable trust in conjunction with a pour-over will permits passing substantial amounts of property by will without making the identity of the beneficiaries and the nature of the beneficial interests a matter of public record.

Many persons who have neither inherited wealth nor accumulated wealth depend heavily on life insurance and employment-related death benefits to provide for surviving family members in the event of death at an early age. Just as a revocable trust created by a settlor during life can be used to receive probate assets at death under a pour-over will, so too it can be used to receive the proceeds of insurance on the settlor's life or death benefits attributable to employment. This is accomplished by designating the trustee of the revocable trust as the beneficiary of the life insurance or death benefits. It is true that by taking advantage of available settlement options under a life insurance policy, the insured decedent might direct the payment of the proceeds of the policy over time (as differentiated from a lump-sum payment), on terms resembling those of a trust. But settlement options are a matter of contract, not trust, and the insurer making payments under a settlement option does so in the performance of a contractual duty, not in the performance of a fiduciary duty as trustee. Generally speaking, administration of the proceeds of life insurance through a trust affords more flexibility than payment under a settlement option. (For example, a trustee can be given discretion to make or withhold distributions.) In any event, the revocable trust funded with life insurance proceeds or death benefits at the settlor's death offers many of the advantages commonly associated with the revocable trust funded with probate assets under a pour-over will.

Although the revocable inter vivos trust is now accepted in all American jurisdictions, and serves many useful purposes, it is not always immune from attack. Notwithstanding its validity for many other purposes, the transfer is treated as "testamentary" for death tax purposes. In many jurisdictions the revocable trust is also treated as "testamentary" for purposes of computing the surviving spouse's elective share (and as a consequence, the spouse can reach the trust property if necessary to satisfy the elective share). By statute or by judicial decision, if the settlor of a revocable trust incurs debts which cannot be paid from his or her own assets, the settlor's creditors generally can reach the trust property to satisfy their claims, both during the settlor's lifetime and (in many jurisdictions) after the settlor's death, irrespective of whether the debts were incurred before or after the creation of the trust. If the settlor (in a nonfiduciary capacity) retained essentially unlimited power to control the administration of a purported revocable trust, the arrangement might conceivably be vulnerable to attack by the settlor's successors in interest (under the intestacy laws, or under the settlor's will) on the ground that it was a mere agency that terminated at the settlor's death. Put briefly, a revocable inter vivos trust may be treated as testamentary for some purposes and under some circumstances, merely by virtue of the settlor's power of revocation. It does not inevitably follow that the trust itself will fail. For example, although a revocable trust created by a deceased settlor is treated as testamentary for death tax purposes, the settlor may direct by will that all taxes payable in connection with the settlor's death, including those attributable to the revocable trust, be paid from the probate estate (assuming the probate estate is sufficient to satisfy the direction). On the other hand, a successful attempt by the surviving spouse to treat the revocable trust as testamentary for purposes of claiming an elective share may result in a depletion of assets in the inter vivos trust. And if revocability combined with other facts induces a court to label an inter vivos trust arrangement a mere agency, the arrangement ceases at the settlor's death.

§ 8.4 INCORPORATION BY REFERENCE

The law in most jurisdictions permits a writing in existence at the time a will is executed to be "incorporated by reference" into the will. For example, § 2–510 of the Uniform Probate Code provides as follows:

> A writing in existence when a will is executed may be incorporated by reference if the language of the will manifests this intent and describes the writing sufficiently to permit its identification.

Compliance with the statute might take this form:

> All the rest, residue, and remainder of my estate, including failed or lapsed gifts, I give, devise, and bequeath to T, in trust, to hold, administer, and distribute in accordance with the terms of an existing trust instrument executed by me and agreed to by T, as trustee, on July 1, 20__, the terms of which trust are hereby incorporated into and made a part of this will as if fully set forth herein.

Although it is conventional to say that a will is "ambulatory" or that it "speaks" at the testator's death, it is a part of the accepted doctrine on "incorporation by reference" that material incorporated into a will by reference takes the form that it had at the time when the will was executed. This aspect of incorporation by reference is of particular importance where the incorporated writing is itself a revocable instrument such as a revocable inter vivos trust created by the testator or a will executed by another living person. Such an instrument may in fact be modified in important respects before the death of the testator who executed the incorporating will. To incorporate by reference a revocable instrument that has been modified with respect to its dispositive provisions after execution of the incorporating will may be, and often is, intent-defeating. The testator may well have assumed that the will would incorporate the terms of the writing as it stood at the testator's death, but that assumption is unwarranted. For example, A creates a revocable, amendable inter vivos trust with B as the beneficiary. A then executes a will, disposing of her residuary estate in accordance with the terms of the inter vivos trust instrument, which she incorporates by reference into her will. Subsequently, finding the attitude or conduct of B unsatisfactory, A amends the trust and replaces B with C as the beneficiary. A, the settlor-testator, then dies, survived both by B, who was removed as the beneficiary of the trust, and by C, who was substituted as the new beneficiary. Under the standard doctrine of incorporation by reference, the trust amendment made after the execution of the will cannot be given effect in disposing of A's residuary estate; it is the original trust instrument, as it existed when the will was executed, which is incorporated by reference in the will. Accordingly, B, the original beneficiary of the inter vivos trust, is the beneficiary of the testamentary trust of the residuary estate arising at A's death. (Note, however, that the result might be different if the will itself were reexecuted or republished by codicil subsequent to the amendment of the inter vivos trust.)

Because incorporation by reference may frustrate intention, it should be used with great caution. But there are other aspects of the matter. Often, if a writing is worth incorporating, it is worth reproducing in the will. Reproduction in the will obviates preliminary inquiry into state law requirements regarding incorporation by reference. (Must the incorporated matter itself be attested? Must the will expressly refer to the incorporated matter as being in existence at the time of execution of the will? Must the incorporated matter be offered for probate together with the will itself?) And aside from these considerations, reproduction in the will resolves questions that otherwise might arise concerning precisely which matter is incorporated. Put briefly, in the planning and drafting of wills, extrinsic written matter should be incorporated by reference only if there are good reasons for doing so.

§ 8.5 FACTS OF INDEPENDENT SIGNIFICANCE AND THE POUR-OVER WILL

The technique of combining a pour-over will with an inter vivos revocable trust traditionally rests on the doctrine of "facts of independent significance." The doctrine is recognized by statute or judicial decision in most jurisdictions. For example, § 2–512 of the Uniform Probate Code provides in part as follows:

> A will may dispose of property by reference to acts and events that have significance apart from their effect upon the dispositions made by the will, whether they occur before or after the execution of the will or before or after the testator's death. . . .

For many years, general acceptance of the pour-over will technique turned on whether the revocable, amendable inter vivos trust constituted a "fact of independent significance" for purposes of the wills act.

In this connection, an act or event has "independent" (nontestamentary) significance if it has a purpose or effect other than attempting to dispose of property at death without complying with the requirements of the local wills act. (The wills act typically requires that the terms of a will be set forth in a written instrument duly executed by the testator in the presence of at least two persons who also sign the instrument as attesting witnesses.) For example, suppose that A keeps cash in a safe-deposit box to which she has sole access, and in her will she leaves "all the cash in my safe-deposit box at my death to my daughter Mary." Upon A's death survived by Mary, the cash in the box passes to Mary under A's will. It is true that the amount of the cash legacy is not fully specified on the face of the will, and that the amount can be determined only by looking beyond the will to extrinsic circumstances existing at A's death (namely, the contents of the safe-deposit box). It is also true that in the interval between the execution of A's will and the time of her death, A may add cash to that already in the safe-deposit box, or she may withdraw cash from the box, and either act affects the amount of cash that passes to Mary at A's death under her will. But, as courts routinely point out in upholding such testamentary provisions, the safe-deposit box is maintained for the purpose of safeguarding valuables, and that purpose has a significance that is independent of any attempt to make or modify a testamentary disposition without complying with the requirements of the wills act.

Much the same reasoning has been used to give effect to a pour-over will that adds probate assets to an existing inter vivos trust at the settlor's death. For example, A creates a revocable, amendable, inter vivos trust, with B as the beneficiary. The trust is funded with assets contributed by A. A then executes a pour-over will leaving her residuary estate to the trustee of the inter vivos trust, to be added to the property already held in trust and administered as a part of that trust (including any subsequent amendments to the terms of the trust). Subsequently, finding the attitude or conduct of B unsatisfactory, A amends the trust and replaces B with C as the beneficiary. The trust amendment is made in accordance with the procedural requirements set forth in the trust instrument, but does not conform to the requirements of the wills act. A, the settlor-testator, then dies, survived both by B, who was removed as the beneficiary of the trust, and by C, who was substituted as the new beneficiary. When A dies, her residuary estate passes by will to the trustee of the inter vivos trust and becomes an integral part of the corpus of that trust as it exists at A's death. The trust operated as a valid arrangement for managing and disposing of property from the time it was created and funded during A's lifetime. Thus, the trust (like the safe-deposit box in the example given above) has a "significance" that is "independent" of its effect on A's testamentary disposition of her residuary estate.

Note that an inter vivos trust has "independent significance" only if it is validly created and funded with property before the settlor-testator's death.

(Under the law of trusts, a trust cannot come into existence until there is at least some property set aside in the hands of the trustee to be administered for the benefit of the beneficiaries.) Accordingly, it has become common practice for a settlor to create an inter vivos trust with a nominal corpus (say, ten dollars), and simultaneously to execute a pour-over will directing that probate assets be added to the trust at the settlor-testator's death. Despite its minimal funding, such a trust nevertheless has sufficient "independent significance" to govern the ultimate disposition of property transferred under the pour-over will at the settlor-testator's death.

In order to simplify and clarify the use of pour-over wills, many states have enacted legislation based on the Uniform Testamentary Additions to Trusts Act (which also appears as § 2–511 of the Uniform Probate Code). The uniform act provides in part as follows:

> A will may validly devise property to the trustee of a trust established or to be established (i) during the testator's lifetime by the testator . . ., or (ii) at the testator's death by the testator's devise to the trustee, if the trust is identified in the testator's will and its terms are set forth in a written instrument, other than a will, executed before, concurrently with, or after the execution of the testator's will . . ., regardless of the existence, size, or character of the corpus of the trust. . . .

The uniform act goes on to state that unless the testator's will provides otherwise, the property transferred by a pour-over will "is not held under a testamentary trust of the testator," but instead "becomes a part of the trust to which it is devised, and must be administered and disposed of in accordance with the provisions of the governing instrument setting forth the terms of the trust, including any amendments thereto. . . ."

Compliance with such legislation might take the following form:

> All the rest, residue, and remainder of my estate, including lapsed or failed gifts, I give, devise, and bequeath to T, in trust, to hold, administer, and distribute as provided in a trust instrument executed by me and agreed to by T, as trustee, on July 1, 20__, as the same may be amended in accordance with its terms, to be added to the corpus of the trust, and to be held, administered, and distributed as a part thereof.

In jurisdictions that have legislation based on the uniform act, it is no longer necessary to go through the formal step of funding the inter vivos trust with nominal assets during the settlor's life. As long as the terms of the trust are set forth in a written instrument and the trust is identified in the will, the uniform act allows a settlor-testator to create an inter vivos trust at death and fund it entirely with probate assets passing under the pour-over will. Of course, the assets passing under the pour-over will are subject to probate administration and creditors' claims. The pour-over will is not used to avoid probate. The principal advantages of using a pour-over will in combination with a revocable inter vivos trust are that the ultimate disposition of the probate assets can be established and amended up until the settlor-testator's death without executing a new will or codicil, and that the terms of the trust need not be disclosed as part of the probate record. Moreover, the inter vivos trust can be used to coordinate the disposition not only of assets passing under the pour-over will but also of life insurance proceeds, death benefits, and other non-probate assets.

It should also be noted that the assets that "pour over" by will at the settlor-testator's death are treated as part of an inter vivos trust. An inter vivos trust is generally administered by the trustee without court supervision, and in the absence of litigation the terms of the trust will generally remain confidential. (By way of contrast, when a trust is incorporated by reference in a will, the assets passing under the will are held in a testamentary trust, which in some jurisdictions must be administered under the supervision of a probate court.)

§ 8.6 REVOCABLE TRUSTS UNDER ELECTIVE SHARE STATUTES

In many states a decedent's surviving spouse is entitled by law to an elective share of the decedent's estate, and the surviving spouse cannot be deprived of his or her elective share by the decedent's will. A surviving spouse who is dissatisfied with the provision, if any, made for him or her in the decedent's will might elect under statute to "take against the will" of the decedent and thereby acquire an elective share in the estate.

Suppose that A, while married to B, transfers property irrevocably in trust to pay the net income to A for life, and on A's death to distribute the trust corpus to C. A dies survived by B and C, and leaves a will that makes no provision for B. The corpus of the irrevocable trust is not a part of A's estate for probate purposes, nor in many states is it viewed as a part of A's estate for purposes of determining B's elective share if B elects under statute to take against A's will. (The corpus is includible in A's "gross estate" for federal estate tax purposes, however, under § 2036 of the Internal Revenue Code.)

Suppose that A, instead of creating an irrevocable trust as described in the preceding paragraph, creates a revocable trust with beneficial interests identical to those just described. A dies survived by B and C, and leaves a will that makes no provision for B. The corpus of the revocable trust is not a part of A's estate for probate purposes. (The corpus is includible in A's gross estate for federal estate tax purposes, however, under §§ 2036 and 2038 of the Internal Revenue Code.) Whether the trust corpus is viewed as a part of A's estate, if B elects to take against A's will, turns on state law. In most states, by statute or judicial decision, the revocable trust is likely to be viewed as a will substitute for purposes of determining B's elective share, with the result that B may be able to reach all or a portion of the trust property to satisfy her elective share. (This is also the result under § 2–205 of the Uniform Probate Code.) In a few states, however, the revocable trust is not viewed as a will substitute for purposes of the elective share statute. In such states, the revocable trust may be used to insulate property from the claims of a surviving spouse who might be dissatisfied with the provisions of the decedent's will.

Even if the law of the settlor's state of domicile treats the revocable trust as testamentary for purposes of the elective share statute, the settlor might attempt to insulate property from a potential claim under the elective share statute by creating a revocable trust in another state where the revocable trust is not so treated, fixing the administration of the trust in that other state and making that other state the situs of the trust. However, in this connection it bears emphasis that the courts of the domiciliary state may be inclined to apply that state's law, rather than the law of the other state, in order to uphold a strong public policy of protecting the surviving spouse against disinheritance. In other words, it is by no means certain that the settlor can successfully circumvent the elective share statute of the domiciliary state simply by establishing a revocable trust in another state.

§ 8.7 PROTECTING BENEFICIARIES FROM THEMSELVES

Of the protective devices available to the settlor of a trust, the "spendthrift" clause is the best known. Where fully accepted, the spendthrift clause protects a beneficiary's interest against both involuntary alienation (forced sale to satisfy the claims of the beneficiary's creditors) and voluntary alienation (transfer by the beneficiary of his or her right to receive future distributions of trust income or principal). A spendthrift clause does not affect a beneficiary's interest after it has been distributed to him or her in the form of trust income or principal. (In this connection, the term "spendthrift" is something of a misnomer, for the protection of such a clause is not limited to spendthrifts, minors, or incompetent beneficiaries.)

No particular words are required to create a spendthrift restraint, but the formula has become somewhat standardized and ordinarily the lawyer intending to create interests subject to a spendthrift clause should use language such as the following:

> Before its actual receipt by a beneficiary of this trust, no income or principal payable or to become payable under this trust instrument shall be subject to anticipation, assignment, sale, or other disposition by such beneficiary, or to control or interference by any creditor of such beneficiary, or to attachment, execution, garnishment, or other legal or equitable process available to a creditor to satisfy any debt or liability of such beneficiary.

Although the spendthrift clause has achieved general acceptance, one should not assume that it is recognized everywhere. Where recognized, it may be effective with respect to equitable interests in income but not equitable interests in corpus. Certain favored types of creditors, such as a spouse or a minor child seeking to enforce a claim against the trust beneficiary for delinquent support payments, may be able to reach the beneficiary's interest notwithstanding the existence of an otherwise effective spendthrift clause. Moreover, in most jurisdictions, in the absence of a statutory provision to the contrary, the rule is well established that the settlor of a trust cannot shield any interests retained by the settlor in income or corpus from claims of his or her own creditors, irrespective of whether those claims arise before or after the creation of the trust. In other words, a spendthrift clause is ineffective against the settlor's own creditors. More importantly, the protection provided by a spendthrift clause applies only to undistributed income or corpus in the hands of the trustee. Once the beneficiary receives a distribution from the trust, the distribution can be reached by the beneficiary's creditors in the same way as the beneficiary's other assets, even though at that time the beneficiary may stand most in need of protection.

The Uniform Trust Code generally recognizes spendthrift trusts, subject to exceptions for support claims of a beneficiary's child or spouse, for claims of creditors who provided "services for the protection of a beneficiary's interest in the trust," and for certain governmental claims. UTC §§ 502 and 503.

Another protective device, which operates somewhat differently from a spendthrift trust, is a "discretionary" trust. The following language is typical of that used to create a discretionary trust:

> . . . to T, in trust, and as long as any child or children of mine are alive, to pay to or apply for the benefit of such child or children as much of the net income and principal of the trust as T in

T's absolute and uncontrolled discretion deems advisable. . . .

The beneficiary of a discretionary trust has no fixed right to receive any specified amount or portion of trust income or corpus. Instead, distributions depend on the trustee's exercise of a broad discretionary power. The trustee's power might be limited by a standard in the trust instrument relating to (say) the beneficiary's "comfortable maintenance" or "needs," but the underlying principle is the same: It is the trustee, and not the beneficiary, who determines whether to make distributions from the trust, to which beneficiaries, at what times, and in what amounts. (A court of equity has inherent power to control a trustee who acts arbitrarily or from improper motives, but courts are ordinarily reluctant to second-guess a trustee who exercises discretion reasonably and in good faith.) In effect, the trustee holds a special power of appointment—a power to designate the beneficiaries who will receive distributions of trust income or corpus, within the limitations imposed by the terms of the trust and subject to basic fiduciary duties of fairness, honesty, and good faith. Because the beneficiary cannot compel the trustee to distribute any fixed amount of trust income or corpus, the beneficiary's creditors or assignees stand in no better position, even if they step into the beneficiary's shoes upon a forced sale or a voluntary transfer.

Discretionary trusts are generally recognized, even in jurisdictions and in situations where a spendthrift trust is not recognized. A discretionary trust may also contain a spendthrift clause, and within a single trust a particular beneficiary's interest may be subject to either or both of these protective devices. In most jurisdictions, however, in the absence of a statutory provision to the contrary, the protection provided by a discretionary trust is subject to one important limitation: The settlor of a trust cannot shield any interests retained by the settlor in income or corpus from claims of his or her own creditors, irrespective of whether those claims arise before or after the creation of the trust. Courts generally hold that the settlor's creditors can reach the maximum amount that the trustee, in the exercise of fiduciary discretion, could properly distribute to the settlor. For example, suppose that A creates an irrevocable trust and gives T, the trustee, a power to distribute trust income or corpus "to any one or more of A, her spouse or her issue living from time to time, in such amounts and at such times as T in T's absolute and uncontrolled discretion deems advisable." Although A was solvent when she created the trust, she subsequently incurs debts that exceed her remaining resources. Under the prevailing doctrine, A's creditors can reach all of the property in the irrevocable trust, because the trustee has a discretionary power to distribute all of the trust income and corpus to A. This is an application of the general rule which allows the settlor's creditors to reach trust property to the extent of the settlor's retained beneficial interest in a "self-settled" trust.

The Uniform Trust Code recognizes the general rule concerning discretionary trusts, as well as the exception for self-settled trusts. UTC §§ 504 and 505.

Thus, "[w]hether or not the terms of a trust contain a spendthrift provision," a creditor or assignee of the settlor of an irrevocable trust can reach "the maximum amount that can be distributed to or for the settlor's benefit." UTC § 505(a)(2).

Because private express trusts are means of making gifts, and donors are permitted, within rather broad limits, to fashion their gifts as they wish, there is considerable variety in the protective devices available to the settlor who wishes to insulate a beneficiary from the distasteful consequences of the beneficiary's own bad judgment or lack of foresight. In addition to the spendthrift trust and the discretionary trust, there are "protective" trusts, "blended" trusts, and "support" trusts. Under the terms of a protective trust, B might be given an income interest for life that ceases automatically in the event that any creditor of B seeks to reach B's income interest to satisfy a claim. On the happening of such an event, the trust becomes discretionary and the trustee is empowered to apply income for B's benefit. In a blended trust for B and B's issue, the trustee might be given unlimited discretion to distribute income or corpus to any one or more beneficiaries to the exclusion of the others, thereby ensuring that no beneficiary has an enforceable right to any ascertainable share of income or corpus. In a support trust, the trustee might be directed to make distributions of income or corpus to a beneficiary in such amounts as the trustee deems necessary for the beneficiary's support and maintenance. The effectiveness of blended trusts and support trusts, like that of the discretionary trust, is based on the limited nature of the beneficiary's interest.

§ 8.8 TRUST TERMINATION

In most cases, a private express trust terminates upon some event or occurrence provided for in the terms of the trust. For example, a trust instrument might direct that income be paid to one or more beneficiaries for their lifetimes (or for a term of years), and that at the death of the last of the income beneficiaries (or at the end of the term, as the case may be), the trust corpus be distributed to the remainder beneficiaries. In the case of a revocable trust, the settlor might terminate the trust by exercising a reserved power of revocation. (A charitable trust may be so created that it can endure indefinitely, but it, too, can be created to end by its own terms.) A trust may also terminate if all of its purposes have been accomplished, or if the purposes of the trust have become unlawful, contrary to public policy, or impossible to achieve.

If A transfers property to T, as trustee, and directs T to pay the net income to B for life and then at B's death to distribute the trust corpus to C, A might logically assume that the mere existence of the trust is sufficient to assure that B's income interest will be enjoyed by B over a lifetime, and that payment to B over time will assure to B protection against improvidence not assured by (say) an outright gift of $10,000 to B in cash. However, A's assumption may prove to be erroneous. If B and C, having agreed to a division of the trust assets, request that the trustee terminate the trust and pay over the assets to them, the trustee might do so voluntarily. If the trustee refuses, B and C may be entitled to a court order of termination, because it is generally accepted that if all of the beneficiaries of a trust are in being, all of them are competent adults, all of them consent to termination, and no material purpose is served by continuing the trust, then the beneficiaries, acting together by unanimous consent, can compel a termination or modification of the trust. In this connection, the law might well have developed otherwise, but the rule being well established, any person involved in the planning or drafting of a trust should take account of it.

The rule permitting early termination is subject to two important limitations. One limitation arises from the requirement that there be no material purpose that would require continuation of the trust. In this connection, the "material purpose" in question is that of the settlor or testator who created the trust and established its terms. The mere existence of a trust with successive interests in different beneficiaries does not indicate that the settlor intended to prohibit early termination. However, courts have traditionally been quick to discover a material purpose (and therefore to deny a request for early termination) in many commonly-encountered situations—for example, in the case of a spendthrift trust, or a discretionary trust, or a trust for the "support" of one or more living beneficiaries. Today, trust instruments drafted by lawyers commonly include discretionary powers or protective provisions which would generally be found to indicate a material purpose and would therefore raise an obstacle to early termination.

In the leading case of Claflin v. Claflin, 20 N.E. 454 (Mass. 1889), a testator died leaving property in trust for his son, and directed that the son receive $10,000 upon reaching age 21, another $10,000 upon reaching age 25, and the balance of the trust property upon reaching age 30. After reaching age 21 but before reaching age 25, the son, as the sole beneficiary of the trust, sought to compel the trustee to terminate the trust and distribute the remaining trust property. The court held, however, that the testator's direction to withhold distributions until the time specified in the terms of the trust constituted a material purpose which required the continuation of the trust. "[A] testator has a right to dispose of his own property with such restrictions and limitations, not repugnant to law, as he sees fit, and . . . his intentions ought to be carried out, unless they contravene some positive rule of law, or are against public policy."

The material purpose doctrine (also known as the *Claflin* doctrine) allows the settlor to require that the trust continue until all of its purposes have been accomplished. The settlor can also waive the material purpose doctrine during his or her lifetime. If all of the beneficiaries, being competent adults, consent to a modification or termination, and the settlor also consents, it is generally accepted that the beneficiaries and the settlor acting together can modify or terminate the trust, without regard to the original purposes of the trust. In effect, the beneficiaries are bound by the settlor's original purposes in creating the trust, unless the settlor is willing to allow the trust to be terminated or continued on different terms. After the settlor's death, the original purposes of the trust can no longer be changed or overridden.

Aside from the material purpose doctrine, the second major limitation on the rule permitting early termination involves the requirement that all of the beneficiaries be competent adults. If some of the beneficiaries of a trust are unborn, minor, or incompetent, that inhibits termination but does not necessarily preclude it, because guardians can be appointed for purposes of a termination suit, and a court might order termination if appropriate under the facts of the particular case. If a court refuses termination at a particular time because of possible unborn beneficiaries, it might at a later time order termination in view of changed circumstances. In trust termination cases, the conclusive presumption of fertility that for so long was a part of perpetuities law has been given short shrift. A settlor or testator intent on preserving a trust against forced termination should not rely on the fact of possible unborn beneficiaries to accomplish this purpose.

The material purpose doctrine and its qualifications are codified in a somewhat more flexible form in the Uniform Trust Code. Under § 411(b) of the Code, a private express trust may be terminated with the consent of all of the beneficiaries upon a judicial determination that "continuance of the trust is not necessary to achieve any material purpose of the trust." Similarly, the trust may be modified with the consent of all beneficiaries upon a judicial determination that the proposed modification is "not inconsistent with a material purpose of the trust." For this purpose, a spendthrift clause is not presumed to constitute a material purpose preventing termination or modification, and a court may approve a termination or modification, even without the consent of all of the beneficiaries, if the court is satisfied that the interests of the non-consenting beneficiaries are "adequately protected" and that the material purpose doctrine would not otherwise prevent the proposed termination or modification. UTC § 411(e). Furthermore, the Code authorizes a court to modify or terminate a trust at the request of a trustee or a beneficiary, without the consent of all of the beneficiaries, if, due to "circumstances not anticipated by the settlor," the proposed modification or termination will "further the purposes of the trust." UTC § 412(a).

§ 8.9 TRUSTEESHIP VERSUS GUARDIANSHIP

As a means of making gifts of real or personal property, the trust is especially useful where the intended beneficiary or beneficiaries are persons who are not in a position to assume full responsibility for managing property, by reason of legal disability (such as minority or incapacity) or practical constraint (such as lack of judgment or experience). Suppose that A, married to B, is a relatively young man with several minor children. A has no assets of great value and no prospect of inheriting any. A has insurance policies on his life that name B as primary beneficiary, if B survives A, and their children as contingent beneficiaries if she does not. A's will leaves all of his estate to B if she survives him, or to their children if she does not.

Suppose that B in fact predeceases A, and that A dies thereafter survived by several children, and some of them are minors. That part of A's probate estate passing to his minor children, and that part of the life insurance proceeds payable to minor beneficiaries, will be managed by a guardian. (A guardian, unlike a trustee, does not have legal title. Title is in the minor, who is under legal disability to convey, encumber, or devise.) The guardian may be a person nominated by A in his will, or (if A has made no nomination, or his nominee is unable or unwilling to serve) the guardian may be a person chosen by the court.

If a minor child of A acquires assets at A's death, as just described, and then dies before reaching the age of majority, the child's estate may be of a size sufficient to require administration, and that entails expense. Alternatively, if a minor child of A acquires assets at A's death and thereafter reaches the age of majority, the child will be responsible for handling his or her own affairs, and that includes managing property, regardless of kind, value, or risk of loss or dissipation in the hands of an inexperienced person.

If A wishes to avoid these possible consequences of passing property outright to a young child either by will or in the form of life insurance proceeds, he can use a "pour-over" will combined with an inter vivos trust. The inter vivos trust names A's children as primary beneficiaries, and includes a "gift over" of the share of any child who survives A but dies thereafter before reaching age 21: ". . . and if any child of mine dies under the age of 21, such child's share shall thereupon be added to the shares of those of such child's brothers and sisters who survive such child. . . ." (The existence of the gift over prevents a young beneficiary from initially acquiring an interest that is outright or absolute.) The dispositive provisions of the trust instrument also include a clause postponing possession of a child's share (or perhaps only a part of it) until the child reaches a prescribed age above the age of majority (say, age 25). The trustee has appropriate powers to make distributions for a beneficiary's support, care, and education in the interval between A's death and the time that the beneficiary comes into actual possession of his or her share, free of trust. In connection with the creation of the inter vivos trust, A executes a will that leaves all of his estate to his spouse B if she survives him, and that contains a pour-over clause leaving all of his estate to the trustee of his inter vivos trust if B does not survive him. A names B as primary beneficiary of his life insurance, if she survives him, with the trustee of the inter vivos trust as contingent beneficiary if B does not survive him. Under these arrangements, if B predeceases A, and A dies thereafter survived by a young child or children, the trustee under powers bestowed by A can provide for the young beneficiaries until such time (if at all) as their respective shares are turned over to them free of trust.

Aside from the matter of flexibility with respect to a minor beneficiary's interest, trusteeship as an administrative device with respect to property is generally superior to guardianship. State statutes tend to give to trustees greater administrative powers than are given to guardians. Consequently, an act lawfully performed by a trustee without a court order may require a court order if performed by a guardian. Because the private express trust is a means of making gifts, the settlor of a trust is free within broad limits to enlarge the administrative powers accorded to a trustee by statute or judge-made law. It may be difficult or impossible for a testator to enlarge the administrative powers of the person he or she nominates as guardian of the estate of a minor or an incompetent person.

Guardians ordinarily must furnish bond and must act only on court order. Acting on court order requires representation by an attorney. Both guardians and trustees customarily are paid for their services, but furnishing bond and requiring legal services on a regular basis usually make guardianship more expensive than trusteeship. (The trustee of an inter vivos trust is not under court supervision unless he or she petitions for instructions, or the trust in some other way becomes the subject of litigation. On the other hand, in many jurisdictions, the trustee of a testamentary trust is subject to supervision by the probate court.)

Because statutory investment powers of a guardian may be more restrictive than the powers of a trustee under statute or judge-made rules, property or funds managed by a guardian may be subject to more erosion through inflation than property or funds managed by a trustee. Of course neither the guardian nor the trustee is an insurer of the continuing value of the property or funds under fiduciary management. (Both are under a duty to insure against loss of property by such hazards as fire or theft.) Under either guardianship or trusteeship, property managed by the fiduciary may simply decline in value because of conditions beyond the control of the fiduciary, and without any fault on the fiduciary's part. If so, the loss falls on the beneficiary and cannot be shifted to the fiduciary. To this hazard (which is always present whether property is managed by a fiduciary or by an owner), an element of additional risk exists where a trust instrument gives a trustee sweeping investment powers that permit the trustee to subject the trust estate to greater risks than would otherwise be tolerated under state law. Nevertheless, even the broadest powers of management and investment must be exercised fairly and honestly for the benefit of the beneficiaries.

§ 8.10 THE DURABLE POWER OF ATTORNEY

By means of a power of attorney, one person (the principal) makes another (the attorney-in-fact) an agent for a specified purpose or purposes. A power of attorney that is not by its terms a "durable" power ends when the principal dies or becomes incapacitated. By statute in every state, a principal can create a durable power of attorney—a power of attorney that persists despite the incapacity of the principal. (A power of attorney that becomes effective only upon the disability or incapacity of the principal is sometimes called a "springing" power of attorney.)

Under a durable power of attorney, the attorney-in-fact can be empowered to manage the assets of the principal in much the same way that a trustee of a private express trust manages trust assets. Therefore the durable power of attorney is sometimes used as an alternative to trusteeship or guardianship. If the principal creates an inter vivos trust, the durable power of attorney can be used to complement trusteeship. (For example, the attorney-in-fact can be specifically empowered to fund the inter vivos trust.) However, because the powers and duties of an attorney-in-fact are often not nearly as well defined as those of a trustee, the lawyer who drafts a durable power of attorney should be especially careful to delineate clearly the scope of the attorney-in-fact's authority on the face of the instrument.

A durable power of attorney may expressly empower the attorney-in-fact to make health care decisions on behalf of the principal. (Many states have statutes specifically authorizing a durable power of attorney for health care decisions.) In this connection, a durable power can be used to complement a living will executed by the principal.

§ 8.11 THE LIVING WILL

All states now recognize the "living will"—a document in which the declarant sets forth advance directives for health care (including the administration or withholding of nutrition, medication, and pain-killers) should the declarant become terminally ill or permanently unconscious. Statutes authorizing the living will are not uniform. Because the effectiveness of a living will turns on the cooperation of the declarant's family, friends, and health care providers, executed copies of the living will should be made available to family, friends, and health care providers upon execution of the document.

CHAPTER 9

FUTURE INTERESTS—AN INTRODUCTION

§ 9.1 REVERSIONS, REMAINDERS, AND EXECUTORY INTERESTS

Before the English chancellors laid the groundwork for the modern trust, the common law courts created a scheme of present and future interests in land. That scheme did not include what are now called executory interests. Both executory interests and powers of appointment became a part of the modern array of property devices following the enactment of the Statute of Uses (1536).

Today if A, the owner of land in fee simple absolute, conveys "to B for life," A retains a reversion in fee simple in the land. (One might also say that A has a "fee simple subject to a life estate in B," but that is not the conventional way of characterizing the matter.) B's life estate is a present, possessory interest. A's reversion is a future interest.

If A, the owner of land in fee simple absolute, conveys "to B for life, remainder to C and his heirs," A retains no interest in the land. C's future interest is an indefeasibly vested remainder in fee simple. C's remainder serves the same purpose as A's reversion in the preceding example, and both A's reversion and C's remainder are alienable (transferable inter vivos), descendible (transferable under the intestacy laws), and devisable (transferable by will). If A by her deed were to create an indefeasibly vested future interest in C but retain the life estate herself rather than create it in B, she would be creating in C by her inter vivos transfer the functional equivalent of a fee simple passing to C by testamentary transfer at A's death. (Indeed, for federal estate tax purposes, the transfer is treated as testamentary and the value of the property at A's death is includible in her gross estate under § 2036 of the Internal Revenue Code.)

If A, the owner of land in fee simple absolute, conveys "to B for life, remainder to C and his heirs if C reaches age 21," A retains a reversion because the remainder in C is a contingent remainder, and if C were to die before reaching age 21, survived by B (the life tenant), the remainder would "fail by its own terms." In that event, A (or A's successor in interest) would be entitled to possession of the land on the termination of B's life estate. Although the contingent remainder was created by English judges, they fashioned a rule of "destructibility" which resulted in the destruction of legal contingent remainders in land in some circumstances. In the example just put, if B were to die, survived by C who had not yet reached age 21, C's contingent remainder would fall under the destructibility rule. (And A, or her successor in interest, would be entitled to possession.) The destructibility rule has been abolished in most jurisdictions.

Executory interests are the modern counterparts of "springing" and "shifting" uses that were recognized in equity prior to the enactment of the Statute of Uses. Executory interests commonly displace or divest a prior interest. For example, if A owns land in fee simple absolute and he conveys "to B and his heirs, but if C reaches age 21, then over immediately to C and his heirs," B's fee simple terminates immediately if C reaches age 21. C's executory interest is capable of divesting B's interest.

A retained power in a grantor which somewhat resembles the executory interest is the right of entry for condition broken (or power of termination) which follows the fee simple on condition subsequent. A, the owner of land in fee simple absolute, conveys "to B and his heirs, but if the use of the land for park purposes ceases, A and his heirs may enter and terminate the estate granted." A's power to terminate B's estate precludes B's interest in fee from being absolute, just as C's executory interest did in the example given immediately above. Using slightly different language, the grantor can create a fee simple determinable and a possibility of reverter. For example, if A conveys "to B and his heirs so long as the land is used for park purposes," A retains a possibility of reverter by implication. It is commonly said that the possibility of reverter (unlike the right of entry for condition broken) takes effect "automatically" upon the happening of the event that terminates the fee simple determinable. In that respect the possibility of reverter appears to resemble C's executory interest more closely than the right of entry does.

An executory interest may be created to displace the interest of its creator. If A, the owner of land in fee simple absolute, conveys it "to B and his heirs ten years hence," B acquires an executory interest which takes effect by displacing A's fee simple at the expiration of ten years from the effective date of the deed. There is no evidence that owners of property commonly create such interests.

It should not be assumed on the basis of the "limitations" in the examples given above that a remainder or a reversion must be in fee simple, or that a future interest cannot be classified as an executory interest unless it may displace or does displace a prior possessory fee simple. A remainder may be for life ("to B for life, then to C for life"), and the executory interest is commonly so created that it may displace a remainder ("to B for life, remainder to C and his heirs, but if C fails to survive B, then to D and his heirs"). There are many variations with respect to limitations. Further, it should not be assumed that classification of future interests is always easy and proceeds smoothly. Those who draft dispositive instruments do not always use stylized language that fits neatly within the traditional classification scheme.

One more matter deserves mention at this point. If A grants "to B for life, remainder to C and his heirs," the words "and his heirs" are traditional words of inheritance indicating that the remainder is in fee simple (rather than for life). They are also words of "limitation" indicating the duration of C's interest, as opposed to words of "purchase" indicating the identity of the takers. Words of inheritance were never required to pass a fee simple by will, and they are not required in most jurisdictions today to pass a fee simple by deed. If A grants "to B for life, remainder to C," the remainder is in fee simple nearly everywhere. Generally speaking, therefore, words of inheritance are dispensed with hereafter in this chapter (and in this book).

§ 9.2 HOW FUTURE INTERESTS CHANGE

The nature of a future interest can and often does change as time passes, and this characteristic of a future estate has significance both for the lawyer preparing a dispositive document and for the lawyer working with a document prepared by another. Suppose that A, the owner of land in fee simple absolute, conveys it "to B for life, remainder to C provided C reaches age 35." (At the time of the conveyance C is under age 35.) If C reaches age 35 during B's lifetime, C's contingent remainder "vests" indefeasibly in C, and on B's death, C is entitled to possession of the land. If B dies, survived by C who has not yet reached age 35, A's reversion, being a "vested" interest, entitles A to possession and (assuming that the destructibility rule has been abolished) A then has a fee simple, subject, however, to the future interest in C. (It may seem incongruous, after B's death, to continue to speak of C's future interest as a "contingent remainder" because it will take effect, if at all, by way of divesting a possessory fee simple. Therefore, one might argue that on B's death C's future interest should change from a contingent remainder to an executory interest. The prevailing view, however, is that C's future interest continues to be classified as a contingent remainder.) Logically, there is no more reason for putting A in possession at B's death than for putting C in possession—A's reversion is subject to an implied condition (C's not reaching age 35), just as C's remainder is subject to an express condition. Possession is awarded to A on the basis of characterizing A's interest as "vested." To further demonstrate the importance of the label attached to an interest, consider this case: A, owning securities, bequeaths them in trust "to pay the net income to B for life, and at B's death, to pay principal to C provided he reaches age 35, and if he dies before age 35, then to pay principal to D." (At A's death C is under age 35). B dies, survived by C who has not yet reached age 35. If the limitations at A's death are construed to be a life estate in B, and a vested remainder in C, subject to possible divestment by an executory interest in D, then on B's death survived by C and D, C is entitled to income from the trust, not A's successor in interest, if the rule announced in Phipps v. Ackers, 8 Eng.Rep. 539 (H.L. 1842) is followed. This result flows from the classification of C's interest as "vested."

In the case just stated, classification of interests is used to solve a difficulty created by circumstances that the lawyer could (and should) have anticipated: disposition of income at B's death survived by C who has not yet reached age 35. (One should not infer that there is any requirement that D survive the income beneficiary. D must survive the testator, but having done that, there is no requirement that D survive any other person in order to take possession of the property if C dies before age 35. If D survived the testator, but predeceased the income beneficiary, D's successor in interest, by will or intestacy, stands in D's place.)

The difficulties created by imprecise drafting can be further demonstrated by elaborating somewhat on the case set out above. A, owning securities, bequeaths them in trust "to pay the net income to B for life, and at B's death, to pay principal to C provided he reaches age 35, and if C dies before age 35 without leaving issue surviving him, then to D." At A's death B, C, and D are living, but C has not yet reached age 35. C dies at age 30, survived by issue and devising his entire estate to his surviving spouse E. B dies. Who is entitled to the trust corpus? Clearly not D, whose interest is conditioned both on C's dying before age 35 and on C's dying without any surviving issue. Did A by implication make a gift to C's issue who survive C? Or on C's death, survived by issue, did his remainder become indefeasibly vested in C's estate? (There is some support for the notion that C's interest under such circumstances does vest indefeasibly in C's estate. If so, that interest passed to E under C's will.) The drafting point is clear: If A intends to make a gift to C's issue who survive C, the gift should be made in explicit terms: ". . . and if C dies before age 35 survived by issue, to pay principal to such issue, but if C dies before age 35 without leaving issue surviving him. . . ."

The ability of future interests to change in character is of particular importance to lawyers engaged in trusts and estates work because future interests can and do exist for years before becoming possessory, and during that time, much may have happened to the interests. To resolve disputes between claimants (or merely to locate those persons entitled to property or a fund to which no claim at all has been asserted), it may be important to determine the classification of an interest at its creation, and subsequent changes (if any) in its classification, as well as changes in its ownership over time. Suppose that A, owning land in fee simple absolute, conveys "to B for life, remainder to C provided C survives B." C's future interest is a contingent remainder, and A has a reversion in fee simple by implication. If C executes a will purporting to devise his future interest to D, and dies thereafter, survived by both B and D, the attempted devise is ineffective because C's contingent remainder ceased to exist (it "failed by its own terms") at C's death. Had C granted (as opposed to devised) his contingent remainder to D, the grant in itself would be effective. (The contingent remainder is alienable.) Were D then to die intestate, survived by B and C and leaving E as his sole heir, D's contingent remainder would pass to E under the intestacy laws. (Under these facts, the contingent remainder is descendible.) If C died thereafter, survived by B and E, the contingent remainder in E would "fail by its own terms." By way of contrast, if B died, survived by C and E, the contingent remainder in E would be transformed into a possessory fee simple absolute in E and A's reversion in fee would be displaced ("divested") by the vesting in possession of E's interest.

For purposes of properly representing others in the preparation, interpretation, or litigation of dispositive documents, it is desirable, then, to keep in mind that classification of a future interest at its creation is frequently no more than a point of departure. Although occasionally important in itself (a contingent future interest is void at its creation under the Rule Against Perpetuities in orthodox form if it might vest at a remote time), initial characterization of an interest is much more often a matter preliminary to solving a problem, not a solution to a problem.

§ 9.3 USING FUTURE INTERESTS

It is well known that transferors can use future interests to extend control over property for extended periods of time. Dispositions that create future interests usually involve some variation of the standard pattern of a life estate followed by a remainder, or a life income interest with a power of appointment followed by a remainder. However, relatively simple limitations can give rise to complicated legal problems. If A's will creates a testamentary trust to pay "income to my wife for life, then income to my children for their lives, then corpus to my grandchildren," and A dies survived by his wife and several children, he has violated no rule of law. (The gift of corpus to the grandchildren must vest or fail no later than the death of A's last surviving child, who is necessarily a life in being at A's death. Thus, the gift does not violate the Rule Against Perpetuities in orthodox form, even though it may include grandchildren unborn at A's death.) However, if A creates an irrevocable inter vivos trust (as opposed to a will) to pay "income to my wife for life, then income to my children for their lives, then corpus to my grandchildren" (the same words as those used in the will just described), the gift of corpus violates the Rule Against Perpetuities in orthodox form if "children" is given its customary construction of "children whenever born." (The trust takes effect at its creation, and includes secondary gifts of income to A's children, some of whom may not yet be born. Those gifts are valid under the Rule. But the gift of corpus, including as it does a gift to an "unborn child of an unborn child," is bad under the rule of Leake v. Robinson, 35 Eng.Rep. 979 (Ch. 1817)—a gift bad as to some members of the class is bad as to all.)

Even future interests that are free from legal defects can give rise to other kinds of problems. Suppose that A owns land in fee simple absolute and devises it "to my wife B for life, remainder to my child C." B takes a present, possessory life estate, and C takes an indefeasibly vested remainder. But from the fact that it is easy to create future interests, it does not follow that it is wise. A simple life estate may prove to be inadequate to meet B's needs (and if the inadequacy of the life estate does not become evident until after the right to elect has expired, it will be useless to point out that B could have elected to take against the will). Furthermore, aside from the matter of the adequacy of a life interest, splitting ownership of land between B and C inhibits sale of the fee simple. Even though the interests of both are alienable, either the life tenant or the remainderman may be reluctant to sell. ("Dad wanted it this way, and I think we should leave things as they are.") Statutes facilitating sale may offer relief in this connection, but requiring a beneficiary to seek statutory relief is a poor substitute for thinking through the consequences of a disposition of property before it is made.

We live in a time of successive marriages, and often the testator fears that after his or her death the surviving spouse may find a new mate who will eventually enjoy the testator's bounty. The testator may therefore hesitate to make an absolute gift of the entire estate to the surviving spouse, and the spouse may instead receive an absolute gift of a fractional share of the estate or, alternatively, a life estate or an income interest for life, with future interests created in the testator's children or issue. If the testator is a person of substantial wealth, so that the limited gift to the surviving spouse is adequate under the circumstances, the arrangement is both common and defensible.

If a simple life income interest appears to be inadequate for the surviving spouse, it can be made both more palatable to the beneficiary and more workable as a dispositive device by making it a part of a trust in which the trustee has a discretionary power to invade corpus of the trust for the support of the income beneficiary. Unquestionably persons at times may reasonably differ on what level of support is appropriate. Nonetheless, giving the trustee a power of invasion provides some assurance that the needs of the primary object of the testator's bounty will be met, while at the same time protecting the interests of the other beneficiaries. Here again, even in the absence of a power of invasion, statutes may afford relief to the income beneficiary who finds income inadequate for proper support. However, the availability of statutory relief does not relieve the lawyer of the obligation to advise the testator that powers to invade corpus might, in an appropriate case, be created by the dispositive instrument.

Contingencies or conditions can be attached to future interests, and they often are. Probably the most common constructional problems involve the question of whether a particular beneficiary must survive until the time for possession of his or her interest. If A devises property "to B for life, remainder to C," the courts have traditionally held that C has an indefeasibly vested remainder and need not survive B in order to receive the property. If C dies survived by B, C's remainder interest passes by will or intestacy to C's successor in interest, who will be entitled to possession of the property at the termination of B's life estate. Similarly, if the devise is "to B for life, remainder to B's children," each child of B living at A's death or born thereafter is entitled to a share of the property at B's death, irrespective of whether he or she survives B. If one of B's children dies before B, the deceased child's share passes by will or intestacy to the child's successor in interest. By way of contrast, if the devise is "to B for life, remainder to B's issue," the courts have traditionally held that the remainder is to be allocated by some form of representation among B's issue who are living at B's death. (In the case of a class gift to "issue," "heirs" or the like with beneficiaries in multiple generations, any method of representation implicitly requires that a beneficiary be living at the time for possession and reallocates the share of a deceased beneficiary among the other living beneficiaries.)

In some jurisdictions, the judicial rules of construction have been modified by statute. For example, § 2–707 of the Uniform Probate Code raises a general presumption that "[a] future interest under the terms of a trust is contingent on the beneficiary's surviving the distribution date." Although judicial or statutory rules of construction may be available to resolve questions concerning survival requirements, a lawyer involved in the planning or drafting of dispositive instruments should not rely on rules of construction but should clearly state whether a beneficiary is required to survive until the time for possession of his or her interest (and, if so, how the interest is to be disposed of if the beneficiary fails to survive).

Sometimes the conditional nature of the gift is emphasized by the explicit creation of an alternative gift: "to B for life, remainder to C provided he reaches age 35, and if he does not, then to D." A gift of this sort, which will shift to an alternative taker if the condition of survival is not met, should be distinguished from a gift that is indefeasibly vested in an ascertained taker with possession or payment postponed: "to B for life, remainder to C, with net income payable annually and one-third of the principal payable at age 21, one-half of the remaining principal payable at age 25, and all of the remaining principal payable at age 30." Even if C dies before reaching the specified ages, C's interest passes to his successor in interest. (C's interest is alienable, devisable, and descendible.)

In the case of a gift "to B for life, remainder to C provided he reaches age 35, and if he does not, then to D," the conditional nature of the gift to C is clear. However, a gift "to B for life, then to C at age 35" invites controversy. Must C survive to age 35 in order to qualify for the intended gift? Or does C take an indefeasibly vested remainder with possession or payment merely postponed until C reaches age 35? Courts have occasionally found fine distinctions based on slight differences in language which may or may not carry out the disposition intended by the transferor. (For example, under the rule in Clobberie's Case, 86 Eng. Rep. 476 (Ch. 1677), a gift to C "at age 25" may fail if C dies before reaching age 25, while a gift to C "to be paid at age 25" may pass by will or intestacy to C's successor in interest.) There is nothing to be said for creating gifts that leave the terms of the disposition in doubt, for the costs of a construction proceeding may significantly diminish the value of the intended gift to the beneficiary.

§ 9.4 THE RULE IN SHELLEY'S CASE AND THE DOCTRINE OF WORTHIER TITLE

Two doctrines that trace their origins back to feudal times may affect the work of a property lawyer today. They are the Rule in Shelley's Case and the Doctrine of Worthier Title.

If A, the owner of land in fee simple absolute, conveys "to B for life, remainder to the heirs of B," applying the Rule in Shelley's Case to the intended remainder results in treating A's deed as if it had read "to B for life, remainder to B and his heirs." (The remainder intended by A for B's heirs is changed by operation of a rule of law into a remainder in B himself.) If A, the owner of land in fee simple absolute, conveys "to B for life, remainder to my [A's] heirs," applying the Doctrine of Worthier Title to the intended remainder results in treating A's deed as if the intended future interest had been omitted from the instrument altogether. (Consequently, A has a reversion by implication.)

Simes's statement of the Rule in Shelley's Case is in part as follows:

> If a life estate in land is conveyed or devised to [B], and by the same conveyance or devise, a remainder in the same land is limited, mediately or immediately, to the heirs of [B], . . . and the life estate and remainder are of the same quality, then [B] has a remainder in fee simple. . . .*

The Rule in Shelley's Case applies only to remainders (legal or equitable) in land.

Gulliver's statement of the Doctrine of Worthier Title is:

> A provision for the intestate successors of the transferor is void if it would give them the same interest as they would take if the provision were omitted from the instrument and the interest

* Simes, Handbook of the Law of Future Interests 45 (2d ed. 1966).

> remaining in the transferor as a result of such omission passed to them by intestacy.*

Note that Gulliver's statement suggests a hypothetical situation: Imagine that the intended future interest was omitted from the deed or instrument of trust. If immediately thereafter the transferor died intestate, would the retained interest passing to the transferor's heirs be the same as that which they were intended to take under the deed or instrument of trust? If so, this is the kind of limitation to which the Doctrine of Worthier Title can be applied. Although the Doctrine is applicable to both legal and equitable interests, in realty or personalty, it is not confined to remainders.

To the extent that it exists today in the United States, the Doctrine of Worthier Title (unlike the Rule in Shelley's Case) is a rule of construction. That is, its applicability is said to turn on the intention of the transferor. The Rule in Shelley's Case, being a rule of law, or a rule of property, applies without regard to the transferor's intention. In most jurisdictions the Rule in Shelley's Case has been abolished by statute. The status of the Doctrine of Worthier Title in some jurisdictions may be unclear if there is neither a statute on the Doctrine nor an authoritative judicial decision dealing with it. The state of New York, commonly credited with resurrecting the Doctrine in the United States, abolished it by statute in 1966.

---

* Gulliver, Cases and Materials on the Law of Future Interests 98 (1959).

Where the Doctrine of Worthier Title exists, it creates a rebuttable presumption that a provision in a deed or trust instrument purporting to create an interest in the transferor's "heirs" or "next of kin" does not in fact do so. The presumption can be overcome by evidence of a contrary intent. (The transferor not only wrote a limitation down, but also meant it.) Determining whether there is sufficient evidence of contrary intent is just as difficult as one would expect it to be. The decided cases on this matter are unmanageable.

If the presumption created by the Doctrine of Worthier Title is not overcome, the transferor has a retained interest by way of reversion or resulting trust. The transferor might or might not still hold that interest at death. If the transferor does hold the interest at death, it might or might not pass by intestacy to his or her heirs.

A lawyer does not use the Rule in Shelley's Case or the Doctrine of Worthier Title in the same sense that he or she uses (say) powers of appointment. Rather, being aware of them, the lawyer takes account of them. Applying the Doctrine of Worthier Title rationally requires reading "heirs" of the transferor to mean "such person or persons who would be the successors in interest of the transferor at death if the transferor were to die intestate still owning the subject matter of the transfer." This ordinary meaning of "heirs" can be avoided by drafting: A grants "to B for life, and then to such person or persons who would be my heirs, or would have been my heirs, as the case may be, were I to die, or had I died, when B dies." Under this language, the identity of the takers of the future interest is fixed at B's death (not at A's death, which might occur before or after B's death).

Aside from the matter of drafting, both the Rule in Shelley's Case and the Doctrine of Worthier Title are relevant in connection with such matters as analyzing limitations to determine what interests in property are created, identifying beneficiaries of those interests, determining creditors' rights, and taxing transfers of interests in property. Both the Rule and the Doctrine are feudal in origin, but their impact has been a continuing one that has not altogether disappeared from the law.

§ 9.5 THE LANGUAGE OF CLASS GIFTS

Future interests are commonly created in the form of a gift to a group (or "class") of beneficiaries that may increase or decrease in number over time. In general, when property is to be divided among the members of a class, it is necessary first to determine who is included (or not included) in the class and then to determine how the property is to be allocated among the class members.

The language of class gifts is well established, but it is not altogether precise. To say that a class "closes" at a particular time means simply that a person born after that time cannot share in the class gift. In effect, the time of class closing establishes the maximum membership of the class. Suppose that at the execution of her will, A has a child B, and B has several children. A's will devises property "to the children of B." The class remains "open" until A's death to admit other children that may be born to B, but the class "closes" at A's death. Thus, a child conceived by B after A's death and born alive does not share in the gift. (The rule of construction need not have worked out that way, but it did.) Had A's will read: "I give $100,000 to such of the children of B as reach age 21" and B, having four children, survives A, the class closes at A's death if a child of B has reached age 21 at A's death. Closing the class at A's death makes it possible to ascertain the maximum number of children who will share and to distribute a share without delay to the child who meets the age requirement. However, closing the class does not necessarily establish the ultimate or final number of the shares. If at A's death a child of B is alive but under 21, such child might or might not reach the prescribed age. If only one of B's four children has reached age 21 at A's death, such child is entitled to an immediate distribution of his or her one-fourth share of $100,000 (that is, $25,000). That child also has a vested interest in the balance of the gift ($75,000), subject to possible divestment as the other children reach age 21.

A class gift is said to be "postponed" when it follows a "particular estate." A, survived by her child B, devises property "to B for life, remainder to the children of B." The class gift is a future interest—a postponed gift. If a child of B is in existence at A's death, that child has a vested interest subject to possible partial divestment by the birth of additional children to B. The class closes at B's death. Suppose instead that A's will devises property "to the children of B." The gift is an "immediate" gift, rather than a postponed gift, and the class closes at A's death. Any children of B who are alive at A's death will share in the gift, to the exclusion of any children conceived by B after A's death. However, if B is childless at A's death, all children of B, whenever born, share. (Any children born to B will take by way of an "executory devise.")

§ 9.6 HOW CLASS GIFTS WORK

The substantive law on class gifts consists of rules of construction that have developed to give effect to the presumed intention of the transferor. Because the rules of construction developed over a long period of time, and because they reflect competing principles, they sometimes work at cross purposes. Some of the rules of construction that are now well established might have been formulated in a different way, but they were not. Of course it is true that once the general operation of the rules of construction has been grasped, one can speculate on how the rules might work by analogy in similar but nonetheless distinguishable cases, but one should not assume that the rules worked out by established precedent fit neatly and seamlessly into a logically consistent scheme. The precedent might well take a different tack because it reflects a different competing principle.

For example, if A devises property "to B for life, remainder to the children of B," and B and several of B's children survive A, any children conceived by B after A's death (and born alive) share in the gift of the remainder. Here there is no compelling reason to close the class at A's death (that is, to exclude afterborn children of B), although one could argue that A might have intended to benefit only children who were personally known to her. Although B has children alive at A's death, they are in no position to call for an immediate distribution because there is an outstanding life estate in B. So the class remains "open" at A's death to admit afterborn children of B on the assumption that A intended to include as many of B's children as possible. (The class "closes" at B's death, when the life interest in B ceases and the remainder becomes a possessory interest.)

By way of contrast, if A devises "to the children of B," and A then dies survived by B and several of B's children, no child of B who is conceived after A's death (and born alive) is entitled to share in the devise. The class closes at A's death. Again, one could argue that A might have intended to include all children of B, whenever born, but the well established rule of construction worked out otherwise. Closing the class at A's death fixes the number of children who share, and permits an immediate distribution to the existing objects of A's bounty who in every respect meet the description of the intended beneficiaries of the gift. Closing the class facilitates sale of the subject matter of the gift (an "indefeasibly vested" interest in property is likely to be more attractive to a buyer than a "vested interest subject to open"). Nevertheless, if A devises "to the children of B," and B survives A but has not yet had any children, all children of B, whenever born, are entitled to share, under the rule of Weld v.

Bradbury, 23 Eng.Rep. 1058 (Ch. 1715). (Here, the gift might have failed entirely, or the subject matter of the intended gift might have been given in its entirety to the first-born child of B, to the exclusion of children born to B thereafter, but the rule of construction worked out otherwise.)

If A devises "to B for life, remainder to the children of B who reach age 21," and A then dies survived by B and several of B's children, the class does not close at A's death even if one of B's children has reached age 21 at A's death. (That child cannot call for immediate distribution because there is an outstanding life estate in B.) The class closes at B's death. Even at B's death the final or ultimate number of shares might not be determinable because one or more of B's children then living might not yet have reached age 21. Only those who reach age 21 will share in the class gift.

Suppose that A bequeaths "$10,000 apiece to each child of B." The only other dispositive clause of A's will is a gift to C of the residuary estate. A dies survived by both B and C. If B has five children at A's death, each takes $10,000. No child of B who is conceived after A's death (and born alive) is entitled to share. To permit afterborn children to take would require a delay in distributing A's residuary estate until B's death, because until that time it is not possible to determine how much of the estate must be set aside to pay a $10,000 legacy to each of B's children. It is presumed, therefore, that afterborn children of B are excluded from the class gift.

Whether the death of a class member defeats his or her interest in a class gift depends on the words of the gift. If A devises property "to B for life, remainder to the children of B," and A then dies survived by B and several of B's children, the class remains open at A's death. At A's death the remainder vests "subject to open" in the children of B then alive. A child of B alive during the life tenancy has an alienable, devisable, and descendible interest in the remainder. If a child of B who was alive at A's death dies before B, without having transferred his or her remainder interest during life, the deceased child's share passes to his or her successor in interest by will or by intestacy. At B's death, the person who then owns that interest becomes entitled to possession of the deceased child's share.

By way of contrast, if A devises property "to B for life, remainder to such of B's children who survive B," an express survival requirement is attached to the gift in remainder. A child of B who was alive at A's death but dies before B receives nothing. Only those children of B who survive B are entitled to share in the class gift.

The class closing rules are referred to as "rules of convenience"—they facilitate administration of the testator's estate and permit beneficiaries to receive possession or distribution of their shares without undue delay. (Understandably, however, a potential taker who is excluded from sharing by the operation of the rules may not view them as a "convenience.")

Because the rules of construction on class gifts are just that—rules of construction, not "rules of property" or "rules of law," they give way to expressions of contrary intent. Suppose that A is considering leaving property "to the children of B," and B is a person alive at the execution of the will who might still be alive at A's death. A does not wish the class to "close" at her death if B is then alive. If so, A might leave the property "to the children of B, whether born before or after my death, share and share alike." Under this language, all of B's children, whenever born, are entitled to share. (Children of B alive at A's death have a fee simple, subject to possible partial divestment.) Persons might reasonably differ on the wisdom of a gift of this kind. The point here is that if the rules of construction are distasteful, they can be avoided by drafting.

§ 9.7 DRAFTING

Because natural objects of a donor's bounty often occur in groups, it is natural, and at times desirable, to use group language in identifying beneficiaries. But group language should be used with care. For example, suppose that A is married to B and has three children—C, D, and E. A devises property to B for life and "then to my children, C, D, and E, or the survivor or survivors of them." If C, D, and E (as well as B) all survive A, but C dies before B, survived by issue, do D and E take all of the property at B's death to the exclusion of C's issue? What did A mean by "my children, C, D, and E, or the survivor or survivors of them"? Although the substantive law on construction of limitations and class gifts, including anti-lapse statutes, may shed some light on these questions, the careful lawyer should not rely on construction to effect intention. Rather, the lawyer should ascertain intention, and express it. Ascertaining intention may not be easy. Expressing intention is often time consuming and difficult.

If it is A's intention that his children be required to survive only A himself (as opposed to surviving both A and B), the lawyer might write: "To B for life, remainder to my children," or (making explicit what is implicit under the substantive law on class gifts) "to B for life, remainder to those of my children who survive me," or (anticipating birth or adoption of a child) "to B for life, remainder to those of my children now alive or thereafter born to or adopted by me who survive me."

But the testator may have a child, alive at the execution of the will, who dies before the testator, leaving issue who survive the testator. Or a child of the testator may have died before the execution of the will, leaving issue who survive the testator. If the lawyer has used the language of the preceding paragraph in creating limitations, such surviving issue are not included in the express terms of the class gift, for they are not children of the testator. Whether or not under any of the limitations a gift by substitution exists under an anti-lapse statute is a matter of local law. For example, if the words of A's will are "to B for life, remainder to my children," and C, a child of A alive at the execution of the will, predeceases A, leaving issue who survive A, an anti-lapse statute may create a gift by substitution in C's issue who survive A. Thus, if A was survived by his spouse B and by his two other children, D and E, the remainder following B's life estate would be divided into three equal shares for D, E, and C's issue living at A's death. (If D, or E, or any of the above-mentioned issue predeceased B, their shares would pass to their respective successors in interest by will or by intestacy.)

Anti-lapse statutes are often construed to apply to class gifts where a member of the class dies after the execution of the will and before the testator's death. And some anti-lapse statutes (including the Uniform Probate Code) expressly provide that a person who fails to survive the testator but who would have taken under a class gift, had he or she survived the testator, is treated as a devisee, whether that person died before or after the execution of the will.

Nonetheless, a testator interested in achieving substantial equality of gifts to issue should not rely on an anti-lapse statute. Determining whether an anti-lapse statute applies to a particular set of facts might require a lawsuit. To provide explicitly for the surviving issue of a child of the testator who is alive at the execution of the will but who might predecease the testator, the limitations might be worded in this way: "to B for life, remainder to those of my children now alive or hereafter born to or adopted by me who survive me; provided, however, should any child predecease me, leaving issue who survive me, the share of such deceased child shall pass to such surviving issue by right of representation."

Just as the drafting lawyer may make explicit what is implicit in a class gift to which an anti-lapse statute is applied, so too the lawyer may avoid the impact of an anti-lapse statute if that is consistent with intention. Within broad limits, a testator is free to dispose of property at death as he or she wishes. Anti-lapse statutes reflect presumed intention. It is conceivable that a testator may wish to make a gift only to living descendants in the first generation. If it is A's intention to include only those of his children (if any) who survive both him and his spouse, the lawyer might write: "to B for life, then in fee simple to those of my children, C and D, who survive both me and my spouse, and if none of my children survive both me and my spouse, then in fee simple to. . . ." If A anticipates birth or adoption of additional children, the lawyer might write: "to B for life, then in fee simple to those of my children now alive or hereafter born to or adopted by me who survive both me and my spouse, and if. . . ." To make avoidance of the anti-lapse statute explicit, the lawyer might direct that the anti-lapse statute not apply to a particular gift or to gifts in general under the will.

Just as the lawyer should avoid using "my children, or the survivor or survivors of them" to describe the beneficiaries of a future interest after a life estate, so too the lawyer should eschew "my children or their issue." If the intention is simply to keep the property in the family and divide it among the testator's issue at the termination of the life estate, the disposition might read as follows: "to B for life, if she survives me, remainder at B's death (or at my death, if B does not survive me) to my issue then living, by right of representation." This language makes the interest of each remainder beneficiary contingent on surviving the life tenant, and also preserves a share of the property for the surviving issue (if any) of a deceased beneficiary. For example, suppose that A (the testator) is survived by his spouse B (the life tenant) and by two children, C (who predeceases B) and D (who survives B). At B's death, C's surviving issue (if any) will become entitled to share the property with D; if C left no issue who survive B, then D will take the entire property. (In any event, no interest passes from C by will or by intestacy, because C's interest failed when C died during B's lifetime.)

Perhaps the testator intends to impose a more limited survival requirement, while preserving equality among children and representatives of deceased children and permitting children who die without issue to dispose of their shares by will or intestacy. In this case, the lawyer might consider the following language:

> I devise Blackacre to B for life, remainder to those of my children now alive or hereafter born to or adopted by me who survive me, in equal shares; provided, however,
>
> (a) should any child of mine now alive or hereafter born to or adopted by me predecease me, leaving issue who survive me, the share of such deceased child shall pass to such surviving issue by right of representation;
>
> (b) should any child of mine now alive or hereafter born to or adopted by me survive me but predecease my spouse, survived by issue, the

share of such deceased child shall pass to such surviving issue by right of representation; and

(c) should any child of mine now alive or hereafter born to or adopted by me survive me but predecease my spouse, not survived by issue, the share of such deceased child shall thereupon be indefeasibly vested in such child.

This language would produce somewhat different results in the preceding example. At the death of the testator (A) survived by his spouse (B), the children (C and D) would each take a vested remainder subject to divestment. Upon C's subsequent death during B's lifetime, C's interest would fail, and C's issue then living (if any) would take an indefeasible one-half share of the remainder (by way of divesting gift); they would not be required to survive B. Moreover, if C died without issue, C's one-half share of the remainder would become indefeasibly vested and would pass to C's successors in interest by will or by intestacy. Upon B's subsequent death survived by D, D would take an indefeasibly vested one-half share of the property in fee simple.

Drafting to anticipate contingencies that are likely to occur is tedious, time-consuming, and ill-paid. Therefore lawyers may be tempted to rely on the substantive law on construction of limitations, class gifts, lapse, the acceleration of remainders, and on the operation of anti-lapse statutes to achieve what can be achieved more reliably through careful drafting.

§ 9.8 THE BASIC LANGUAGE OF POWERS

The language used with respect to powers is fairly well developed, but it continues to evolve. Because powers of appointment are commonly created in connection with a transfer of property, the person who creates a power is often referred to as the "donor" and the holder of the power as the "donee." (Often the donor and the donee may be the same person, as in the case of a settlor who retains a power to appoint interests in property held in trust.) By its terms, a power may be exercisable in favor of a broad or narrow group of persons, or even a single person. Prior to exercise of a power, the potential takers are called the "objects" of the power; once a power is exercised to create beneficial interests in one or more persons, those persons are called "appointees." If a power is not exercised and expires (or "lapses") by its own terms, the property subject to the power passes to the "takers in default." The subject matter of a power is the "appointive property" or "property subject to the power" (as distinguished from property actually owned by the holder of the power).

If a power is exercisable by deed during the lifetime of the holder, it is an "inter vivos" power; if exercisable only by will, it is a "testamentary" power. (A power can be both inter vivos and testamentary: "to such person or persons as B by deed or will appoints.")

It is conventional to classify powers as "general" or "special." Following the usage in the Internal Revenue Code, a general power is defined as one which may be exercised in favor of the holder, the holder's estate, the holder's creditors, or creditors of the holder's estate. In other words, a general power is one that the holder can exercise for his or her own personal benefit, either during life or at death. Any other power is classified as a special (or "limited" or "non-general") power. Thus, if A creates a trust to pay income to B for life, and gives B a power of appointment which can be exercised in favor of anyone in the world—other than B, B's estate, or creditors of B or B's estate—B holds a special power. (If B, B's estate, or the creditors of B or B's estate were included as objects, B would have a general power.)

One intended to have a power of appointment may decline to accept the power by "renouncing" or "disclaiming" it. Once a power of appointment has come into existence, the holder may extinguish the power by "releasing" it. The distinction between renunciation (refusal to accept a power) and release (destruction of an existing power) may be significant for federal gift and estate tax purposes. For example, under the federal gift tax, release of a general power to appoint by deed or will results in a deemed gift from the holder of the power to the person or persons who benefit from the release. In contrast, renunciation of such a power (like renunciation of a devise or bequest under a will) does not result in a deemed gift. A special power of appointment is releasable unless it is a power in trust.

Although the traditional law on powers of appointment was developed by judges in deciding cases, some jurisdictions have detailed statutes governing the classification of powers, the manner of their creation, and the consequences of their exercise (or non-exercise). The Uniform Powers of Appointment Act, promulgated in 2013, codifies much of the traditional law of powers. Even a state without a statutory system of powers may have specific statutory provisions dealing with particular matters arising under the law of powers, such as whether a testamentary power of appointment, not otherwise expressly exercised, is impliedly exercised by a residuary clause in the will of the donee. For example, § 2–608 of the Uniform Probate Code provides in relevant part that "a general residuary clause in a will . . . expresses an intention to exercise a power of appointment held by the testator only if (i) the power is a general power exercisable in favor of the powerholder's estate and the creating instrument does not contain an effective gift if the power is not exercised or (ii) the testator's will manifests an intention to include the property subject to the power." A testator who intends to exercise a testamentary power of appointment in connection with a residuary gift might use the following language: "All the rest, residue and remainder of my estate, including lapsed or failed gifts, I give, devise, and bequeath to . . ., and all property over which I have a power of appointment under the will of A, dated . . ., I hereby appoint in its entirety to. . . ."

§ 9.9 THE ORIGIN OF POWERS

The power of appointment originated in the English system of "uses" (the old counterpart of the modern trust). Prior to the enactment of the Statute of Wills, the power to devise freehold interests in land was not recognized at common law. But substantially the same thing could be accomplished by means of a "use." If A, the owner in fee simple, enfeoffed "B and his heirs to the use of A for life and thereafter to such person as A should by last will appoint," at A's death B could be compelled in a court of equity to convey to A's appointee, who took by way of a "shifting use." Although this device for circumventing the rules of the common law became superfluous after the enactment of the Statute of Wills in 1540, the possibilities of the "power" continued to be recognized, and powers are frequently created today. For example, suppose that A by his will creates a testamentary trust of his residuary estate and directs the trustee "to pay the net income to my spouse B for life, and at her death to pay principal to such person or persons as my spouse B by deed or will appoints, and in default of appointment to pay principal to my issue then living, by right of representation." A is survived by B and by several children. A (the "donor") has created a general power of appointment in B (the "donee")—a power under which B can lawfully designate any person, including B herself, as the owner of the trust property. (For federal estate tax purposes, mere possession of such a power by B at her death is sufficient to cause the trust property to be included in her gross estate under § 2041 of the Internal Revenue Code.) To the extent that B does not effectively exercise the power of appointment, the trust property will go to A's surviving issue as "takers in default."

§ 9.10 WHAT MOTIVATES THE CREATION OF POWERS?

A power of appointment permits a property owner to project control over wealth into the future, often for many years after his or her death. But the power differs from other methods of creating future interests in that an owner of property who creates a power of appointment gives to another person a discretionary power to direct the devolution of wealth in the light of subsequent events and changed circumstances. Thus, if A devises property "to B for life, remainder to those of B's children who survive B," all of B's children who are living at B's death are treated equally. But if A devises property "to B for life, remainder to such of B's children who survive B, to one or more to the exclusion of others, and in such shares and proportions, as B by her last will appoints," B may favor those of her children who are diligent, or impecunious, or ill. In a sense, B is making a testamentary disposition on behalf of A—filling in terms that were deliberately left open in the original will—at a time when A himself can no longer act.

One who owns property may make an inter vivos transfer of the property, either in trust or not, and retain (or "reserve") a power of appointment with respect to the property transferred, or some part of it. But the most useful power of appointment is not one retained by the original owner of the property subject to the power, but one created in another person, as described in the preceding paragraph. A general power or a special power created in someone other than the original owner of the property may be exercisable long after the original owner has died, in light of circumstances which could not be foreseen at that time. Adjusting interests in income or principal in accordance with the needs of beneficiaries as they exist from time to time is the most important function of the power of appointment.

Although the creation of powers is customarily justified on the ground that powers permit flexibility in the disposition of property, powers sometimes serve other purposes as well. A special power may be framed so broadly that the holder can use the appointive property for virtually any purpose other than his or her own pecuniary benefit ("a power in B to appoint the property to any one or more persons other than B, B's estate, B's creditors, or the creditors of B's estate"), yet the appointive property cannot be reached by the power holder's creditors to satisfy their claims. This is true even if the special power is held by the same person who created it. Moreover, in the absence of statute, even a general power of appointment, if unexercised, does not subject the appointive property to claims of the holder's creditors, unless the general power is held by the same person who created it. (However, if the holder of a general power exercises the power while insolvent, the holder's creditors can reach the appointive property to satisfy their claims, after exhausting the holder's own assets.) General powers of appointment are commonly used for tax planning reasons—for example, to obtain a marital deduction for property left in trust by a decedent for a surviving spouse, or to obtain an annual exclusion for gift tax purposes. If A dies leaving property to his surviving spouse B for life, "remainder to such person or persons as B by deed or will appoints, and in default of appointment, to my issue who survive B, by right of representation," A can confidently predict that the trust property will escape federal estate tax at his death by virtue of the marital deduction, that B, as life income beneficiary and holder of a general power, will have access to the property if she needs it, though it is beyond the reach of her creditors, and that in all probability the trust property will pass at B's death to A's issue then living because B is unlikely to exercise the power in favor of anyone else. Here, "flexibility" in the usual sense does not motivate creation of the power.

§ 9.11 HOW POWERS WORK

Because a general power of appointment so closely approximates ownership of the appointive property, the substantive law on general powers is less strict than the law on special powers. By way of example, if A, owning land in fee simple absolute, grants or devises it "to B for life, remainder to such person or persons as B by will appoints," and B executes a will purporting to appoint the remainder in its entirety to her child X, who predeceases B, it is conceivable that a statute may create a gift by substitution in X's issue who survive B. An anti-lapse statute that makes no reference to testamentary gifts by way of appointment may be construed to cover this kind of case because the general power in B so closely approximates ownership that it can be treated for purposes of an anti-lapse statute (as it is for federal estate tax purposes) as the equivalent of ownership of the appointive property. Likewise, if the holder of a general testamentary power purports by will to exercise the power by "blending" the appointive property with "owned" assets in a unified scheme of disposition, and the attempted appointment turns out to be ineffective (for example, due to lapse or to a violation of the Rule Against Perpetuities), the appointive property is said to be "captured" for the benefit of the power holder's estate. After all, the power holder could have appointed the property directly to his or her estate.

Because a power enables the holder to effect a shift in property rights from one person to another through exercise of the power (the happening of an event), it is part of the accepted substantive law of powers that an appointee taking property as a result of an exercise of a power takes from the creator of the power (the "donor") rather than the holder of the power (the "donee"). For example, suppose that A, owning land in fee simple absolute, grants it "to B for life, remainder to such of the children of B, to one or more to the exclusion of others, and in such shares and proportions, as B by deed or will appoints." Because A has created merely a life estate and a special power of appointment, A has a reversion in fee. If B appoints the remainder in its entirety to her child X, the appointment displaces A's reversion. (If the deed contained an express gift in default of appointment (for example, "and in default of appointment, to my child C"), B's appointment to X would displace the remainder in C.) And X takes from A, the donor, not from B, the donee.

The notion that the appointee takes from the donor and not from the donee has not been pushed to the extreme. Suppose that A by deed creates a life estate in B and a special power to appoint, as just described, and thereafter A dies, survived by B and several children of B, including X. B executes a will purporting to appoint the remainder in its entirety to X, but X predeceases B. B dies and her will takes effect. Is B's appointment to X effective because X takes from the donor, not the donee, and X was alive when A died? Long ago it was decided that when a power is exercised by will, the appointee must survive both the creator and the holder of the power in order to take, with the result that the intended appointment is likely to fail. (Some anti-lapse statutes may create a gift by way of substitution in the surviving issue of the deceased appointee, even though such issue are not included as objects under the literal terms of the power.)

§ 9.12 DRAFTING

Because the power of appointment is a somewhat unusual device, problems encountered in connection with powers are many. A lawyer creating powers or exercising powers cannot reasonably be expected to anticipate all problems, but the lawyer can (and should) anticipate some. In the case stated in the preceding paragraph, when B executes a will purporting to exercise the special power created by A, B can create an alternative provision to take effect should her child X predecease her, just as B can create an alternative gift should an intended beneficiary of a testamentary gift of B's "owned" (as opposed to "appointive") property predecease B: "and with respect to the land situated at . . . over which I have a power of appointment under a deed recorded in . . ., I appoint such property in its entirety to my child X; if my child X does not survive me, I appoint such property in its entirety to my child Y."

Similarly, problems involving "powers in trust" and "illusory appointments" can be avoided by making an express gift in default of appointment, and by making explicit the right of the holder of a special power to prefer one or more of several objects of the power over others to whom an appointment might be made. For example, suppose that A devises land "to B for life, remainder to such of the children of B, to one or more to the exclusion of others, and in such shares and proportions, as B in her absolute discretion by deed or will appoints, and in default of appointment, remainder to C." B then dies survived by her children X, Y, and Z, and by will appoints the land in the following shares: one-half to X, four-tenths to Y, and one-tenth to Z. Can Z plausibly argue that the appointment to him is "illusory," and that A intended that all of B's children were to take "substantial" shares by way of appointment? No, because the special power in B is clearly "exclusive" or "exclusionary." The drafter of the power has effectively precluded use of the "illusory" appointment notion. (B could have excluded Z altogether.) Now, suppose that B dies survived by her children X, Y, and Z, and that B never attempted to exercise the power. A power of appointment is said to be "personal" to the holder—the power lapses if the holder dies without having exercised it. Can X, Y, and

Z plausibly argue that B's power was "in trust," and that in the absence of an effective exercise of the power by B, there is an implied gift to X, Y, and Z? No, because there is an express gift in default of appointment, and furthermore, the power is "exclusive" or "exclusionary." When B dies without having exercised the power, the express gift in default becomes a fee simple absolute in C. The drafter of the power has effectively precluded use of the "power in trust" notion.

When can an "illusory appointment" or a "power in trust" be argued? Suppose that A devises land "to B for life, remainder among the children of B as B by deed or will appoints." B dies survived by her children X, Y, and Z, and by will appoints the land in the following shares: one-half to X, four-tenths to Y, and one-tenth to Z. Alternatively, B dies survived by her children X, Y, and Z, and B never attempted to exercise the power. In these circumstances, an argument might be made concerning an "illusory appointment," on the one hand, or a "power in trust," on the other.

Suppose that A creates a trust to pay the net income "to B for life, remainder to such of the children of B, to one or more to the exclusion of others, and in such shares and proportions as B by deed or will appoints, and in default of appointment, remainder to the children of B in equal shares." There is a vested remainder subject to open at the creation of the trust if a child of B is then alive. If B dies without having exercised the power, survived by her children, X, Y, and Z, the children take the trust property in equal shares as beneficiaries of the express gift in default of appointment, and this is true even if one or more of them fail to survive B. (The gift in default is not conditioned on surviving the income beneficiary, although it is subject to diminution by birth of additional children to B and subject to diminution or complete extinguishment by the exercise of the power by B.) Now suppose that B did exercise the power to this extent: By will she appointed one-half of the trust principal to X, who (along with Y and Z) survives B. Does X take not only by appointment, but also as one of the takers in default? If the creator of a power wishes to preclude X from taking both as an appointee and as a taker in default in these circumstances, the drafting lawyer can anticipate the problem by providing as follows:

> No child of B to whom an appointment is made by B may share in the gift in default of appointment unless the property appointed to such child is added to the property to be distributed in default of appointment.

In the case just put, X would not, of course, want to contribute because her gift by way of appointment is larger than that which she would receive were she to contribute. The clause set out is called a "hotchpot" clause.

It bears emphasis, then, that in creating as well as in exercising powers of appointment, a lawyer should use the same care as in drafting a devise or bequest in a will. Any formal requirements imposed by the creator of the power concerning the manner of exercise should be scrupulously adhered to. For example, the power may by its terms be exercisable only by an instrument that makes "express" or "specific" reference to the power, in order to prevent an inadvertent exercise by a general reference to appointive property (for example, a gift by the power holder of "all property owned by me or subject to a power of appointment exercisable by me"). In exercising such a power, the holder should clearly identify the power: "All property over which I have a testamentary power of appointment under the will of A, dated . . ., I hereby appoint in its entirety to . . . ." More generally, to avoid confusion, exercise or non-exercise of the power, as the case may be, should be explicit: "And with respect to the property over which I hold a testamentary power of appointment under the will of A, I expressly refrain from exercising the power by this my last will, and any reference to my estate or my residuary estate or my property in this will does not refer to property over which I have merely a testamentary power of appointment."

CHAPTER 10
CHARITABLE TRUSTS

§ 10.1 CHARITABLE TRUSTS

A trust is "charitable" if it is created to support religion or education, to promote health, to relieve poverty, or to perform an act that the general government itself might perform (such as maintaining a park for public use). Although individuals can and do benefit from charitable trusts, such trusts are both condoned and encouraged because of the benefits they provide to the general public. A characteristic common to charitable trusts is the absence of personal profit—charitable trusts exist to promote the general good, not to enrich individual beneficiaries. It does not follow at all that the charitable trust device (or the non-profit charitable corporation) has never been abused. On the contrary, there are numerous reported cases documenting misuses of the charitable trust. But it has worked reasonably well over several centuries, and it imparts a richness and diversity to American life that would be sorely missed if charitable trusts disappeared.

Listing generally accepted charitable purposes such as "supporting religion" or "promoting health" fails to reveal the wide range of purposes that judges have found to be "charitable." It is true that a valid charitable trust could be established by a simple testamentary statement: "I leave all of my estate in trust for charity." But only an extensive (and not very rewarding) examination of cases gives one an appreciation of what is "charitable" for legal purposes. Although there is much general agreement on the matter, it is hardly surprising that once outside the core area of general agreement, one finds that an activity deemed charitable in one state is viewed differently in another, or that what is charitable for purposes of applying "cy pres" is not necessarily charitable for purposes of tax exemption.

Much of the law of trusts applies across the board to private express trusts, charitable trusts, trusts for unincorporated associations, and even "honorary" trusts. (An honorary trust is not a trust at all, in the usual sense. Rather, it is a device by which a donor achieves a purpose considered not altogether anti-social, such as caring for a pet for some reasonable length of time after the donor's death, or maintaining a private cemetery plot. Trusts for such purposes are enforceable under §§ 408 and 409 of the Uniform Trust Code.) The law on fiduciary administration applies to all trustees, although there is evidence that it is somewhat more relaxed with respect to trustees of charitable trusts. Just as there can be no private express trust unless there is identifiable trust property, there can be no charitable trust unless there is identifiable subject matter of the trust.

But there are some differences in doctrine. The beneficiaries of a private express trust are one or more individuals, whereas the beneficial interest of a charitable trust is in the public. Individual beneficiaries enforce private trusts. The Attorney General, or a similar state official, enforces charitable trusts (and as a consequence, enforcement tends to be uneven). A trust created exclusively for charitable purposes, unlike a private express trust, is exempt from the Rule Against Perpetuities; such a trust may endure indefinitely. With the passage of time and changes of circumstances, however, the original specific purposes of a charitable trust may become impracticable or impossible to achieve. A prudent lawyer should anticipate failure of the original purpose and provide a secondary gift for another charitable purpose ("for charitable purpose A, but if that purpose fails for any reason, then for charitable purpose B"). Even in the absence of a specific direction, judicial reformation may be available, under the doctrine of "cy pres," to give effect as nearly as possible to the settlor's general charitable intent. However, if cy pres is not available (for example, because the settlor lacked a general charitable intent), a resulting trust may arise for the settlor's successors in interest (residuary beneficiaries under the settlor's will, or heirs under the intestacy laws, as the case may be). In this way, the settlor's successors may affect the enforcement of charitable trusts. Because costs of litigation over trusts are frequently borne by the trust fund itself, it is important that litigation be discouraged by anticipating events that might lead to a lawsuit. To the extent that costs are payable from trust assets, the donor's gift (whether for private or public purposes) is diminished.

The indirect enforcement of charitable trusts by beneficiaries or intestate successors of the settlor has its counterpart with respect to trusts for unincorporated associations and honorary trusts. A disappointed heir who believes (and perhaps with reason) that the amount set aside by the decedent for the care of (say) a favorite race horse is excessive, might challenge the disposition either at the time of the decedent's death or thereafter.

Unlike a private express trust, a charitable trust may lawfully endure forever. A trust for an unincorporated association may by its terms lawfully endure beyond the perpetuities period, although it cannot remain indestructible beyond the perpetuities period. Honorary trusts must be so created that their duration is limited to the perpetuities period. (For example, the lawyer might explicitly set the term of the honorary trust at 20 years from the death of the testator.)

However, just as the settlor of a private express trust should not ordinarily push the duration of the trust to its outermost permissible limits, so too the creator of a charitable trust (or a trust for an unincorporated association, or an honorary trust) should consider the purpose of the gift, and limit the duration of the trust accordingly. Wealth should not be tied up for a long period of time unless there is a persuasive reason for taking it out of commerce. Furthermore, pushing doctrine to its limits tends to antagonize the natural objects of the settlor's bounty. It is one thing to attach a spendthrift restraint to the beneficial interest of a child or grandchild known by the settlor to lack judgment. It is another to attach it to beneficial interests of the unborn. A beneficiary who might not otherwise attack a trust may be goaded into doing so by the existence of restraints on possession that appear capricious or vindictive, or by an unreasonably extended trust duration.

§ 10.2 TAX CONSIDERATIONS

Although as a matter of the traditional substantive law on charitable trusts, a great variety of activities have been deemed charitable under state law, there is currently a factor at work that unquestionably affects both the language by which gifts to charity are created, and the characteristics attached by donors to such gifts. Under the federal income, gift, and estate taxes, deductions are available to donors with respect to qualified charitable gifts. The income of charitable trusts and foundations may be wholly or partially exempt from income tax. Under state law, charities may be eligible for property tax exemptions. Donors are aware that just as the general law of trusts (and nonprofit corporations) favors gifts to charity, the tax laws encourage such gifts as well. Preferential tax treatment may induce donors to make larger or more frequent charitable gifts than they would otherwise have done, and the requirements of tax law may have an important bearing on the terms, size, and nature of gifts to charity.

Here it bears emphasis that what is charitable for purposes of state law is not necessarily charitable for purposes of federal tax law. Of course there is substantial overlap, but the Internal Revenue Code has its own intricate requirements concerning the eligibility of charitable organizations for tax-exempt status and the allowance of tax deductions for gifts to such organizations. For example, an organization does not qualify as charitable for federal tax purposes if a "substantial part" of its activities consists of "attempting to influence legislation." Moreover, the specific terms of a gift to charity at times may be of crucial importance. If a donor creates a remainder interest for charity in property other than a farm or a personal residence, the arrangement must take the form of a "charitable remainder annuity trust" or a "charitable remainder unitrust" or a "pooled income fund," if the gift of the remainder is to qualify for the charitable deduction.

§ 10.3 MORTMAIN ACTS

At one time several states had statutes called "mortmain" acts which imposed rigid limitations on testamentary gifts to charity. Charitable gifts, especially those made by a will executed within a relatively short period before the testator's death, were thought to pose a special risk of overreaching on the part of the charitable donee at the expense of the natural objects of the testator's bounty. The mortmain acts were not uniform, and have nearly all been repealed or declared unconstitutional. Nonetheless, in an attempt to curb a more modern pattern of abuse, several states have enacted statutes restricting testamentary gifts to the owner or operator of a nursing home or residential home where the testator was a resident shortly before death.

§ 10.4 COMMUNITY FOUNDATIONS

Occasionally a donor attempts to achieve a charitable purpose with inadequate resources. The testator in Lippincott Estate, 17 Pa.D. & C.2d 80 (Orphans' Ct. 1959), left her residuary estate in trust to use the annual income "for the purpose of paying entrance fees into homes and institutions for the blind or other homes in . . . Pennsylvania, of persons qualified as hereinafter provided . . . ." The trustees were authorized by the will to advertise periodically for applicants and were directed to notify "all organizations within . . . Pennsylvania interested in . . . relief of the blind as to the function of the Fund . . . ." Income not expended in paying entrance fees was to be used to start the blind in business. As an incident to an accounting proceeding, a trustee of the Lippincott trust petitioned for discharge, appointment of a substitute trustee, and modification of the terms of the trust. In disposing of the petition, the court said:

> When we consider the many responsibilities placed upon the trustees in administering this small trust, its impracticability comes into sharp focus. The average income which this fund can be expected to produce is approximately $750 a year. The trustees' joint compensation for administering the trust would be about $37.50 annually. With these minuscule earnings, and for this negligible compensation, they are expected to carry out the ambitious program defined by testatrix.

The trust intended by the testator in *Lippincott Estate* was impracticable from its inception. In some localities there are "community foundations" or "community trusts"—usually nonprofit corporations created for the express purpose of receiving contributions and channeling them to charitable organizations. A donor wishing to make a charitable gift, but lacking either adequate resources or a particular charitable purpose (or both) might sensibly turn to the community foundation as a means of carrying out a general charitable intent, and lawyers should be aware of the fact that such a facility for making charitable gifts exists. Making gifts through the community foundation helps to ensure that the donor's charitable intention can be carried out at a reasonable administrative cost. Because a community foundation or community trust is itself a charity, making gifts through such a facility does not jeopardize the charitable deduction.

CHAPTER 11
THE RULE AGAINST PERPETUITIES AND RELATED DOCTRINES

§ 11.1 THE RULE AGAINST PERPETUITIES

The Rule Against Perpetuities (in orthodox or wait-and-see or cy pres form) regulates the creation of future interests. The Rule Against Accumulations regulates directed accumulations of income, and an analogous rule limits restraints on the destructibility of trusts. All of these rules are "rules of law" or "rules of property"—they apply without regard to the transferor's intention. In operation they are intent-defeating.

Under the Rule Against Perpetuities in its orthodox common law form, an interest is invalid unless it is so created that it must vest, if it vests at all, within a period measured by some life in being at the creation of the interest and 21 years.

The Rule Against Perpetuities applies to interests created in private beneficiaries, subject to a narrow but significant exception for successive gifts to charity. Specifically, a charitable gift that is limited to take effect upon the failure or termination of a preceding charitable gift does not violate the Rule. However, the Rule applies with full force to a charitable gift following a gift to a private beneficiary, or vice versa.

A lawyer engaged in trusts and estates work should know enough about the Rule Against Perpetuities to avoid violations of the Rule in drafting instruments, and to recognize violations of the Rule when examining instruments drawn by others. In both connections, the lawyer should be informed about relevant changes in the Rule brought about by legislatures or judges in recent years, but he or she should not assume that modification of the Rule in orthodox form appreciably affects the matter of drafting. Regardless of modification, the prudent lawyer drafts to comply with the requirements of the Rule in orthodox form. A limitation that is bad under the Rule in orthodox form may be saved under a "wait and see" or "cy pres" version of the Rule, but compliance with the Rule in orthodox form makes it unnecessary to test the validity of a disposition under a relaxed form of the Rule and may avoid the expense of litigation.

For purposes of the Rule, "interest" means future interest, and includes the contingent remainder, the contingent executory interest, and the vested remainder subject to open.

Note that the Rule does not require that an interest be so created that it is certain to vest within the perpetuities period. Rather, the Rule requires that an interest be so created that all contingencies that affect the vesting of the interest will be resolved within the perpetuities period (a life in being at the creation of the interest and 21 years). The Rule says "vest, if at all"—a valid interest may fail by its own terms within the perpetuities period and thus never become vested. If A dies survived by B and C, and devises property "to B for life, then to C if C survives B," the contingent remainder in C is good under the Rule Against Perpetuities. (The contingent remainder is so created that it must vest, if at all, within the lifetime of C, who is a "life in being" at A's death, when the interest is created.) But C may ultimately predecease B. If so, the contingent remainder simply fails.

To determine whether an interest created by a deed, a trust instrument, or a will violates the Rule Against Perpetuities in orthodox form, one first looks back to the time the interest was created for perpetuities purposes: the time of delivery, in the case of a deed; the time of execution, in the case of an irrevocable trust; the date of the testator's death, in the case of a will; or the date of the settlor's death, in the case of a revocable trust. (For perpetuities purposes, a revocable trust is treated as if it were a will.)

Next, one examines the instrument to see if it creates any future interests. (The Rule does not apply to present interests because they are fully vested upon creation.) If there is a future interest, it must be classified according to the customary rules of construction. To classify an interest properly one must ascertain relevant facts: Who is alive when the interest is created? If reaching a prescribed age is a condition precedent, has the beneficiary already reached the prescribed age when the interest is created? For example, suppose that when A executes her will her son B has a three-year-old child C. A's will says: "I devise Blackacre to B for life, remainder to C if C reaches age 35." At A's death, she still owns Blackacre and she is survived by B and by C, now age 10. Because the intended gift of the future interest to C is subject to an express condition precedent of reaching age 35, it is contingent, but it is a contingent remainder that does not violate the Rule. (Viewed as of the time of A's death, the remainder must vest, or fail, within C's own lifetime, and C is a "life in being" at A's death.) Alternatively, suppose that at A's death, she still owns Blackacre and she is survived by B and by C, now age 35. Under these facts, the intended gift of the future interest to C is an indefeasibly vested remainder, which automatically complies with the Rule Against Perpetuities.

The Rule Against Perpetuities applies only to future interests that are not already "vested" upon creation. For purposes of the Rule, an interest is "vested" if it is classified as a reversion, a possibility of reverter, a right of entry for condition broken, an indefeasibly vested remainder, a vested remainder subject to divestment, or a vested executory interest. Accordingly, these interests automatically comply with the Rule upon creation and need not be tested further. The interests that must be examined for a possible violation of the Rule are those which are not "vested" upon creation: contingent remainders, contingent executory interests, and vested remainders subject to open. (The matter of powers of appointment under the Rule will be considered separately at a later point.)

Examination of an interest for possible violation of the Rule Against Perpetuities in orthodox form proceeds as follows. The Rule invalidates a future interest that might vest remotely, that is, more than 21 years after the death of every person living at the creation of the interest. The validity of an interest can be demonstrated by showing that the interest must vest, if at all, within the perpetuities period. Conversely, an interest is invalid if there is some sequence of events, no matter how improbable, that might postpone vesting beyond the perpetuities period.

For example, suppose that A devises property "to B for life, remainder to the child of B who first reaches age 35." A dies survived by B, who has no living children. The contingent remainder is invalid under the Rule in orthodox form. At A's death, when the interest is created, the only relevant "life in being" that one might use to attempt to demonstrate validity is B. (All other lives in being can be ignored because they have no bearing on the question whether B will have a child who will reach age 35. If B already had a child (under age 35), that child could not be used to validate the interest because the child might die before reaching age 35, and the interest in question might still remain non-vested for more than 21 years after the child's death.) Now it is true that a child born to B after A's death might reach age 35 within a period measured by B's lifetime and 21 years. (Indeed, such a child might reach age 35 within B's lifetime, even without the additional 21-year period.) But the requirements of the Rule are not met merely because a child of B might reach age

35 within the perpetuities period. The test for validity under the Rule in orthodox form is a possibilities test, not an actualities test. Viewed as of the time of A's death, it must be certain that a child of B will reach age 35, or not, within the perpetuities period. In other words, it must be clear with respect to the gift intended for B's child that the contingency will be resolved within the period.

Suppose that A devises "to B for life, remainder to C if C reaches age 35." A dies survived by B and by C, who is 15 years old. The validity of the contingent remainder in C can be demonstrated in three ways, any one of which is sufficient to satisfy the Rule in orthodox form. First, C will reach age 35, or not, within C's own lifetime, so C's life can be used as the "life in being" at A's death to demonstrate validity. Second, because C is already 15 years old at A's death, C will reach age 35, or not, no later than 21 years after B's death, so B's life (with the 21-year period) can be used to demonstrate validity. Finally, C will reach age 35, or not, within the "period in gross" of 21 years following A's death, so the period in gross can be used to demonstrate validity without identifying any "life in being." (If C is only five years old at A's death, the only method of demonstrating validity is to use C's life—C will reach age 35, or not, within C's own lifetime.)

Now suppose that A devises property "to B for life, remainder to the child of B who first reaches age 21." A dies survived by B. The contingent remainder is valid under the Rule Against Perpetuities in orthodox form, irrespective of whether B has any living children at A's death. Any child of B who reaches age 21 will do so within 21 years after B's death, assuming that the child is born during B's lifetime. (The Rule allows an actual period of gestation, if necessary, in addition to the stated period of lives in being plus 21 years.) If B has no children, or if all of B's children die before reaching age 21, the contingent remainder will fail, but this too will happen within 21 years after A's death. Thus, there is no possible sequence of events that would postpone vesting beyond the permissible period.

Occasionally an interest can be shown to be valid even if there is no single identifiable "life in being" for demonstration purposes. Suppose that A devises property "to my grandchildren who reach age 21." A dies survived by several children. The contingent remainder is valid under the Rule Against Perpetuities in orthodox form, irrespective of whether there are any grandchildren in existence at A's death. All of A's children are lives in being at A's death, and all of her grandchildren, if any, will be born during the lifetimes of her children. Accordingly, all of A's grandchildren who reach age 21, if any, will do so within 21 years after the death of A's last surviving child. (If A will have no grandchildren who reach age 21, that too must occur within the same period.) In other words, under no imaginable sequence of events could any grandchild of A be alive and under age 21, more than 21 years after the death of A's last surviving child. Although it is not possible to know which of A's children will live the longest, it is sufficient for purposes of the

Rule to know that the last surviving child is a life in being at A's death.

§ 11.2 THE "PERPETUITIES PERIOD"

The Rule Against Perpetuities includes the expression "some life in being at the creation of the interest and 21 years." The "perpetuities period" is a short-hand way of describing the time within which a future interest must "vest, if at all," if it is to be valid or "good" under the Rule in orthodox form. Because it is permissible for a lawyer to designate explicitly one or more of the so-called "measuring lives," it is conventional to say that the perpetuities period consists of any reasonable number of lives in being at the creation of the interest and 21 years. For example, A might by will leave property "to such of my grandchildren as are alive 21 years after the death of the survivor of X, Y, and Z." X, Y, and Z are young persons known to A, and A subsequently dies survived by all three. The intended gift to A's grandchildren is unquestionably valid under the Rule. (Note that X, Y, and Z might be wholly "extraneous" lives not related to A or named as beneficiaries in the will.) However, lawyers often do not explicitly identify the "measuring lives," and therefore it is ordinarily necessary to determine which lives in being at the creation of the interest are relevant for purposes of demonstrating validity under the Rule.

For purposes of the Rule, a child who is born alive is considered to be in existence from the time of conception. Accordingly, the perpetuities period may be extended by periods of actual gestation, if necessary to validate an interest. For example, suppose that T leaves property by will "to my grandchildren who reach age 21." T dies leaving an only child X, who is in gestation at T's death and is subsequently born alive. Years later, X dies leaving an only child Y, who is in gestation at X's death and is subsequently born alive. The gift to Y under T's will is valid under the Rule, even though Y is the posthumous child of T's posthumous child.

§ 11.3 CLASS GIFTS AND THE RULE

Under the Rule Against Perpetuities in orthodox form, a "unit rule" applies to a gift to a class: If the interest of any member of the class violates the Rule, the entire class gift fails.

For example, suppose that A devises property "to B for life, then to B's children for their lives, with remainder to B's grandchildren." A dies survived by B, by several children of B, and by several grandchildren of B. "Children" is construed to mean "children of B whenever born," and "grandchildren" is construed to mean "grandchildren of B whenever born." Under these facts, the intended gift to B's grandchildren is a vested remainder "subject to open" to admit grandchildren of B born after A's death. It is bad in its entirety under the Rule because the ultimate or final number of grandchildren sharing in the gift is not certain to be fixed or determined within the perpetuities period. After A's death, B might conceive a child who is born alive and who turns out to be the last surviving child of B. That after-born child might conceive a child who is born alive more than 21 years after the death of B and all of the other relevant persons who were in existence at A's death. Because there is no reason to "close" the class of grandchildren until all of B's children have died, the class of grandchildren might remain open to admit this "unborn child of an unborn child" at a remote time. The possibility that the ultimate number of grandchildren sharing in the gift might not be known until a remote time makes the intended gift to B's grandchildren bad in its entirety.

Similarly, if A devises property "to B for life, with remainder to such of the children of B as reach age 25," the intended gift to the children of B is bad in its entirety under the Rule, if B is alive at A's death and "children" is construed to mean "children of B whenever born." The gift is bad even though one or more children of B alive at A's death have already reached age 25 at A's death. Under these facts, the class gift to B's children remains open until B's death, and each child's interest is contingent on reaching age 25. After A's death, B might conceive a child who is born alive less than four years before B's death. The test for validity under the Rule Against Perpetuities in orthodox form is a possibilities test, not an actualities test. Viewed as of the time of A's death, it is possible that an after-born child of B who is not excluded from the class (because the child is born during B's lifetime while the class is open) might reach age 25 at a time beyond a period measured by B's life and 21 years. (It makes no difference that B's after-born child might actually die within 21 years after B's death, so that the ultimate or final number of children sharing in the gift would be fixed or determined within the perpetuities period.) The intended gift to B's children who reach age 25 is bad in its entirety.

The effects of the unit rule on class gifts are mitigated by the exceptions of Cattlin v. Brown, 68 Eng.Rep. 1319 (Ch. 1853), and Storrs v. Benbow, 43 Eng.Rep. 153 (Ch. 1853), and by the operation of "class closing" rules. But it bears emphasis that limitations like those in *Cattlin* and *Storrs* are not common. The unit rule on class gifts is an ever-present threat to dispositions in trusts and wills that are in no sense unusual.

Limitations like those of Cattlin v. Brown escape the harsh effects of the unit rule on class gifts. *Cattlin* involved a gift to a class of sub-classes, and under the "rule" of Cattlin v. Brown, a gift to a particular sub-class may be valid under the Rule Against Perpetuities in orthodox form even though the gift to another sub-class is void. For example, suppose that A creates a testamentary trust to pay the net income "to B for life, then in equal shares to the children of B for their lives, and on the death of each child, to pay that child's proportionate share of principal to his or her issue then living, by right of representation." A dies survived by B and by several of B's children. "Children" is construed to mean "children of B whenever born." Under the rule of Cattlin v. Brown, the remainder in the issue of each child is treated as a separate gift to a sub-class. Gifts that are bad under the Rule are separated from those that are good, and the latter are permitted to stand. Accordingly, the gifts to the issue of each child of B living at A's death are valid (each child of B living at A's death validates the remainder interest in that child's issue). But if B has any more children born after A's death, the remainder interest in the issue of any such after-born child would be void. If B in fact has no after-born children, the *Cattlin* rule salvages A's intended distribution. But if there are any after-born children, the rule may seriously distort A's dispositive plan. (In such a case, a court might invoke the doctrine of "infectious invalidity" to strike down all of the remainder interests in order to avoid an inequitable result.)

The "rule" of Storrs v. Benbow shows how the class closing rules may avoid a violation of the Rule Against Perpetuities. Suppose that A bequeaths "$1,000 apiece to each child of B who reaches age 30." A dies survived by B and by several children of B. If a child of B, born after A's death, is included in the class gift, the intended gift as to such afterborn child of B is bad under the Rule Against Perpetuities in orthodox form because an afterborn child of B might reach age 30, if at all, at a time beyond the period measured by B's life and 21 years. However, the "class closing" rule precludes after-born children of B from taking at all. The class closes at A's death, and only children of B alive at A's death are permitted to qualify for the legacy. The intended legacies are valid under the Rule as to all children of B alive at A's death, because any such child who is then under age 30 will reach age 30, or not, within that child's own lifetime.

Note that the class closing rule as applied in Storrs v. Benbow also precludes a gift to an after-born child that would not violate the Rule at all: Suppose that A bequeaths "$1,000 apiece to each child of B who reaches age 21." If B is alive at A's death, any after-born child of B would reach age 21, or not, within a period measured by B's life and 21 years. Even so, such after-born child is precluded from qualifying for a legacy by the class closing rule.

§ 11.4 POWERS OF APPOINTMENT AND THE RULE

Both the creation of a power of appointment and the interests that result from its exercise fall within the ambit of the Rule Against Perpetuities in orthodox form.

A general power of appointment that is presently exercisable by the holder from the time of its creation is exempt from the Rule. For purposes of the Rule, a presently-exercisable general power of appointment is comparable to absolute ownership of the property subject to the power.

A general power of appointment that is not presently exercisable at the time of its creation is nonetheless good under the Rule in orthodox form if the power is so created that it must become exercisable, if at all, within the perpetuities period. For example, if A creates a testamentary trust "to pay the net income to B for life, and then to pay the principal to such person or persons as B's surviving spouse by deed or will appoints," and B is an unmarried person at A's death, the general power is good under the Rule because the power must become exercisable, if at all, at the death of B (a life in being at the creation of the power), when it is determined whether B left a surviving spouse.

A general testamentary power of appointment, or a special power of appointment, is void ab initio under the Rule Against Perpetuities in orthodox form if it is so created that it might be exercised at a remote time. It follows that to be valid under the Rule, a general testamentary power or a special power that is intended for a person unborn at the time of creation must be so described that it cannot be exercised beyond the perpetuities period. For example, if A creates a testamentary trust "to pay the net income to B for life, and then to pay principal to such of my grandchildren, namely, X, Y, and Z, as B's first-born child appoints," the special power is good under the Rule even though at the time of A's death B does not yet have any children. Although the special power is intended for a person unborn at A's death (when the power is created), the objects of the power are limited to persons alive at A's death. Therefore the power cannot be exercised beyond the perpetuities period.

In summary, then, if a general power of appointment might not become exercisable until after the perpetuities period, the power is bad under the Rule Against Perpetuities in orthodox form. A general testamentary power of appointment or a special power of appointment is bad under the Rule if it is so created that it might be exercised at a remote time.

Because holding a presently-exercisable general power of appointment is comparable to owning the subject matter of the power, the validity under the Rule of an appointment made by the exercise of such a power is determined by computing or measuring the perpetuities period from the time of the exercise of the power. Suppose that A creates a testamentary trust to pay the net income to B for life, and gives B a general power to appoint the trust property by deed or will. The general power itself complies with the Rule because it is presently exercisable by B from the time of its creation at A's death. B exercises the power by will, and appoints the property in further trust to pay the net income to C for life, with remainder to C's children. Even if C was not born until after A's death, the appointment is nonetheless valid under the Rule Against Perpetuities in orthodox form because C is a person in being at B's death when the power is exercised, and the number of children of C who share in the remainder is determinable within the lifetime of C. For purposes of determining the validity of the appointment made by B, the perpetuities period "runs" from the time of B's death.

To determine the validity under the Rule of an appointment made by the exercise of a general testamentary power or a special power, one "reads back" or interpolates the appointment into the instrument creating the power, and computes or measures the perpetuities period from the time the power was created. In this connection, perpetuities law simply reflects the traditional notion that exercise of a general testamentary power or a special power is an event upon the happening of which the subject matter of the power passes from the creator of the power (the "donor") to the appointee. (The appointee takes from the creator of the power, the "donor," not from the holder of the power, the "donee.") Nonetheless, facts existing at the time the appointment is made are taken into account when determining the validity of the appointment (this is referred to as taking a "second look" at the facts). For example, suppose that A leaves property in trust "to pay the net income to B for life, and then to pay the principal to such of the children of B, to one or more to the exclusion of others, on such conditions, and in such shares and proportions, as B by will appoints, and in default of appointment, to pay the principal to B's issue then living, by right of representation." B survives A. B has never had any children. The special power created in B is good under the Rule in orthodox form because it is exercisable only by B, a person alive at A's death when the power is created. (The contingent remainder in default of appointment is also good under the Rule because it will vest, if at all, at B's death.) Suppose that B by will appoints the trust property "to such of my [B's] children as reach age 25." B is survived by several children, the youngest of whom is four years old. B's appointment is valid under the Rule because, "read back" into A's will, it is as if A's will had directed the trustee "to pay the net income to B for life, and then to pay the principal to such of the children of B as survive B and reach age 25 no later than 21 years after B's death." B is a person in being at A's death when the special power was created and the perpetuities period began to run. Because B's youngest child is four years old at B's death, the number of B's children who will ultimately reach age 25 and share in the appointment will be determinable within 21 years after B's death.

§ 11.5 DRAFTING UNDER THE RULE

Taking account of the statement of the Rule Against Perpetuities, and keeping in mind both the "perpetuities period" and the complexities involved in applying the Rule to powers of appointment, the lawyer can avoid some obvious (and some not so obvious) pitfalls by observing a few rules of thumb in preparing dispositive documents:

(1) Because the Rule applies only to future interests, do not create future interests unless they are essential to the plan of disposition. Generally speaking, persons of modest means seldom have occasion to make use of elaborate dispositions involving future interests, powers of appointment, or trusts (other than a simple revocable trust that functions as a will substitute). The lawyer preparing the dispositive instrument should use the simplest and most efficient means available to carry out the client's intended disposition.

(2) Do not create gifts extending to the third generation unless the testator is willing to treat like kinds of persons in an unequal way. Suppose that A has a child B and devises property "to B for life, then to B's children for their lives, remainder to the grandchildren of B." "Children" is construed to mean "children whenever born," and "grandchildren" is

construed to mean "grandchildren whenever born." If B survives A, the gift to B's grandchildren is bad under the Rule in orthodox form, even if B has one or more children, as well as grandchildren, alive at A's death. (The gift is a gift to a class that might include an unborn child of an unborn child of B. Under the "unit rule" on gifts to a class, a gift bad as to any member of the class is bad as to all members of the class.) The secondary gift of income to B's children is good under the Rule although it includes an unborn child of B. (The interest of that child will vest, at the latest, at B's death.) The gift to grandchildren is good if the lawyer writes "to B for life, then to B's children for their lives, remainder to grandchildren of B alive at my [A's] death or born thereafter to a child or children of B alive at my [A's] death." (Under this language, a child of B born after the execution of the will and before A's death might have children who are eligible to share in the remainder.) The gift to grandchildren is also good if the lawyer writes "to B for life, then to B's children for their lives, remainder to grandchildren of B alive at my death or born thereafter during the lifetime of the survivor of B's children alive at my death." (Under this language, a child of B born after A's death might have children who are eligible to share in the remainder.) But limitations of the kind just suggested might result in inequality of treatment with respect to A's great-grandchildren, depending on the turn of events. The inequality would not result from a "per stirpes" distribution among the grandchildren of B; rather, it would originate in excluding some grandchildren of B from sharing at all.

(3) Do not condition gifts on reaching an age greater than 21 unless the gift is to a person or persons specifically identifiable by the express words of the dispositive instrument at the time the interest is created for perpetuities purposes. Suppose that A devises property "to B for life, remainder to such of the children of B as reach age 25." B survives A, and "children" is construed to mean "children whenever born." The remainder is bad under the Rule in orthodox form, even if B has a child who has reached age 25 at A's death. (Because the class is "open" at A's death and does not "close" until B's death, a child might be born to B less than four years before B's death and reach age 25 beyond the perpetuities period.) By way of contrast, had A intended to give only to children of B personally known to her, the devise might have read "to B for life, remainder to such of X, Y, and Z as reach age 25." Suppose that A is survived by B, and by X, Y, and Z, none of whom has yet reached age 25. The lives of X, Y, and Z can be used to demonstrate the validity of the contingent remainder under the Rule. Or had A intended to include only children of B alive at A's death, the devise might have read "to B for life, remainder to such of the children of B alive at my [A's] death as reach age 25." Children of B alive at A's death are specifically identifiable persons whose lives can be used to demonstrate the validity of the remainder under the Rule.

(4) Because the Rule applies only to a narrow category of cases, do not create an interest that raises perpetuities questions of the more difficult kind where that serves no purpose. Suppose that A has an

adult child B who is married to C. The lawyer learns that A wishes to create a life estate in B, followed by a life estate in C and a remainder at the death of the survivor of B and C to B's issue then living. The lawyer could write "to B for life, then to B's spouse for life, with remainder to B's issue who survive B and B's spouse." A then dies survived by B, by C, and by their several children. Although the facts at the execution of the will may be such that the future interests can be confined as a matter of construction to a life estate in C and a remainder in B's issue who survive B and C, the open-ended phrase "B's spouse" invites treating the ultimate remainder as a gift to a class that might remain "open" (and subject to a condition precedent of survival) beyond the perpetuities period, resulting in a violation of the Rule in orthodox form. (The violation can be illustrated by the following sequence of hypothetical events: B might survive C and marry X, a person born after A's death; then B might die, still married to X, and X might survive B and all of B's children who were alive at A's death by more than 21 years. In this situation, X is sometimes referred to as an "unborn widow." Note that X's life estate complies with the Rule because it must vest, if at all, at B's death. The violation occurs only with respect to the remainder in B's issue, which by its terms will not become vested until the takers are ascertained at X's death.) The validity of the remainder could be assured if the lawyer wrote what the testator probably intended: "to B for life, then to C for life, with remainder to B's issue who survive B and C." If the stability of B's marriage is in doubt, C's life estate could be made subject to an express condition: "to C for life, if C is B's surviving spouse . . . ." Or, if the testator actually contemplated the possibility of B's remarriage, the lawyer could avoid a violation of the Rule by an appropriate saving clause: "if B dies survived by a spouse who was born during my [A's] lifetime, to such spouse for life, with remainder at the death of such spouse (or at B's death, if B is not survived by such spouse) to B's issue then living."

(5) A special power of appointment that is exercisable beyond the perpetuities period is void from inception under the Rule in orthodox form. This aspect of the Rule has become increasingly important as professional trusteeship has shifted from individuals to trust companies. "Sprinkling," "spraying," and "discretionary" trusts involve special powers, and frequently the power is intended by its creator to permit an appointment among a class that includes persons unborn when the perpetuities period begins to run. Where a special power is given to an identified natural person, it cannot be exercised beyond the perpetuities period because it is personal to the holder. But if a special power is created in a corporate trustee to appoint among a class including unborn objects, the power is intended to be exercisable at a time that might be remote. Do not create a special power in a corporate trustee unless exercise of the power is limited either explicitly or implicitly to the perpetuities period (for example, by confining permissible appointees to persons alive at the creation of the power).

(6) When testing the validity of an appointment made by the exercise of a special power or a general testamentary power, the appointment must be "read back" or interpolated into the instrument creating the power, and the perpetuities period is measured from the time the power was created. (The appointee takes from the donor, not the holder of the power.) In exercising a special power or a general testamentary power, the lawyer should reconstruct the instrument creating the power so that it contains the contemplated appointment, for only in this way can the effectiveness of the appointment be determined. If A by will created a life estate in B, with a general testamentary power of appointment in B, and the draft of B's will purporting to exercise the power reads in part "I appoint to my children for their lives, remainder to my grandchildren," the contemplated appointment might in part be bad under the Rule. Interpolated into A's will, the appointment takes this form: "to B for life, then to B's children for their lives, remainder to B's grandchildren." The appointment to B's children will be good, because all of B's children are identifiable within B's lifetime, and B is in being at A's death. But the attempted appointment to B's grandchildren will be bad if any child born to B after A's death survives B.

(7) Either expressly limit the duration of a private express trust to the perpetuities period, or include a "saving clause" in the dispositive document. The former requires that a trust end by its own terms within the perpetuities period. The latter directs an overriding disposition in order to avoid a potential

violation of the Rule. For example, a saving clause might read as follows:

> Unless sooner terminated by its own terms, this trust shall terminate 21 years after the death of the survivor of the settlor, the settlor's spouse, and the settlor's issue living at the time this trust was created, and at that time the trustee shall pay over the remaining trust property to the settlor's issue then living, by right of representation, notwithstanding any provision in this trust to the contrary.

Note that the saving clause identifies the relevant "lives in being" when the perpetuities period starts to run ("the survivor of the settlor, the settlor's spouse, and the settlor's issue living at the time this trust was created"), and also directs the disposition of the trust property upon termination ("to the settlor's issue then living, by right of representation").

§ 11.6 REFORMING THE RULE

Reforming the Rule Against Perpetuities in orthodox form has taken two principal forms: (1) adopting a "wait and see" version of the Rule, or (2) authorizing "cy pres" to reform a disposition that violates the Rule. Some jurisdictions have adopted a combination of "wait and see" and "cy pres."

A state that adopts "wait and see" abandons the possibilities test for validity of a non-vested future interest under the Rule, and instead tests validity by the actualities test: Does the interest in fact vest within the perpetuities period? If so, it is valid or "good" under the Rule Against Perpetuities in "wait and see" form. Only if it does not in fact vest within the perpetuities period does the interest fail. For example, suppose that A devises property "to B for life, remainder to B's children who reach age 25." B survives A, but no child or children of B are alive at A's death. "Children" is construed to mean "children whenever born." If all of B's children who reach age 25 in fact do so within 21 years after B's death, the future interest is valid under the Rule in "wait and see" form. Note that under the Rule in "wait and see" form, it may be necessary to wait until B's death (or even longer, if B dies survived by a child under the age of four) to determine the validity of the remainder in B's children. In contrast, under the Rule in orthodox form, the entire gift to B's children would be void from inception.

A state that adopts a "cy pres" approach first uses the possibilities test of the orthodox Rule to check the validity of a non-vested future interest under the Rule, and then, if a violation is found, reforms the disposition (if possible) to ensure compliance with the Rule. For example, suppose that A devises "to B for life, remainder to that child of B who first reaches age 25." A dies survived by B, who has no children. Under the Rule in orthodox form, it is possible that the child (if any) of B who first reaches age 25 might do so more than 21 years after B's death. The intended contingent remainder is therefore void from inception under the Rule in orthodox form. In contrast, under a "cy pres" approach, the disposition might be reformed to read "remainder to that child of B who first reaches age 21."

The Uniform Statutory Rule Against Perpetuities, enacted in a number of states, sets out the Rule in orthodox form, but also provides a 90-year "wait and see" period, coupled with "cy pres" reformation if necessary to avoid a violation of the Rule. Section 1 of the Uniform Statutory Rule provides in part as follows:

> A nonvested property interest is invalid unless:
>
> (1) when the interest is created, it is certain to vest or terminate no later than 21 years after the death of an individual then alive; or
>
> (2) the interest either vests or terminates within 90 years after its creation.

If a future interest is not vested at the end of the 90-year period, § 3 of the Uniform Statutory Rule authorizes a court to reform the disposition "in the manner that most closely approximates the transferor's manifested plan of distribution" and is within the 90-year wait and see period.

In some jurisdictions the Uniform Statutory Rule has been modified to expand the 90-year wait and see period to several hundred years or even 1,000 years. In other jurisdictions the Rule Against Perpetuities has been made optional or repealed altogether by statute. In these jurisdictions, it is possible (though perhaps not advisable) to create a perpetual trust, often referred to as a "dynasty" trust, which may postpone the vesting of the beneficiaries' interests indefinitely.

§ 11.7 DESTRUCTIBILITY AND DURATION OF TRUSTS

The Rule Against Perpetuities is concerned only with the remote vesting of future interests. The Rule does not impose any direct limitation on the duration of private express trusts. Because a trust may continue after all future interests of the beneficiaries have become vested, the trust may endure beyond the perpetuities period. For example, suppose that A devises property in trust to pay the net income to B for life, then to B's children for their lives, and at the death of B's last surviving child, to pay the principal to C. A dies survived by B, by several children of B, and by C. The interests of all of B's children (including any who might be born after A's death, assuming that "B's children" is given its usual construction of "B's children whenever born") will become fully vested at B's death. Moreover, C's remainder is indefeasibly vested from the creation of the trust. Thus, the entire disposition is valid, even though the trust may last beyond the perpetuities period. (The survivor of B's children might be a child born after the creation of the trust, and might be alive more than 21 years after the deaths of B, C, and all of B's children who were alive at the creation of the trust.)

Although the Rule Against Perpetuities does not directly limit the duration of the trust in the example just given, an analogous rule does prevent the trust from being made indestructible beyond lives in being and 21 years. This rule has implications for the operation of the *Claflin* doctrine, which generally prevents the beneficiaries from modifying or terminating a trust if a "material purpose" requires continuation of the trust. Returning to the example given above, suppose that all of the income interests in the trust are subject to a "spendthrift" clause. (Courts have traditionally found that a protective device such as a spendthrift clause indicates a "material purpose" sufficient to prevent early termination.) After B's death, B's children, all of whom are competent adults, join with C and unanimously request an early termination of the trust. Should their request be granted? Some courts have held that a restraint on termination is void ab initio if it is created to last beyond the perpetuities period, while other courts have taken the more lenient view that the restraint cannot be enforced beyond the perpetuities period. Under either view, a lawyer should avoid using a protective device that might last more than 21 years after lives in being at the time of creation.

Similar considerations apply to discretionary trusts in which the trustee is given a special power to appoint income or principal among the beneficiaries. A special power of appointment that purports to be exercisable beyond the perpetuities period is void ab initio under the Rule Against Perpetuities in orthodox form.

Careful drafting to avoid violations of the Rule Against Perpetuities and analogous rules concerning the duration of "indestructible" trusts can be supplemented by a "saving clause" in the trust instrument which provides for termination of the trust and directs distribution of the remaining trust property at the end of the perpetuities period.

§ 11.8 THE RULE AGAINST ACCUMULATIONS

If a private express trust requires that income be accumulated beyond the perpetuities period, the directed accumulation is void ab initio in its entirety under the common law Rule Against Accumulations.

A mandatory accumulation of income for charity may endure indefinitely, but it is subject to control by a court (and it follows that the direction may be modified or abrogated if circumstances so warrant).

Under the Rule Against Accumulations, the perpetuities period is used as a measuring device, just as it is with respect to restraints on the destructibility of trusts. A directed or mandatory accumulation that by the terms of the trust instrument will last no longer than the life of an identified person alive at the effective date of the instrument and 21 years is a permissible accumulation under the common law. Some states have statutes on directed or mandatory accumulations, and here, as in other connections, one should check for the existence of a statute. Both common law and statutory versions of the Rule Against Accumulations are little known. Because an occasional settlor is taken with the notion that a dream impossible of immediate fulfillment may be realized ultimately through miracles wrought by compound interest or shrewd investment policy, a lawyer preparing or examining a trust document should be aware that a directed or mandatory accumulation of income may be invalid.

Even if the law of the jurisdiction governing the trust does not include a Rule Against Accumulations, the lawyer should not conclude that it is safe to direct an accumulation for a private purpose for the perpetuities period. Courts have traditionally taken a dim view of a trust settlor's direction to accumulate income over extended periods of time. Therefore, if an accumulation of income is to be required at all, the period should be kept as short as possible consistent with attaining the settlor's objectives. An accumulation that is required to last for the full perpetuities period might, indeed, be upheld as valid. But a shorter period, if acceptable to the settlor, might arouse less antagonism on the part of those in a position to challenge the validity of the settlor's dispositive scheme.

CHAPTER 12
SOME ASPECTS OF FIDUCIARY ADMINISTRATION

§ 12.1 ADMINISTRATIVE POWERS

The personal representative (executor or administrator) of a decedent's estate, like the trustee of an inter vivos trust or a testamentary trust, is a fiduciary who holds and administers property that belongs to others. A lawyer aware of the substantive law on (say) trusteeship, is prepared in a general way to cope with problems arising out of administration of an estate. Moreover, a lawyer who never serves as a trustee or as the personal representative of a decedent's estate may nonetheless advise or represent a trustee or a personal representative.

The functions of a personal representative differ in several respects from those of a trustee. A personal representative finds and collects the decedent's assets, preserves them during the time needed to determine and pay creditors' claims and death taxes (if any), and ultimately distributes the net probate estate to the beneficiaries under the decedent's will (or to the heirs in the case of an intestate estate). In the absence of special problems (arising from, say, a dispute concerning the validity or interpretation of a will or a contested creditor's claim or tax liability), administration of a decedent's estate is ordinarily concluded within one or two years after the decedent's death.

By way of contrast, a private express trust normally lasts for a substantially longer period of time, often for the lives of one or more beneficiaries. (A charitable trust may be created to endure indefinitely.) At the creation of the trust, the trustee ordinarily knows precisely what the subject matter of the trust is, and throughout the period of trust administration, the trustee's only contact with creditors may be with creditors of the beneficiaries of the trust (as distinguished from the settlor's creditors). More importantly, the trustee's duties with respect to the subject matter of the trust generally go beyond mere conservation. The trustee generally has a duty to make the trust property productive. And the trustee ordinarily is authorized or directed to make distributions to beneficiaries throughout the term of the trust, as well as at the termination of the trust. In sum, administration of a decedent's estate tends to be a short-term process, with ultimate distribution to the beneficiaries of the estate; administration of a private express trust tends to be a long-term process, with periodic distributions to beneficiaries of the trust.

Nonetheless, the powers and duties of a decedent's personal representative closely resemble those of the trustee of a private express trust in many important respects. The substantive law concerning the scope of fiduciary duties and remedies for breach applies interchangeably in both contexts, and the basic principles of fiduciary administration have a common core. Therefore it is convenient to consider at the same time the powers and duties of both kinds of fiduciaries.

Administrative powers exist in fiduciaries as a matter of state law, and that law is not uniform throughout the United States. Administrative powers that fiduciaries hold as a matter of state law may be enlarged by the testator in the will, or by the settlor in the trust instrument. Because state law on fiduciary administration is sometimes underdeveloped or unclear, it is common to find a detailed enumeration of specific fiduciary powers in a will or a trust instrument. Even if state law on fiduciary administration is relatively well developed, a lawyer may nonetheless insert in the will or the trust instrument fiduciary powers in addition to those provided by law because the nature of the property to be administered and the family circumstances of the testator or settlor make additional powers desirable. (The broad general powers granted to trustees under § 815 of the Uniform Trust Code are supplemented and elaborated by a comprehensive list of administrative powers in § 816.) The lawyer might also insert in the instrument the same powers provided by law, as a matter of convenience, to assist the fiduciary in dealing with persons who may be unfamiliar with the general law on administrative powers.

Administrative powers included in wills and trusts reflect the fact that the law on fiduciary administration varies somewhat from one state to another, and that the property and family circumstances of the testator or settlor often call for powers tailored to meet particular needs. Moreover, with respect to certain matters many lawyers believe that the fiduciary powers provided by law are inadequate and should ordinarily be displaced or supplemented in the will or the trust instrument.

Language introducing the administrative powers given to an executor by will might read as follows:

> In addition to and not by way of limitation of such powers as executors and administrators have by common law or by statute, I give to my executor hereinafter named, and any successor executor, the following powers, all of which may be exercised without application to any court.

The language "all of which may be exercised without application to any court" frees the executor from securing a court order that otherwise might be required under state law to perform an administrative act.

State law regulating fiduciary administration has traditionally provided only limited powers to dispose of assets. If a fiduciary is trustworthy and a person of good judgment, it is ordinarily advisable to give the fiduciary powers that permit using judgment for the benefit of the estate:

> To retain any property, real or personal, that my executor receives as a part of my estate, even though such property by reason of its kind, amount, or proportion to the total amount of my estate, would otherwise be considered inappropriate. To sell, exchange, lease, partition, give options upon, or otherwise dispose of any property, real or personal, in my estate, at public or private sale or otherwise, for

cash or credit, upon such terms and conditions, and at such prices as my executor deems fit.

Because a personal representative may need cash (to pay taxes or routine expenses of administration), and a forced sale of assets to yield cash might be inadvisable, the representative should be empowered to borrow, and to use property in the estate as security for loans:

To borrow money, and to mortgage or pledge any property in my estate, real or personal, as security therefor.

To facilitate transfer of property, it may be desirable that title to property be held in a form other than the customary fiduciary form (Estate of X, by Y, executor):

To keep any property in the name of the executor or in the name of a nominee without disclosure of the fiduciary relationship in any instrument of ownership, or in bearer form.

The decedent may have been engaged in controversy at death, or controversy with respect to the estate may arise after death. Claims both by and against the estate may exist or arise. It is ordinarily desirable to give the executor power to exercise judgment with respect to such matters, and to compromise rather than litigate:

To collect, pay, contest, compromise, settle, renew, or abandon claims by or against my estate, wherever situated, on whatever terms my executor deems advisable.

A fiduciary should be empowered to employ others without being subject to the charge of improper delegation of authority:

> To employ attorneys, accountants, bankers, brokers, and investment counsel, and to rely on their advice without making further inquiry, and to hire agents, custodians, and depositaries.

Actual distribution of the net probate estate is at times made easier by giving some discretion to the executor:

> To distribute my estate among beneficiaries in cash or in kind, or both, in divided or undivided interests, and in proportionate or disproportionate shares, at such values as my executor deems appropriate, with such valuation to be final and conclusive as to the distributees.

The function of the executor or administrator of a decedent's estate tends to be short-term. The function of the trustee of a private express trust tends to be long-term, and ordinarily involves investing and reinvesting trust assets. Because state law on investments has traditionally restricted the trustee to a relatively narrow range of investments, the settlor of the trust may enlarge investment powers:

> To invest and reinvest the trust estate in any property, real or personal, including securities of domestic and foreign corporations, common stocks, preferred stocks, bonds, mortgages, mortgage participations, investment trusts, mutual funds, and common trust funds,

> irrespective of any common law or statutory rule on investments by trustees, and irrespective of any common law or statutory rule requiring diversification of investments by trustees.

Inserting language in a trust instrument that expands or restricts the powers of the trustee has its dangers. It bears emphasis that the line dividing administrative powers from dispositive powers is not always clear. Creation of a power considered by the lawyer to be administrative may carry adverse federal tax consequences if that dividing line for tax purposes has been crossed. Or the settlor of an inter vivos trust in the trust instrument may deprive the trustee of powers otherwise available to such an extent that the trust is thereafter attacked as a mere agency or a sham. In short, varying the powers of the trustee should be given careful thought, just as exempting a fiduciary from the requirement of furnishing bond should be a matter of informed choice, not a matter of routine.

§ 12.2 DUTY OF LOYALTY

The duty of loyalty is often overlooked or misunderstood, and in application it may come as a shock to an unsuspecting trustee. The duty of loyalty has been called "the most fundamental duty" owed by the trustee to the beneficiaries. Under the standard formulation, codified in § 802 of the Uniform Trust Code, a trustee is required to administer the trust "solely in the interests of the beneficiaries." By implication, the trustee is generally not permitted to derive any personal gain (other than compensation for fiduciary services) for administering the trust. Moreover, the trustee is prohibited from engaging in transactions where self-interest conflicts with a duty to the beneficiaries.

The duty of loyalty is violated if the trustee sells a trust asset to himself or herself as an individual, or if the trustee buys his or her own property for the trust. In this connection it is irrelevant that the price is the same as it would have been had the trustee in each instance dealt with a stranger rather than with himself or herself as an individual. The transaction in either case is voidable by the beneficiaries. The trustee has no defense to such an act of "self-dealing," unless the transaction was authorized by the terms of the trust or by court order, or the transaction was entered into in good faith, on fair terms, and with the consent of the beneficiaries after full disclosure of the material facts.

Enforcing the duty of loyalty may lead to harsh results. Suppose that a trustee in good faith uses trust funds to buy personally owned securities for the trust. The securities are "prudent" trust investments which would be perfectly proper had they been purchased from a stranger. The securities suddenly plummet in value because of an unforeseeable change in economic conditions. The beneficiaries then discover the breach of trust, repudiate the purchase, and demand that the trustee restore to the trust fund the purchase price of the now worthless securities. Had the securities been purchased from a stranger, the loss in value would have been borne by the beneficiaries, for a trustee is not a guarantor of the investment outcomes for the trust fund. In this instance, however, the loss is borne by the trustee because the trustee violated the duty of loyalty. It makes no difference that the trustee may have acted in good faith or that the purchase price may have been fair and reasonable.

The duty of loyalty crops up in many different situations. For example, the executor in Hall v. Schoenwetter, 686 A.2d 980 (Conn. 1996), discovered a stolen Stradivarius violin among the decedent's possessions. The executor negotiated the return of the violin to Lloyd's of London (which had acquired legal title from the original owner upon payment of the instrument's insured value following the theft), in exchange for a substantial finder's fee. The court held that the executor was required to account for the finder's fee as an asset of the estate. As a fiduciary, she could not appropriate for herself an asset that properly belonged to the estate. "No matter how the [violin] was obtained, it was a possession of the decedent's estate, and once the [executor] chose to negotiate with Lloyd's for the finder's fee her fiduciary duty required that she negotiate on behalf of the estate, not herself."

Even an apparently routine business transaction may give rise to potential difficulties. Suppose that a bank or trust company has a private trust department as well as a commercial banking department. As a fiduciary, the bank serves as trustee of numerous trusts; as a commercial bank, it is engaged in the business of accepting deposits and lending money. Is it proper for the bank as trustee to deposit trust funds in accounts with the bank's own commercial banking department? Technically, such a transaction constitutes a form of self-dealing because the bank would in effect be lending trust funds to itself. However, assuming that the terms of the transaction are "fair" (that is, the same as those prevailing in similar transactions between parties dealing at arm's length), it seems pointless to require the trustee to deposit its trust funds with a different commercial bank. Accordingly, by statute in many states, a corporate trustee is expressly authorized to deposit trust funds with a commercial bank owned by or affiliated with the trustee. (Such deposits are expressly authorized by § 802(h)(4) of the Uniform Trust Code.)

Consider a slightly different case. T, a professional trustee, administers numerous trusts. T determines that it is desirable as a matter of prudent trust administration for one trust administered by T to acquire shares of a particular company as an investment and for another trust administered by T to divest itself of shares in the same company. T, as trustee of the one trust buys the shares from herself as trustee of the other trust. Thereafter the purchased security plummets in value because of an unforeseeable change in economic conditions. Is T liable for breach of trust, specifically, for breach of the duty of loyalty? Here T is not purchasing from herself as an individual. If the transaction was fair to both trusts, there is no breach of trust and therefore no liability. But to avoid having "fairness" established through a lawsuit, this kind of transaction can be anticipated by the settlor when creating the trust:

> I hereby authorize the trustee hereinafter named, and any successor thereto, to enter into any transaction authorized by this article with the trustee or trustees of any other trust, even if one or more beneficiaries of such other trust have beneficial interests hereunder, and even if one or more trustees of such other trust is the trustee named herein or any successor thereto.

A trustee has numerous duties. Clauses in trust instruments enlarging the trustee's administrative powers are sometimes supplemented by an "exculpatory" clause:

> Neither the trustee hereinafter named, nor any successor trustee, shall be liable for loss to the trust estate or to any beneficiary of this trust unless the loss was caused by the willful neglect or default of the trustee.

Judges considering the effectiveness of exculpatory clauses often scrutinize them closely to guard against overreaching on the part of the trustee. Thus, § 1008 of the Uniform Trust Code provides that an exculpatory clause is unenforceable to the extent that it purports to relieve the trustee of liability for a breach of trust committed "in bad faith or with reckless indifference to the purposes of the trust or the interests of the beneficiaries." The same provision also makes an exculpatory clause unenforceable to the extent that it was inserted "as the result of an abuse by the trustee of a fiduciary or confidential relationship to the settlor." It does not follow that it is either improper or unwise to insert exculpatory language into a document. Rather, in drafting or reviewing an exculpatory clause, the lawyer should make sure that the clause is fair under the circumstances and that its existence and contents are fully explained to the settlor.

§ 12.3 TRUST INVESTMENTS

Because the trustee of a private express trust holds and manages property that in equity belongs to the beneficiaries of the trust, the trustee is subject to fiduciary duties grounded in statute and in case law. Some of these duties are what one would expect—for example, the duty to preserve and protect trust property. Others are what one might expect on reflection. Because a trust may endure for a substantial period of time, the trustee is much more than a mere caretaker. The trustee is under a duty to make the trust property productive. Making trust property productive often includes making investments.

By statute or judicial decision, trustees have traditionally been constrained in choosing from a range of permissible investments. The "prudent man" rule on investments, announced by the court in Harvard College v. Amory, 26 Mass. 446 (1830), is couched in highly general terms:

> All that can be required of a trustee to invest, is, that he shall conduct himself faithfully and exercise a sound discretion. He is to observe how men of prudence, discretion, and intelligence

> manage their own affairs, not in regard to speculation, but in regard to the permanent disposition of their funds, considering the probable income, as well as the probable safety of the capital to be invested.

Although the prudent man rule appears to allow the trustee considerable flexibility with respect to investments, over the years courts applying the rule have often appeared to approve certain kinds of investments (for example, federally insured bank deposits, high-quality government or corporate bonds, notes secured by first mortgages on real property, and common stock of "seasoned" corporate issuers) while rejecting others as categorically imprudent.

In some states there are statutory "legal lists" which prescribe permissible types of fiduciary investments (and by implication exclude all other investments). It should be noted, however, that a particular investment is not necessarily appropriate merely because it is included in a legal list. For example, the legal list might include "bonds issued by municipalities in this state," but a bond issued by the City of X (a municipality within the state) might nevertheless be improper as a matter of fiduciary administration if the circumstances indicate that the City of X is likely to encounter difficulty in making full and timely bond payments.

Both the prudent man rule, as applied by the courts, and the statutory "legal lists" have encouraged trustees to confine their choice of investments to a limited range of "safe" categories and to eschew any kind of "risky" investment. Accordingly, trustees have tended to pursue a markedly conservative investment strategy geared primarily toward producing regular current income and avoiding principal loss rather than maximizing total return or managing risk.

Because a trustee is under a duty to make the trust property productive, and because income beneficiaries, in particular, are likely to challenge investment practices that fail to produce a level of current income that they deem satisfactory, the trustee working under any rule on trust investments may be placed in an awkward position. The problem is especially severe where the terms of the trust limit the trustee to an unduly narrow range of permissible investments. Although it is possible to seek a judicial order permitting or requiring the trustee to "deviate" from the investment restrictions, such relief is granted only in exceptional situations where strict compliance with the settlor's directions would substantially impair the purposes of the trust due to an unanticipated change of circumstances. To avoid the expense and uncertainty of judicial proceedings, it is preferable (if possible) to provide sufficiently broad investment powers in the trust instrument to enable the trustee to pursue a sensible investment strategy in response to changing economic circumstances. Indeed, an individual or corporation considering serving as trustee will often review the terms of the trust in advance, and may well condition acceptance of the job on an explicit grant of broad powers of investment and management. Such powers may be essential to allow the trustee to administer the trust effectively.

In light of changing investment practices and evolving financial theories, many states have adopted the Uniform Prudent Investor Act, which embraces "modern portfolio theory" and encourages a flexible approach to investments, emphasizing the tradeoff between risk and return. Section 2(a) of the uniform act sets forth the basic "prudent investor" rule as follows:

> A trustee shall invest and manage trust assets as a prudent investor would, by considering the purposes, terms, distribution requirements, and other circumstances of the trust. In satisfying this standard, the trustee shall exercise reasonable care, skill, and caution.

Under the prudent investor rule, a trustee's investment and management decisions with respect to individual assets are to be evaluated "not in isolation but in the context of the trust portfolio as a whole and as a part of an overall investment strategy having risk and return objectives reasonably suited to the trust." UPIA § 2(b). Categorical restrictions on permissible investments are removed; the trustee may invest in "any kind of property or type of investment" consistent with the statutory standards. UPIA § 2(e). Moreover, the trustee generally has a duty to diversify the trust investments, which can be satisfied either by constructing a portfolio of individually selected investments or by means of pooled investment vehicles such as mutual funds. UPIA § 3. The trustee is under a duty to control investment costs, incurring only "costs that are appropriate and reasonable in relation to the assets, the purposes of the trust, and the skills of the trustee." UPIA § 7. Finally, the uniform act gives the trustee broad authority to delegate investment and management functions, subject to a duty to exercise reasonable care, skill, and caution in the selection, direction, and monitoring of agents. UPIA § 9. (This represents a substantial change from the traditional judge-made restrictions on delegation of fiduciary administrative functions.)

§ 12.4 DUTY OF IMPARTIALITY

Trusts commonly have multiple beneficiaries, and the trustee has a fundamental duty to treat all of them fairly and evenhandedly. This does not mean that all beneficiaries must receive precisely equal treatment, which is often neither possible nor desirable, but it does require that the trustee "act impartially in investing, managing, and distributing the trust property." UTC § 803. The trustee may not arbitrarily favor any particular beneficiary or class of beneficiaries over any other.

The duty of impartiality raises special concerns in connection with trust investments because many types of investments tend to favor either income beneficiaries or principal beneficiaries. For example, a portfolio of municipal or corporate bonds may produce relatively high current income while allowing the real value of the principal to be eroded by inflation. Conversely, a portfolio of "growth" stocks may generate substantial capital appreciation but little or no current income. To permit the trustee to pursue a sensible investment strategy without violating the duty of impartiality, the lawyer drafting a trust instrument might consider giving the trustee discretion to adjust the shares of the respective beneficiaries, either directly (by accumulating income or invading principal) or indirectly (by making adjustments between income and principal). Often, however, the trustee may prefer not to have an open-ended discretionary power of adjustment because disgruntled beneficiaries might be prompted to challenge the trustee's fairness and impartiality in exercising (or not exercising) such a power.

To simplify the trustee's task and provide an objective standard for distributions, the drafting lawyer might consider defining the beneficiaries' successive interests in a way that operates independently of the traditional trust accounting concepts of income and principal. For example, instead of requiring annual distributions of net income, the trust instrument might provide for annual distributions of a fixed amount payable from either income or corpus (that is, an "annuity"), with any remaining trust property to be distributed upon termination of the trust to the remainder beneficiaries. Alternatively, the trust instrument might provide for annual distributions of a fixed percentage of the value of the trust property, determined annually (that is, a "unitrust"), with any remaining trust property to be distributed upon termination of the trust to the remainder beneficiaries. In an annuity trust, the current beneficiary receives fixed payments, with the result that the remainder beneficiaries bear the risk of investment gain or loss. By way of contrast, in a unitrust, the current beneficiaries and the remainder beneficiaries participate proportionately in the total investment return on the trust property. In both cases, the trustee can be given broad investment powers to achieve the best possible total return, irrespective of whether the return takes the form of current income or capital appreciation.

§ 12.5 CONTRACT AND TORT LIABILITY OF THE FIDUCIARY

Although a trust or a decedent's estate may be treated as an "entity" for purposes of federal income taxation, the traditional view was, and largely still is, that neither the trust nor the estate of a decedent is an artificial person. Traditionally, a person who contracted with a trustee dealt with the trustee as an individual, not as a representative of the beneficiaries. If a trustee committed a tort during the administration of the trust, the trustee was personally liable to the injured person. Of course if a trustee properly entered into a contract for the benefit of the trust, and was held individually liable on the contract, the trustee could lawfully shift the burden of liability to the trust (and ultimately to the beneficiaries) through the right of "indemnity." Similarly, if a trustee was held liable for a tort committed during administration of the trust, the trustee in some circumstances could shift the burden of liability to the trust.

For example, suppose that A is the sole proprietor of a thriving business. A dies, leaving her entire estate (including the business) to her friend T, in trust. A's will expressly authorizes T to continue operating the business. As operator of the business, T enters into a contract with P. Viewed from the standpoint of the beneficiaries of the trust, the making of the contract is within T's powers and is appropriate. Performance of the contract does not proceed smoothly. P sues T as an individual for breach of contract, and secures judgment against T. Because the contract was properly entered into by T, and because it was made for the benefit of the trust, the burden of the judgment should not be borne by T personally or individually. Through the right of indemnity, T can shift the burden from himself by paying the judgment from trust assets in the first instance (the right of "exoneration") or by reimbursing himself from trust assets after having paid the judgment (the right of "reimbursement"). If T wishes to avoid judgment against himself as an individual, he can petition at the outset of the lawsuit to be "exonerated" from personal liability, and to have any judgment be against him solely in his representative capacity, that is, as trustee.

A fiduciary may derive little comfort from the right to indemnity in a particular case. If a trustee is entering into an authorized contract for the benefit of the trust, the trustee sensibly contracts to avoid personal liability altogether. In this connection it would be foolish for the trustee to rely simply on the designation "trustee" in the contract. That may be brushed off in litigation as merely "descriptio personae" or "surplusage." Rather, the contract should be more explicit: "T, as trustee of the XYZ Trust, in his representative capacity, and not as an individual," or "the XYZ Trust, by T, trustee, in his representative capacity and not as an individual." Further, the contract should state explicitly that the other contracting party looks solely to the trust assets, and not to the trustee, for satisfaction of any claim arising out of the contract.

Viewed from the standpoint of one contracting with the trustee, it might seem that it is always preferable to contract in such a way that the trustee is personally liable on a contract that is within the trustee's authority and properly entered into, for then one might in an appropriate case secure a judgment against the trustee as an individual. But that assumption may be ill-founded. It might be the case that trust assets are ample, but that the trustee has little property which could be reached to satisfy a judgment against the trustee personally. Under such circumstances, if a judgment were secured against the trustee personally, satisfaction of the judgment would depend on gaining access to trust assets through the trustee's right to indemnity. Gaining access to trust assets might occur through action by the trustee or by a proceeding in equity brought by the unpaid judgment creditor.

One who contracts with the trustee only in the trustee's representative capacity, and who expressly agrees to look only to trust assets for satisfaction of any contract claim, does not reach trust assets through the trustee's right to indemnity, because the trustee is not personally liable on such a contract. Not relying on the right to indemnity is important not only where the trustee personally has little property, but also where the trustee has committed a breach of trust in connection with some other transaction.

Traditionally, a trustee's right to indemnity is affected by the state of accounts between the trustee and the trust. For example, the trustee might be liable to the beneficiaries for a breach of trust that has no connection at all with the contract made by the trustee. If so, the right to indemnity in connection with contract claims is diminished or even extinguished completely, as the case may be. Suppose that T, the trustee of a private express trust, has committed a breach of trust by using trust assets to pay his personal creditors. For the breach of trust, T is liable in money damages to the beneficiaries of the trust. In administering the trust, T properly enters into a contract with P that is within T's authority. Performance of the contract does not proceed smoothly. P sues T as an individual for breach of contract, and secures judgment against T. The traditional view is that T's right to indemnity with respect to P's judgment is diminished to the extent that T is liable to the beneficiaries for breach of trust (that is, using trust assets to pay his personal creditors). Because P's rights with respect to reaching trust assets are in these circumstances traditionally viewed as derivative in nature (that is, dependent upon T's right to indemnity), satisfaction of P's judgment is jeopardized.

The traditional view of the trustee's personal liability and the right to indemnity still prevail in some jurisdictions, but the modern trend is to relieve the trustee of personal liability on contracts properly entered into in a fiduciary capacity, and to allow contract creditors to reach the trust assets, irrespective of the state of accounts between the trustee and the trust. For example, § 1010(a) of the Uniform Trust Code provides as follows:

> Except as otherwise provided in the contract, a trustee is not personally liable on a contract properly entered into in the trustee's fiduciary capacity in the course of administering the trust if the trustee in the contract disclosed the fiduciary capacity.

Furthermore, under § 1010(c) of the Uniform Trust Code, a claim based on a contract entered into by the trustee in the trustee's fiduciary capacity "may be asserted in a judicial proceeding against the trustee in the trustee's fiduciary capacity, whether or not the trustee is personally liable for the claim."

With respect to tort liability and the right to indemnity, the trustee should take account of the fact that this is an age of insurance. Just as the trustee may have a duty to procure insurance against loss of trust assets by fire or other casualty, the trustee may have a duty to procure insurance against depletion of trust assets resulting from tort claims against the trustee. In consequence, the right of indemnity may be diminished or extinguished if the trustee was negligent in failing to procure liability insurance. For example, suppose that A is sole proprietor of a thriving business. A dies, leaving her entire estate (including the business) to her friend T, in trust. A's will expressly authorizes T to continue operating the business. T as trustee uses due care in selecting B as an employee for the business. In the course of the employment, B negligently causes injury to the person and property of P. P sues T on a respondeat superior basis, and obtains a judgment against T. Because T used due care in selecting B as an employee, and is liable to P only on a respondeat superior basis, the burden of the judgment prima facie ought not to be borne by T, but by the trust. But if as a matter of prudent trust administration, T should have procured liability insurance to protect trust assets from depletion through tort claims, T is not entitled to indemnity as to the amount of insurance that he should have obtained (but failed to obtain).

In connection with tort liability, as with contract liability, it is the traditional view that the trustee's right to indemnity is affected by the state of accounts between the trustee and the trust. And again, the modern trend is to relieve the trustee of personal liability for torts committed in the course of administering the trust unless the trustee is "personally at fault," and to permit a tort claimant to reach the trust assets, irrespective of the state of accounts between the trustee and the trust, if the tort was committed in the course of administering the trust. UTC § 1010(b) and (c).

CHAPTER 13
FEDERAL ESTATE AND GIFT TAXATION

§ 13.1 INTRODUCTION

Gratuitous transfers of wealth, whether made during life or at death, are generally not subject to the federal income tax. Instead, such transfers are subject to one or more of the federal estate, gift, and generation-skipping transfer taxes. Taken together, these three taxes constitute a separate system of wealth transfer taxation which operates for the most part independently of the income tax. A lawyer engaged in estate planning should be familiar with the basic structure of the wealth transfer taxes and should understand how ordinary contractual and property devices for transmitting wealth are treated for tax purposes.

The central component of the wealth transfer tax system is the federal estate tax, which is imposed on the privilege of transferring property at death. Many states also have their own "death" taxes, generally in the form of an estate tax or an inheritance tax. An estate tax, as its name implies, is imposed on the transfer of property by a decedent at rates graduated according to the size of the decedent's estate. By way of contrast, an inheritance tax is imposed on the receipt of property from a decedent, and is typically graduated for each beneficiary according to the beneficiary's relationship to the decedent and the size of his or her share. Although an estate tax differs from an inheritance tax in the method of computation and collection, the burden of both taxes is generally viewed as ultimately falling on the beneficiaries whose shares are reduced by the tax imposed on the transfer.

The federal estate tax reaches not only transfers which are "testamentary" in the usual sense of the term (that is, property passing from a decedent by will or intestate succession), but also various non-probate transfers occurring at death and certain inter vivos transfers that are treated for tax purposes as testamentary substitutes. For example, the estate tax reaches property transferred by means of a revocable inter vivos trust or a joint tenancy with right of survivorship, as well as a joint-and-survivor annuity and proceeds of life insurance on the decedent's life.

To prevent easy avoidance of the estate tax by means of inter vivos gifts, the federal gift tax reaches gratuitous transfers of property made by a donor during his or her lifetime. The gift tax is imposed on an annual basis, but its rates are graduated according to the amount of the donor's cumulative taxable gifts, with the result that successive lifetime transfers are subject to tax at progressively higher rates. The gift tax functions primarily as a backstop to the estate tax.

For many years the estate and gift taxes operated as components of a "dual" system, with each tax having its own separate exemption and rate schedule. Because the gift tax rates were substantially lower than the estate tax rates, the dual system encouraged wealthy donors to make large lifetime gifts. Since 1976 the two taxes have been part of a "unified" system which applies a single graduated rate schedule to all cumulative taxable transfers, whether made during life or at death, above a specified exempt amount. Under the unified system, a donor's taxable gifts in each year are cumulated with his or her taxable gifts for previous years and are taxed at progressively higher rates under the graduated rate schedule. At death, the taxable estate is cumulated with the decedent's lifetime taxable gifts and is taxed under the same rate schedule.

Transfers made by one spouse to the other, during life or at death, are generally sheltered from gift and estate tax by a marital deduction. The marital deduction was originally intended to allow married couples in separate property states to enjoy the benefits of gift and estate "splitting" on roughly the same basis as couples in community property states. The amount of the marital deduction was originally limited to one half of the value of separate property transferred by one spouse to the other. In 1981, however, this limitation was removed, and today spouses can make unlimited transfers of property to each other during life or at death without incurring any gift or estate tax liability. Effective use of the marital deduction is of central importance in modern estate planning for married couples.

There is also an unlimited charitable deduction for transfers made during life or at death to qualifying charitable organizations. As a result, such transfers escape gift and estate tax altogether.

The final component of the federal wealth transfer tax system is the generation-skipping transfer (GST) tax. As its name implies, the GST tax is intended to ensure that wealth does not escape tax as it passes from one generation to the next. The GST tax reaches transfers that shift property to beneficiaries two or more generations below the transferor without attracting a gift or estate tax at the level of the intervening (or "skipped") generation. The GST tax functions as a supplement to the estate and gift taxes, but it has its own separate exemption and rate structure. In large estates, the GST tax can have a significant impact on the planning and drafting of long-term trusts for successive generations of beneficiaries.

The wealth transfer taxes have no direct effect on the vast majority of the population—less than one percent of decedents each year leave taxable estates large enough to incur an estate tax liability. For those who do incur tax liability, however, the impact can be significant, both in terms of reporting and paying the taxes actually owed and in terms of planning to avoid or minimize those taxes.

The wealth transfer taxes enjoy at best only lukewarm popular support, and for many years they have encountered vigorous opposition from business owners, farmers, and other interest groups. Beginning in the 1990s, opponents of the wealth transfer taxes have mounted a concerted campaign to eliminate the taxes altogether. Although the ultimate goal of complete and permanent repeal remains elusive, anti-tax sentiment has gathered considerable political momentum. Since 2001 Congress has enacted a series of tax cuts which have drastically curtailed the scope of the wealth transfer taxes, reducing the top marginal rate from 55 percent to 40 percent and increasing the exemption from $1 million to $15 million (indexed for inflation). In sum, after years of legislative tinkering, the impact of the federal wealth transfer taxes is considerably diminished, but the essential structure of the taxes remains largely unchanged.

§ 13.2 CORRELATIVE INCOME TAX CONSEQUENCES

Although gratuitous transfers of property generally are not subject to federal income tax, they may have important collateral income tax consequences, especially with respect to the recipient's "basis" in the property. The Internal Revenue Code prescribes different rules depending on whether property is transferred by gift during life or passes from a decedent at death.

In the case of property transferred by gift, the donee generally has a "carryover" basis in the property equal to the donor's basis (except that for purposes of determining loss on a subsequent disposition, the donee's basis is limited to the value of the property at the time of the gift). I.R.C. § 1015(a). In the case of a gift of appreciated property, the donee's basis is increased by the amount of gift tax, if any, paid with respect to the gift and attributable to the unrealized appreciation. I.R.C. § 1015(d). In the case of gifts between spouses, the donor's basis carries over in the hands of the donee without limitations or adjustments. I.R.C. §§ 1015(e) and 1041.

In the case of property passing from a decedent, the property in the beneficiary's hands generally takes a "fresh start" basis equal to the fair market value of the property at the time of the decedent's death. I.R.C. § 1014(a). (This is often referred to as a "stepped-up" basis, even though the basis may actually be stepped down if the value of the property at the decedent's death is less than its basis in the decedent's hands.) The fresh start basis rule applies not only to property acquired by bequest, devise, or inheritance, but also to other property that is includible in the decedent's gross estate. I.R.C. § 1014(b). (Moreover, in the case of community property, the entire property receives a fresh start basis even though only half of the property is included in the decedent's gross estate. I.R.C. § 1014(b)(6).) Note that a stepped-up basis may be available in some cases even though no estate tax is actually payable with respect to the property in question (for example, because the estate is fully covered by the estate tax exemption, or because the property passes to the decedent's surviving spouse and qualifies for the marital deduction).

The fresh start basis rule for property acquired from a decedent encourages individuals to retain appreciated assets until death, in order to pass them on with a stepped-up basis and eliminate income tax on the appreciation accrued before death. Suppose that A owns appreciated stock and gives it to her elderly parent B, who dies shortly afterwards and bequeaths the stock back to A. Does A take the stock with a stepped-up basis? To prevent this sort of basis "laundering," the statute requires that A take a carryover basis in the stock if B dies within one year after A's initial gift. I.R.C. § 1014(e). If B survived for more than one year, however, A would be entitled to a stepped-up basis.

The fresh start basis rule is subject to one important limitation. It does not apply to tax-deferred retirement accounts, accrued but unpaid earnings, or other items of "income in respect of a decedent." Such items are subject to income tax in the hands of the beneficiary, who steps into the decedent's shoes and takes a carryover basis. I.R.C. §§ 691(a) and 1014(c).

§ 13.3 ESTATE AND GIFT TAXES—COMPUTATION AND PAYMENT

The estate and gift taxes are "unified" in the sense that they share a cumulative base, a single graduated rate schedule, and a single exemption. Nevertheless, the two taxes remain formally separate. The estate tax appears in Chapter 11 of the Internal Revenue Code (I.R.C. §§ 2001 et seq.); the gift tax appears in Chapter 12 (I.R.C. §§ 2501 et seq.). Moreover, largely for historical reasons, the two taxes are not perfectly correlated with each other, and they occasionally overlap in their application to a single transfer.

The gift tax is imposed annually on the "transfer of property by gift" by an individual donor during the calendar year. I.R.C. § 2501. Although the concept of a "gift" is defined broadly for gift tax purposes, not all gifts are taxable. The total amount of gifts made by the donor is reduced by allowable exclusions and deductions to arrive at the donor's "taxable gifts" for the year. I.R.C. § 2503. (For example, pursuant to the "annual exclusion," a donor may make tax-free gifts each year up to a specified amount—$19,000 in 2026—per donee. Amounts covered by the annual exclusion are completely removed from the donor's gift tax base and do not count against the gift tax exemption described below. Gifts to a spouse or charitable organization that qualify for a marital or charitable deduction are also removed from the donor's gift tax base.)

The donor's taxable gifts for the current year are cumulated with his or her taxable gifts for all previous years, in order to ensure that successive gifts are taxed at progressively higher rates under the unified rate schedule. This is accomplished by computing a "tentative tax" under the rate schedule on the total amount of the donor's cumulative taxable gifts for the current year and all previous years, and then subtracting a "tentative tax" computed under the same rate schedule on the donor's taxable gifts for all previous years. I.R.C. § 2502. In effect, each year's taxable gifts are "stacked" on top of those made in previous years and then subjected to tax under the unified rate schedule.

Each individual donor is allowed a gift tax exemption in the form of a "unified credit." I.R.C. § 2505. The unified credit is a dollar-for-dollar reduction in the tax computed under the unified rate schedule, and it applies automatically to offset the tax that would otherwise be payable on taxable gifts up to a "basic exclusion amount" of $15 million (indexed for inflation). The unified credit is functionally equivalent to a lifetime exemption of $15 million (indexed for inflation), and the basic exclusion amount is commonly referred to as the "exemption" or the "exclusion." Because the exemption takes the form of a credit rather than a deduction, it applies at the lowest brackets of the graduated rate schedule and provides a uniform benefit to all donors, regardless of their marginal rate brackets.

In effect, the unified credit establishes a zero rate bracket for the first $15 million (indexed for inflation) of taxable gifts, and gifts over that amount are subject to tax at a flat rate of 40% under the unified rate schedule set forth in I.R.C. § 2001(c). (The unified rate schedule nominally establishes graduated rates for taxable gifts up to $1 million and a 40% rate for gifts over that amount, but as a practical matter the unified credit eliminates the tax on gifts up to $15 million (indexed for inflation).)

In general, a donor who makes any taxable gifts during a calendar year is required to file a gift tax return and to pay any resulting gift tax by April 15 of the following year. A gift tax return must be filed even if the tax is entirely offset by the unified credit, in order to document the cumulative amounts of taxable gifts made and credit used by the donor. However, no return is required if all of the donor's gifts are fully covered by the annual exclusion.

The federal estate tax is imposed on the "transfer" of a decedent's "taxable estate." I.R.C. § 2001. The starting point for the estate tax computation is the "gross estate," which includes property actually owned by the decedent at death as well as other enumerated types of transfers that are deemed for this purpose to occur at death (including, for example, revocable trusts, joint tenancies with right of survivorship, joint-and-survivor annuities, and life insurance proceeds). I.R.C. §§ 2031–2044. From the gross estate, certain deductions are allowed for items such as administration expenses, creditors' claims, and amounts passing to a surviving spouse or charity, in arriving at the "taxable estate." I.R.C. §§ 2051–2058.

The estate tax computation resembles the cumulative gift tax computation described above. The decedent's taxable estate is cumulated with all "adjusted taxable gifts" (defined as taxable gifts made after 1976 that are not otherwise includible in the gross estate), and a "tentative tax" is computed under the unified rate schedule. This tentative tax is then reduced by the amount of gift tax that would have been payable on the total amount of the decedent's post-1976 taxable gifts, computed under the same rate schedule. I.R.C. § 2001(b). In effect, the taxable estate is treated as a single, final deathtime transfer which is "stacked" on top of the decedent's post-1976 taxable lifetime gifts and then subjected to tax under the unified rate schedule.

The final step in determining the amount of estate tax payable is to apply any available credits against the tax computed under the unified rate schedule. The most important credit is the unified credit, which is allowable to the extent not already used during life. I.R.C. § 2010. In addition to the unified credit, the estate tax allows credits for estate taxes paid on certain prior transfers to the decedent (I.R.C. § 2013) and for foreign death taxes imposed on property included in the gross estate (I.R.C. § 2014). The credit formerly allowed under I.R.C. § 2011 for state death taxes has been replaced by a deduction for such taxes under I.R.C. § 2058.

An estate tax return must be filed if the decedent's gross estate (combined with any adjusted taxable gifts) exceeds the estate tax exemption. Accordingly, a return may be required even if no estate tax is due—for example, where allowable deductions reduce the taxable estate to an amount that is fully sheltered from tax by the unified credit. The decedent's personal representative is primarily responsible for filing the estate tax return and for paying any tax. The deadline for filing the estate tax return and paying the estate tax, if any, is nine months after the decedent's death, though extensions for filing and payment are available in some circumstances.

§ 13.4 TRANSFERS OF PROPERTY BY GIFT

Section 2501(a) of the Internal Revenue Code imposes the gift tax on the "transfer of property by gift." The statute does not offer a specific definition of what constitutes a gift for this purpose, but provides that the gift tax applies "whether the transfer is in trust or otherwise, whether the gift is direct or indirect, and whether the property is real or personal, tangible or intangible." I.R.C. § 2511(a). The regulations state that "any transaction in which an interest in property is gratuitously passed or conferred upon another, regardless of the means or device employed, constitutes a gift subject to tax." Reg. § 25.2511–1(c)(1). Thus, a gift subject to tax may arise from "the creation of a trust, the forgiving of a debt, the assignment of a judgment, the assignment of the benefits of an insurance policy, or the transfer of cash, certificates of deposit, or Federal, State or municipal bonds." Reg. § 25.2511–1(a). The tax applies only to a "transfer of a beneficial interest in property"; it does not apply to a "transfer of bare legal title to a trustee." Reg. § 25.2511–1(g)(1).

For gift tax purposes, there is no gift unless there is a transfer of property. A person named as a beneficiary of property in a will or trust or other instrument of transfer may disclaim the property and let it pass to an alternative taker under the terms of the instrument or applicable state law. Under the federal disclaimer statute, if a person makes a "qualified disclaimer" of an interest in property, the estate, gift, and GST taxes apply as if the disclaimed interest "had never been transferred to such person."

I.R.C. § 2518(a). As a result, the disclaimed interest is treated for federal tax purposes as passing directly from the original transferor to the ultimate recipient in a single transfer, without passing through the hands of the disclaimant. Note that I.R.C. § 2518 controls only the federal tax treatment of the qualified disclaimer; the devolution of the disclaimed interest is governed by state law. A qualified disclaimer must be made in writing within nine months after the date of the transfer creating the interest (or, if later, the date on which the disclaimant reaches age 21). The disclaimant must not have accepted the disclaimed interest, and as a result of the disclaimer the disclaimed interest must pass, without any direction on the part of the disclaimant, either to the original transferor's spouse or to some person other than the disclaimant. I.R.C. § 2518(b). A qualified disclaimer may be especially useful in adjusting a decedent's estate plan after death, in order to fine-tune the amount of a marital or charitable deduction. For example, if the decedent's surviving spouse disclaims a bequest, which passes instead to other beneficiaries, the disclaimed interest will not be eligible for a marital deduction. (If the disclaimed interest passes to a grandchild or more remote descendant of the original transferor, the transfer may become subject to the GST tax.)

The gift tax applies only to completed transfers of property. For gift tax purposes, a transfer generally becomes complete when the donor relinquishes dominion and control, retaining no power to revoke the transfer or change the interests of the beneficiaries in the underlying property. Reg. § 25.2511–2(b). Conversely, a transfer remains incomplete to the extent that the donor retains control over the beneficial enjoyment of the transferred property. Reg. § 25.2511–2(c). If the donor initially retains sufficient control to prevent the transfer from becoming complete and subsequently relinquishes or terminates the retained power during life, the transfer will become complete upon the relinquishment or termination of the power; if the donor retains control until death, the transfer will generally be included in the donor's gross estate. Reg. § 25.2511–2(f). Thus, for example, the creation of an ordinary revocable trust is not a completed transfer for gift tax purposes, irrespective of whether the donor or another person serves as trustee. Less obviously, a retained power that allows the donor to name new beneficiaries or to change the interests of the original beneficiaries (but not to recover beneficial ownership) is also sufficient to prevent a completed gift. In any case, amounts of income or principal that are actually distributed to other beneficiaries while the trust remains subject to the donor's retained power constitute completed gifts at the time of distribution, and a relinquishment by the donor of the retained power during his or her life constitutes a completed gift of the remaining trust property.

If the donor's retained power is held in a fiduciary capacity and is limited by a "fixed or ascertainable standard," the power is deemed to be sufficiently circumscribed that it does not rise to the level of dominion or control and is disregarded for gift tax purposes. Reg. § 25.2511–2(c). For example, if A declares herself trustee of an irrevocable inter vivos trust for the benefit of her adult children B and C, and A (in her capacity as trustee) retains a power to invade principal as needed for the "support" or "education" or "health" of the beneficiaries, the creation of the trust constitutes a completed gift. (The result would be different, however, if A retained a power to invade principal for the "welfare" or "happiness" of the beneficiaries.) The "ascertainable standard" rule is often useful to a donor who wishes to retain a restricted power without being treated as having retained dominion and control for gift (or estate) tax purposes.

Powers held solely by a person other than the donor generally do not prevent a transfer from being complete for gift tax purposes. For example, if A creates an irrevocable inter vivos trust for the benefit of B and C, and names T as trustee, with discretionary power to distribute trust income and principal to either or both of the beneficiaries, A has made a completed gift of the entire trust property. (However, if A retained an unlimited power to remove T and substitute herself as trustee, the trustee's powers would be attributed to A and the gift would be incomplete.) Powers held jointly by the donor and another person are treated as if they were held by the donor alone, unless the other person has a "substantial adverse interest" in the underlying property or the income therefrom. Reg. § 25.2511–2(e). The rationale for this rule is that any person selected by the donor to exercise a joint power can ordinarily be expected to be responsive to the donor's wishes, unless the other person stands to lose a substantial beneficial interest in the underlying property or its income.

A gift may be partially complete and partially incomplete. Thus, a donor may make a completed gift of certain interests in property while retaining other interests in the same property. Reg. § 25.2511–1(e). For example, if A uses her own funds to purchase land and takes title in the names of herself and B as joint tenants with right of survivorship, A has made a completed gift of one half of the value of the property. (By way of contrast, if A with her own funds opens a joint bank account in the names of herself and B, under circumstances such that A can regain the entire fund without B's consent, there is no completed gift until B withdraws funds without obligation to account to A.)

If A creates an irrevocable inter vivos trust to pay income to herself for life, with remainder at her death to B, A has made a completed gift of the remainder interest. Suppose instead that A creates an irrevocable inter vivos trust to pay income to B for life, and at B's death to pay principal to A if living, or if A is not living to B's issue then living. Here there are completed gifts of a life income interest to B and a contingent remainder to B's issue. (In both cases, if the other beneficiaries are members of A's family, the transferred interests are valued under the special valuation rules of I.R.C. § 2702, resulting in a taxable gift of the entire value of the underlying property. If the special valuation rules do not apply, the transferred interests are valued under the actuarial tables promulgated pursuant to I.R.C. § 7520.) Note that the test of completion focuses on the donor's relinquishment of dominion and control; there is no requirement that the donees be identified or that their respective shares be ascertained.

Overall, the rules concerning gift completion give the donor considerable flexibility. If the donor wishes to transfer property without incurring an immediate gift tax liability, the donor can retain a power of revocation (or some other power that prevents the transfer from being complete), though of course the property will eventually be subject to gift or estate tax when the retained power expires. Alternatively, the donor may prefer to pay a gift tax at the outset in order to avoid a subsequent gift or estate tax liability. This can be accomplished if the donor is careful to tailor any retained powers in a way that will not attract an estate tax at death. It is possible for the same transfer to give rise to both gift and estate taxes, but such an overlap is almost always undesirable and can usually be avoided through careful planning.

In general, a transfer of property by gift is valued at the time the gift becomes complete. The amount of the gift is equal to the value of the transferred property, reduced by any consideration "in money or money's worth" received by the donor. I.R.C. § 2512. If the donor receives "full and adequate consideration in money or money's worth," the gift tax does not apply. Reg. § 25.2511–1(g)(1). Because consideration functions as an offset in measuring the amount of the gift, it must enhance the donor's net worth in some way. It is not enough that the donee relinquishes a benefit or incurs a detriment in reliance on the donor's transfer, nor that the donee reciprocates with gratitude and affection. If A transfers $100,000 to B in exchange for B's promise to marry A or to refrain from smoking and drinking, A has made a gift of $100,000. In this connection, it makes no difference that the transaction is enforceable as a contract under state law or that A lacks donative intent.

A payment made to discharge an enforceable obligation founded on a promise or agreement is ordinarily not a gift, if the obligation was "contracted bona fide and for an adequate and full consideration in money or money's worth." I.R.C. § 2053(c)(1)(A). Thus, a borrower who repays his or her own debt does not make a gift; the repayment merely discharges an existing liability and leaves the borrower's net worth unchanged. Similarly, there is no gift when a person pays money or property to satisfy his or her own legal obligation to support a spouse or a minor child; the discharge of a legal support obligation is treated as the receipt of consideration in money's worth.

The relinquishment by one spouse of the right to claim an elective share or similar "marital rights" in the other spouse's property or estate is not treated as consideration in money's worth for gift tax purposes. Reg. § 25.2512–8. Accordingly, a transfer of property in exchange for a release of marital property rights pursuant to an antenuptial or postnuptial agreement is generally subject to gift tax. For example, if A pays her husband B $100,000 for B's release of his right to claim an elective share in A's estate at her death, A has made a gift to B of $100,000; the transfer may qualify for the marital deduction, but it is a gift nonetheless. (The rule disqualifying inchoate marital property rights does not apply to a right of support or an interest in community property.)

There is a special statutory exemption for marital property settlements incident to divorce. Under I.R.C. § 2516, if one spouse transfers property to the other pursuant to a written agreement relating to their marital and property rights, and divorce occurs within two years after (or one year before) the date of the agreement, the transfer is deemed to be made for full money's-worth consideration and therefore is not subject to gift tax. Divorce settlements are commonly structured to come within the statutory exemption, in order to avoid the need to determine the values of transfers actually made or received by the respective spouses. Note that the statutory exemption applies only if divorce actually occurs within the specified time period, but § 2516 does not preclude a finding of a nongratuitous transfer in cases falling outside its terms. If a husband and wife enter into a written marital property settlement, and divorce occurs more than two years thereafter, transfers made pursuant to a decree incorporating the terms of the settlement may escape gift tax on the ground that they are founded on the court decree rather than on the parties' agreement. Harris v. Commissioner, 340 U.S. 106 (1950). A separation agreement, without more, does not provide automatic protection from the gift tax, although transfers between spouses during marriage may qualify for the marital deduction.

§ 13.5 THE ANNUAL EXCLUSION

The "annual exclusion" set forth in I.R.C. § 2503(b) allows a donor to make tax-free gifts in a specified dollar amount to an unlimited number of donees each year. The statutory amount of $10,000 is indexed for inflation; in 2026, the annual exclusion was $19,000. This is the maximum amount of excludable gifts that the donor can make to a particular donee in a single year. However, there is no limit on the permissible number of donees, nor on the number of successive years in which excludable gifts can be made to the same donees. Gifts that are fully covered by the annual exclusion do not enter into the donor's taxable gifts, do not absorb any unified credit, and need not be reported on a gift tax return.

The annual exclusion applies on a per-donee, per-year basis. A can make annual tax-free gifts of $19,000 to each of B and C in any calendar year, but if she gives $5,000 to B and $25,000 to C in the same year, the exclusion covers only the gift to B and the first $19,000 of the gift to C. (Similarly, if A gives $5,000 to B in one year and $25,000 to B in the following year, the exclusion covers the first year's gift in its entirety but only the first $19,000 of the second year's gift.)

For married couples, the utility of the annual exclusion is enhanced by the "gift-splitting" provision of I.R.C. § 2513, which treats any gift made by a married donor to a donee (other than the donor's spouse) for gift tax purposes as made one-half by the donor and one-half by the spouse, if both spouses consent. Thus, if a married couple elect to split their gifts for the year, either spouse can give up to $38,000 to any donee without incurring any gift tax liability.

One obvious way to stretch the annual exclusion is to spread a large gift of property over several years. For example, if A wishes to make a tax-free gift to B of property worth $190,000, she can give B a one-tenth undivided fractional interest in the property in the current year and then make similar gifts in each succeeding year until the entire property has been transferred to B. This approach may require periodic appraisals to ensure that the annual gifts are fully covered by the available exclusion. To avoid the need for periodic appraisals and put the entire property in B's hands at once, A might structure the transfer as an arm's-length sale to B, and then return the purchase price to B through a series of annual exclusion gifts. (Occasionally a donor goes too far. If A transfers separate blocks of stock, each worth $19,000, to 20 different friends and family members, and each transferee promptly turns around and retransfers the stock to B, the transaction can easily be recast as a single gift to B of stock worth $380,000, which qualifies for only one annual exclusion.)

The annual exclusion is allowed only if the donee receives an immediate, unrestricted right to the use, possession, or beneficial enjoyment of the transferred property. Reg. § 25.2503–3(b). An outright gift of property ordinarily meets the "present interest" test without difficulty, even if the property consists of a contractual right to future payments (such as a bond or a life insurance policy). Gifts in trust, however, require careful planning. The donees of a gift in trust are the beneficiaries, and the exclusion is available only to the extent that one or more beneficiaries receive immediate, ascertainable, unrestricted rights in the trust property or its income. Suppose that A creates an irrevocable inter vivos trust of income-producing property, and the trustee is required to distribute all of the income to B for life, with principal payable at B's death to C. The income interest given to B is a present interest which qualifies for the annual exclusion (up to the lesser of the exclusion amount or the value of the income interest); no exclusion is allowed for the remainder interest given to C. (Even if the principal is payable at B's death to B's estate, so that B is the sole beneficiary of the trust, only the income interest is eligible for the annual exclusion.)

No exclusion is allowed for a gift of a "future interest," defined as one that is "limited to commence in use, possession, or enjoyment at some future time." Reg. § 25.2503–3(a). This disallowance extends not only to interests commonly classified as future interests under state law (such as remainders and reversions), but also to any gift that imposes restrictions on the donee's immediate right to the use, possession, or beneficial enjoyment of the transferred property. For example, if A creates an irrevocable inter vivos trust and authorizes the trustee to make or withhold distributions of trust income or principal to B and C in the trustee's unfettered discretion, the donor is generally not allowed any annual exclusions because neither B nor C can compel a distribution of any ascertainable amount; each beneficiary has only a "future interest" within the meaning of the statute. Similarly, if A creates an irrevocable inter vivos trust and directs the trustee to accumulate the trust income until B reaches age 40 (or sooner dies) and then to pay the principal and accumulated income to B (or B's estate), the gift to B is a future interest for which no annual exclusion is allowed, even though B, the sole beneficiary, has an indefeasibly vested interest in the subject matter of the trust, subject to a restraint on immediate possession.

The donor can create a present interest where none would otherwise exist, and thereby obtain an annual exclusion, by giving the donee an immediate, unrestricted power of withdrawal. For example, suppose that A creates an irrevocable inter vivos trust and authorizes the trustee to sprinkle trust income or principal to B or C in the trustee's unfettered discretion. If the trust instrument also gives each of B and C a power to withdraw $19,000 from the trust, each beneficiary has a present interest which qualifies for the annual exclusion, whether or not the power is exercised. Such a "demand power" is often referred to as a "Crummey power," after the leading case of Crummey v. Commissioner, 397 F.2d 82 (9th Cir. 1968), which allowed annual exclusions based on unexercised demand powers held by minor trust beneficiaries. Technically, a demand power is a general power of appointment which would ordinarily cause the holder to be treated as the owner of the underlying property for gift and estate tax purposes. However, pursuant to a special rule for powers that lapse during the holder's life, demand powers are customarily designed to remain exercisable for only a brief period—usually 30 or 60 days—before they lapse automatically. As a practical matter, demand powers are almost never exercised; they are used to generate one or more annual exclusions for the donor, not to facilitate withdrawals of trust property by beneficiaries.

A gift made in the form of a custodianship under the Uniform Transfers to Minors Act (or its predecessor, the Uniform Gifts to Minors Act) qualifies as a present interest eligible for the annual exclusion, even though the statute gives the custodian broad discretionary powers over the management and beneficial enjoyment of the property. (Note that if the donor dies while acting as custodian, the custodianship property will be included in the donor's gross estate for estate tax purposes. For this reason, it is generally recommended that the donor consider naming someone else as custodian.)

For large gifts to a minor beneficiary, a trust may be preferable to a custodianship due to its greater flexibility. A gift in trust which would otherwise not meet the present interest test of I.R.C. § 2503(b) may nonetheless be eligible for the annual exclusion under § 2503(c), which treats the donee as having a present interest if the transferred property and its income "may be expended by, or for the benefit of, the donee before his attaining the age of 21 years" and must, to the extent not so expended, "pass to the donee on his attaining the age of 21 years" (or, if the donee dies sooner, "be payable to the estate of the donee or as he may appoint under a general power of appointment"). Section 2503(c) permits the settlor of a trust for a minor beneficiary to lodge control over the trust property in the hands of a trustee without losing the benefit of the annual exclusion. In effect, the minor beneficiary is treated for gift tax purposes as the constructive owner of the trust property, since he or she is entitled to claim absolute ownership upon reaching age 21 and no interim distributions of trust income or principal can be made to any other person.

§ 13.6 EDUCATIONAL AND MEDICAL EXPENSES

In addition to the annual exclusion, there is a separate gift tax exclusion in I.R.C. § 2503(e) for certain educational and medical expenses paid on behalf of an individual beneficiary. The exclusion is unlimited in amount, and covers amounts paid directly to an educational organization as tuition for the beneficiary's education or training, but not for books, room and board, or other incidental expenses. The exclusion also covers amounts paid directly to a medical care provider as payment for the beneficiary's medical care (including expenses incurred for the diagnosis, treatment and prevention of disease, and medical insurance premiums). Reg. § 25.2503–6. In each case, the exclusion applies only to amounts paid by the donor directly to the educational organization or medical care provider for eligible expenses; it does not cover funds set aside in trust for future expenses, nor does it cover amounts paid to reimburse the beneficiary for his or her own payment of current expenses.

§ 13.7 THE GROSS ESTATE: PROPERTY OWNED AT DEATH

The gross estate includes not only property actually passing from the decedent by will or intestacy but also several enumerated types of property, discussed below, which are treated for estate tax purposes as testamentary substitutes. Property in the gross estate is generally valued at its "fair market value" as of the date of death. I.R.C. § 2031. However, in some cases where the gross estate drops in value after death, property may be valued as of an "alternate valuation date" up to six months after death. I.R.C. § 2032. And certain real property used in a farm or a closely held business may be eligible for "special use" valuation. I.R.C. § 2032A.

In most cases, the bulk of the gross estate consists of property owned at death. Under I.R.C. § 2033, the gross estate includes "all property to the extent of the interest therein of the decedent." This provision applies to all kinds of property, real and personal, tangible and intangible, in which the decedent had a transmissible beneficial interest at death. It does not apply to property held by the decedent as a fiduciary for other beneficiaries, nor does it apply to interests that expire at the death of the decedent. For example, suppose that A is the life income beneficiary of a trust created by A's parent, and that at A's death the trust principal is payable to B if living, or to C if B is not living. C dies, survived by A and by B. C's contingent remainder interest passes to her successors by will or intestate succession, and is includible in her gross estate. (The value of the interest is determined under actuarial tables set forth in the regulations.) Later B dies, survived by A. Because B did not survive A, his contingent remainder interest fails by its own terms, and is not includible in his gross estate. Finally, A dies. A's income interest terminates at her death, and is not includible in her gross estate.

§ 13.8 JOINT TENANCY WITH RIGHT OF SURVIVORSHIP

Many people think of a joint tenancy with right of survivorship as a convenient will substitute, without considering how the arrangement is treated for gift and estate tax purposes. While both tenants are alive, either of them can unilaterally sever the joint tenancy at any time and convert it to a tenancy in common. For gift tax purposes, each tenant is treated as owning an equal one-half share of the underlying property. Accordingly, the creation of a joint tenancy may give rise to a completed gift if one tenant contributes a disproportionate share of the consideration for the jointly owned property. Similarly, a deemed gift may occur upon the termination of a joint tenancy if one tenant keeps a disproportionate share of the property or its proceeds. If the joint tenants are a married couple, a gift from one spouse to the other on creation or termination of the joint tenancy has little practical significance, since such gifts are automatically sheltered from tax by the unlimited marital deduction.

The estate tax treatment of property held in joint tenancy (or in tenancy by the entirety) with right of survivorship is governed by I.R.C. § 2040, which differentiates between spousal and nonspousal joint tenancies. If the joint tenants are a married couple, as is frequently the case, each spouse is treated for estate tax purposes as owning an equal one-half share of the underlying property. Accordingly, at the death of the first spouse, one half of the property is includible in the decedent's gross estate. I.R.C. § 2040(b). Since an equivalent amount automatically qualifies for the unlimited marital deduction, the net effect is to remove the decedent's share of the joint tenancy property from his or her taxable estate. Thus, under current law, spousal joint tenancies (and tenancies by the entirety) do not give rise to any gift or estate tax liability. (Nonetheless, the estate tax treatment has collateral income tax consequences. Because one half of the property is includible in the decedent's gross estate, the surviving spouse receives a "fresh start" basis in the one-half share of the property that is treated as passing from the decedent under I.R.C. § 1014.)

If the joint tenants are not a married couple, the estate tax consequences are more complicated. At the death of the first tenant, the statute generally requires that the full value of the joint tenancy property be included in the decedent's gross estate, "except such part thereof as may be shown to have originally belonged to [the surviving joint tenant] and never to have been received or acquired by the latter from the decedent for less than an adequate and full consideration in money or money's worth." I.R.C.

§ 2040(a). For example, suppose that A with her own funds purchases Blackacre in the names of herself and her child B as joint tenants with right of survivorship. The creation of the joint tenancy results in a completed gift of one half of the property (which qualifies as a present interest for purposes of the annual exclusion). Later A dies survived by B, who becomes the absolute owner of the property by right of survivorship. The full deathtime value of Blackacre is includible in A's gross estate, but the resulting estate tax is partially offset by any gift tax that A paid when she created the joint tenancy. In effect, the full value of Blackacre is taxed in two stages, with a portion of the tax payable during life and the balance at death. If B subsequently dies owning Blackacre, the full value of the property will be includible in B's gross estate under I.R.C. § 2033.

Now suppose that in the preceding example A paid only one-third of the purchase price of Blackacre and B paid the other two-thirds. The creation of the joint tenancy would result in a gift of one-sixth of the value of the property from B to A, and at A's death, survived by B, one-third of the deathtime value of the property would be includible in A's gross estate. Note that the burden of proving the surviving joint tenant's contribution lies with the decedent's executor. If evidence of the parties' respective contributions is unavailable, the entire value of the property may be subject to estate tax at the decedent's death.

If the decedent and the survivor originally acquired the joint tenancy property by "gift, bequest, devise, or inheritance," a ratable share of the property is includible in the decedent's gross estate, just as if the joint tenants had made equal contributions toward the purchase price.

The joint tenancy (or tenancy by the entirety) with right of survivorship is widely used as a convenient will substitute. But a survivorship interest carries no tax advantage, and it may have an unexpected and disagreeable tax consequence.

§ 13.9 SURVIVOR ANNUITIES

Under I.R.C. § 2039, a decedent's gross estate includes survivor benefits payable to beneficiaries under a "contract or agreement," if the decedent was entitled under the same contract or agreement to receive an "annuity or other payment" for life. The survivor benefits are includible to the extent attributable to contributions made by the decedent (or on the decedent's behalf by his or her employer) toward the purchase price. This provision is aimed primarily at survivor benefits under employment-related retirement plans, but it also applies to commercial survivor annuities and other contractual arrangements. Suppose that A uses her own funds to purchase an annuity payable to herself for life and then to her husband B for his life if he survives her. Upon A's death survived by B, the value of the survivor annuity payable to B is includible in A's gross estate under § 2039. Likewise, if under A's contract of employment she is entitled to a pension upon retirement, with a survivor benefit payable to her husband B, the survivor benefit is includible in A's gross estate if she dies survived by B. (The survivor benefit will also qualify for the unlimited marital deduction, and therefore will not result in any estate tax liability.)

Section 2039 does not reach life insurance proceeds, survivor benefits under statutory programs such as Social Security, or "pure" death benefits under arrangements that made no provision for payments to the decedent during life. Also, if the decedent purchased a single life annuity payable to himself or herself for life, with no survivor benefits payable to another beneficiary, nothing is includible in the gross estate.

§ 13.10 LIFE INSURANCE

I.R.C. § 2042 governs the estate tax treatment of proceeds of insurance on the decedent's life. If the proceeds are payable to the decedent's estate, they are fully includible in the gross estate under § 2042(1). However, if the proceeds are payable to any other beneficiary (as is typically the case), they are includible only if the decedent possessed at death any one or more of the "incidents of ownership" in the policy. I.R.C. § 2042(2). For example, suppose that A takes out a $100,000 policy of life insurance on her own life and designates B as beneficiary. Later A dies survived by B. The proceeds of the policy are includible in A's gross estate if at the time of her death she held any of the incidents of ownership in the policy. The term "incidents of ownership" is not limited to ownership in the technical legal sense; it refers generally to "the right of the insured or his estate to the economic benefits of the policy," and includes, for example, "the right to change the beneficiary, to surrender or cancel the policy, to assign the policy, to revoke an assignment, to pledge the policy for a loan, or to obtain from the insurer a loan against the surrender value of the policy, etc." Reg. § 20.2042–1(c)(2). The term also includes a reversionary interest in the policy or its proceeds if immediately before death the value of the interest exceeded 5% of the value of the policy.

If a married couple hold a policy on one spouse's life as community property, and the insured spouse dies first, only half of the proceeds are includible in the insured spouse's gross estate. Reg. § 20.2042–1(c)(2) and (c)(5). The noninsured spouse is treated as the owner of the other half of the policy (or proceeds) for gift and estate tax purposes. For example, suppose that A and B, a married couple, own a policy on A's life as community property, with their child C named as beneficiary. A dies survived by B and by C, and the proceeds become payable to C. Half of the proceeds are includible in A's gross estate under § 2042, and B is treated as making a completed gift of the other half of the proceeds at A's death. (If B died first, one half of the value of the policy would be includible in B's gross estate under § 2033 as property owned at death. Section 2042 has no application to policies owned by a decedent on the life of another person.)

A person who holds an insurance policy on his or her own life can put the proceeds beyond the reach of § 2042 simply by transferring the policy and relinquishing all incidents of ownership during life.

Such a transfer could generate large tax savings, especially if the current value of the policy is substantially less than the proceeds payable at death and the insured policy holder expects death to occur relatively soon. To foreclose this gambit, the statute provides a three-year "look-back" rule for life insurance: If a decedent dies within three years after transferring or relinquishing an incident of ownership in a policy on his or her own life, the life insurance proceeds are includible in the gross estate just as if the decedent had retained the incident of ownership until death. I.R.C. § 2035(a). As a result, the policy holder must survive for at least three years after the transfer in order to remove the proceeds definitively from the gross estate. Under current law, it is irrelevant for estate tax purposes whether the premiums on a life insurance policy are paid by the insured person or by someone else. If an insured decedent held no incidents of ownership in a policy at death or during the preceding three-year period, the proceeds are not includible in the gross estate, even if the decedent paid all of the premiums up to the date of death.

The estate tax treatment of life insurance has given rise to the widespread use of irrevocable life insurance trusts which allow an insured settlor to pay all of the premiums during life while keeping the proceeds out of his or her gross estate at death. To illustrate, suppose that A creates an irrevocable inter vivos trust for the benefit of her children and funds the trust with sufficient cash to pay the initial premium on the policy. T, as trustee, procures an insurance policy on A's life, with proceeds to be paid over to the trust at A's death. The trust should be structured to ensure that A has no beneficial interest in the trust, no power to alter the interests of the beneficiaries, and no power to control T or to act as trustee. A makes regular contributions to the trust to cover premiums on the life insurance policy. Such contributions will be completed gifts, which may be eligible for one or more annual exclusions if the trust beneficiaries are given unrestricted powers to withdraw a portion of each contribution as it is made to the trust. (If each beneficiary's demand power is limited to the greater of $5,000 or 5% of the value of the trust property, the lapse of the power during the holder's life will have no gift or estate tax consequences to the holder.) Thus, if properly structured, the trust allows A to make substantial tax-free gifts to cover premiums on the policy during life while avoiding inclusion of the proceeds in her gross estate at death.

§ 13.11 LIFETIME TRANSFERS WITH RETAINED POWERS OR INTERESTS

The estate tax reaches various transfers which, although technically made during life, nevertheless remain "incomplete" in some respect until death due to powers or interests retained by the decedent. Under the statute as originally enacted, the gross estate included transfers "intended to take effect in possession or enjoyment at or after death." Today the same ground is covered in considerably more detail by three separate provisions, each predicated on a transfer made by the decedent during life (for less than full consideration in money or money's worth) which left the decedent holding some specified power or interest. Section 2036 reaches transfers under which the decedent retained a life estate or a life income interest in the transferred property. Section 2037 reaches transfers in which the decedent retained a reversionary interest and the interests of other beneficiaries are conditioned on surviving the decedent. Section 2038 reaches transfers in which the decedent retained a power affecting beneficial enjoyment. These provisions are not mutually exclusive; indeed, they often overlap (for example, where the decedent retained both a life estate and a power to revoke).

Under § 2038, the gross estate includes property transferred by the decedent during life, to the extent that the decedent at death held a power to "alter, amend, revoke, or terminate" beneficial enjoyment of the transferred property. For example, suppose that A transfers property in trust to pay the net income to B for life, and then to pay the principal to C, with a reserved power in A to revoke or amend the trust at any time. If A dies holding the power to revoke or amend, the trust property is includible in her gross estate. Note that for purposes of § 2038, it is not essential that the decedent could have recovered absolute ownership of the property by revoking the transfer; it is sufficient that the decedent held a power to alter the interests of other beneficiaries. If A creates an irrevocable inter vivos trust for the benefit of B and C, retaining a discretionary power to sprinkle trust income or principal among the beneficiaries, and later dies holding the "nonbeneficial" power, the trust property is includible in her gross estate. Indeed, § 2038 applies to "any power affecting the time or manner of enjoyment of property or its income, even though the identity of the beneficiary is not affected." Reg. § 20.2038–1(a). Thus, if A creates an irrevocable inter vivos trust for the sole benefit of her minor child, and retains a power to accumulate trust income or invade principal, the trust property is includible in A's gross estate. Similarly, if A creates a custodianship for a minor child under the Uniform Transfers to Minors Act and then dies while serving as custodian before the child reaches the age of majority, the custodianship property is includible in A's gross estate.

Section 2038 applies to a power held by the decedent alone or "in conjunction with any other person," even if the other person has a beneficial interest that would be adversely affected by consenting to the exercise of the power. Suppose that A creates an inter vivos trust to pay income to B for life with principal payable at B's death to C, and A retains a power to revoke that can be exercised only with B's consent. If A dies holding the power, the trust property is includible in her gross estate. Although B might have refused to consent, thereby nullifying the power as a practical matter, A is treated as holding a power to revoke.

For purposes of § 2038, it generally makes no difference whether the decedent held a power in a fiduciary capacity or as an individual. Nevertheless, the courts have held § 2038 inapplicable where the decedent held a fiduciary power, exercisable in favor of other beneficiaries, that was limited by an "ascertainable standard" enforceable in a court of equity. If A declares herself trustee of an irrevocable inter vivos trust for the benefit of her adult children B and C, and retains a fiduciary power to invade principal as needed for the "support," "education," or "health" of the respective beneficiaries, the retained power will not cause the trust property to be included in A's gross estate. In Old Colony Trust Co. v. United States, 423 F.2d. 601 (1st Cir. 1970), the court observed that "[t]he trust provision which is uniformly held to provide an ascertainable standard is one which, though variously expressed, authorizes such distributions as may be needed to continue the beneficiary's accustomed way of life." (By way of contrast, a power to invade principal for the "best interests" of the beneficiaries, or for their "comfort and happiness," or "as circumstances require," would not be sufficiently limited by an "ascertainable standard.") As in the gift tax context, the ascertainable standard doctrine rests on the premise that a retained power does not amount to dominion or control if it is limited by an objective, external standard and is constrained by fiduciary duties (with the implicit sanction of enforcement by a court of equity).

Section 2038 reaches only powers affecting beneficial enjoyment. It has no application to purely "administrative" powers such as standard fiduciary powers to select trust investments, to sell or exchange trust property, or to allocate receipts and disbursements between income and principal.

Section 2038 does not apply to "a power held solely by a person other than the decedent." Reg. § 20.2038–1(a). In some cases, however, a power held by another person may be attributed to the decedent. For example, if the decedent held an unrestricted power to remove a trustee at any time and appoint himself or herself as a successor trustee, the decedent would be treated as holding the powers vested in the trustee.

Section 2036 requires that property transferred by the decedent during life be drawn back into the gross estate at death if the decedent retained possession or enjoyment of the transferred property, or the right to the income from the property, for life. If § 2036 applies, the amount included in the gross estate is not the value of the decedent's retained interest or right (which ordinarily expires at death), but rather the value of the underlying property in which the decedent retained the interest or right. If A transfers Blackacre to B and retains a life estate in the property for herself, the full value of Blackacre is includible in A's gross estate at her death. For estate tax purposes, A's retained life estate is treated as retained ownership of the underlying property, and the shift in possession and enjoyment at A's death is treated as a transfer of the property.

There is no requirement under § 2036 that the decedent's retained interest be expressly set forth in the terms of the transfer. It is sufficient if the decedent retains actual possession or enjoyment under an informal understanding or agreement at the time of the transfer. For example, if A conveys her house to her child B with the understanding that A may continue to live there as long as she wishes to do so, and A then dies while still in possession, the house is includible in her gross estate under § 2036, even though the lifetime conveyance to B was absolute on its face, because A retained possession for a "period which [did] not in fact end before [her] death." (Note that the lifetime conveyance is a completed gift, and any resulting gift tax is allowed as an offset against the estate tax.)

But the coverage of § 2036 is not confined to this simple kind of case. Suppose that A creates an irrevocable inter vivos trust to pay income to B for life, then to pay income to A for life, and finally to pay the principal to C. If A dies survived by B, the value of C's remainder interest (in other words, the value of the trust property, less the value of B's outstanding income interest) is includible in A's gross estate. The constructive transfer under § 2036 is limited to the remainder interest that follows or depends on A's retained life estate; this is the only interest that takes effect in possession or enjoyment after A's death.

Moreover, a decedent is treated under § 2036 as having retained possession and enjoyment of the transferred property to the extent that the property or its income is to be applied for the pecuniary benefit of the decedent, including the discharge of a legal obligation of the decedent. Reg. § 20.2036–1(b)(2). For example, suppose that A creates an inter vivos trust and directs the trustee to use the income for the support of A's minor child B. If A dies before B reaches the age of majority, the trust property is includible in A's gross estate. If income is required to be used to discharge A's legal obligation to support B, it is as if A had received the income herself and used it to support B.

Section 2036 also applies if the decedent retained a power "to designate the persons who shall possess or enjoy the property or the income therefrom." This provision overlaps to a large extent with § 2038, and the courts have reached identical results under both provisions in cases involving joint powers, powers subject to ascertainable standards, and administrative powers. Nevertheless, the two provisions are not completely congruent. Section 2036 is aimed at powers affecting the beneficial enjoyment of property or income during the decedent's life, while § 2038 reaches powers over the property itself which do not affect the enjoyment of income earned or received during the decedent's life. Reg. § 20.2036–1(b)(3). Because the amounts includible under the two provisions are not necessarily identical, it is important in analyzing the estate tax consequences of retained powers to consider the applicability and effect of each provision separately.

If the decedent made a lifetime transfer of an interest in property that takes effect in possession or enjoyment at or after the decedent's death, subject to a retained future interest in the same property, the transferred interest may be drawn back into the decedent's gross estate under § 2037. This provision applies only if two requirements are met: the holder of the transferred interest must be able to obtain possession or enjoyment of the property "only by surviving the decedent"; and the decedent's reversionary interest must be worth more than 5% of the value of the underlying property immediately before death. I.R.C. § 2037(a).

To illustrate the type of transfer at which § 2037 is aimed, suppose that A creates an irrevocable inter vivos trust to pay income to B for life and then to pay the principal to A if living, or to C if A is not alive. If A dies before B, A's reversion fails by its own terms and C's remainder becomes indefeasibly vested. The "necessary survivorship" requirement of § 2037 is met because C must survive A to obtain possession or enjoyment of the trust property; in no event could C's interest become possessory during A's lifetime. If A's reversion immediately before death was worth more than 5% of the value of the trust property—in other words, if the actuarial probability of A surviving B was greater than one in twenty—then the transfer is subject to § 2037. Under § 2037, if applicable, the includible amount is not the value of A's reversion (which is extinguished at her death), but rather the value of C's remainder which can be possessed or enjoyed "only by surviving the decedent." Reg. § 20.2037–1(e). In the above example, A failed to survive B. Because her reversion failed at her death, nothing is includible in her gross estate under § 2033. Had she survived B, however, her reversion would have become possessory and the property would eventually be includible in her gross estate under § 2033.

Now suppose that A creates an irrevocable inter vivos trust to pay income to B for life and then to pay the principal to C if living, or to A if C is not alive. Here the "necessary survivorship" requirement is not met because C need not survive A to possess or enjoy the property; if C survives B, C will receive the property at B's death, irrespective of whether A is then living.

Section 2037 has far less practical importance than §§ 2036 and 2038. Transferors often wish to retain lifetime possession or enjoyment, or a power affecting beneficial enjoyment, of transferred property, but they seldom have a similar desire to retain a reversionary interest except as a last resort upon the failure of all other interests. As a result, the type of transfer reached by § 2037 has relatively little planning significance.

§ 13.12 TRANSFERS WITHIN THREE YEARS OF DEATH

In its current form, the three-year "look-back" rule of I.R.C. § 2035(a) applies only to a narrow range of deathbed transfers that would otherwise escape inclusion in the gross estate. By far the most important application of § 2035(a) involves insurance policies on the decedent's own life. If A owns a policy on her own life and assigns the policy, retaining no incidents of ownership, and then dies within three years of the transfer, the proceeds of the policy are includible in A's gross estate just as if she had retained ownership of the policy until death. In effect, for estate tax purposes, the deathbed transfer is disregarded. The three-year rule also applies to the transfer or relinquishment of a retained "string" described in §§ 2036, 2037, or 2038. Thus, for example, if A transfers property to B subject to a retained life estate, then transfers her outstanding life estate to B and dies within three years thereafter, the underlying property is includible in her gross estate just as if she had retained possession of the property until death.

In its current form, § 2035(a) has no application to ordinary, outright gifts made within three years of death. If the decedent had held the property until death instead of giving it away, the property would have been includible under § 2033, but that provision is not mentioned in § 2035(a) and accordingly the three-year rule does not apply. Similarly, a termination of a joint tenancy within three years of death falls outside the scope of the three-year rule.

Section 2035(b) requires inclusion in the gross estate of the amount of any gift tax paid by the decedent (or by the estate) on gifts made by the decedent or by the decedent's spouse within three years of death. Note that this provision applies regardless of whether the gift property itself is drawn back into the gross estate. Thus, if A makes an outright gift of $50,000, pays the resulting gift tax of (say) $20,000, and dies within three years after the date of the gift, her gross estate must be increased by the $20,000 gift tax payment. Section 2035(b) is intended to prevent donors from using large deathbed gifts to remove the resulting gift tax permanently from the tax base. Note that the gift tax is imposed on the net value of the transferred property, exclusive of the gift tax, while the estate tax applies to a base that includes the amount of the estate tax. In tax parlance, the gift tax computation is said to be "tax-exclusive" and the estate tax computation is said to be "tax-inclusive." The "gross-up" provision of § 2035(b) neutralizes the advantage of a tax-exclusive computation in the case of gifts made within three years of death, and puts such gifts roughly on a par with transfers occurring at death.

§ 13.13 POWERS OF APPOINTMENT

Unlike I.R.C. §§ 2036–2038, which are concerned with interests or powers retained by a decedent with respect to transfers of his or her own property, I.R.C. § 2041 deals with "powers of appointment" exercisable by the decedent over property that the decedent never actually owned or transferred. Most powers of appointment arise in connection with the creation of a trust. For example, if A, the life income beneficiary of a trust created by her parent, is entitled to withdraw or consume trust principal during life or to designate the beneficiaries who will receive the property at her death, she holds a power of appointment. A power of appointment may also be held in a fiduciary capacity, as in the case of a trustee who has discretion to sprinkle trust income or principal among the beneficiaries.

For both estate and gift tax purposes, a general power of appointment is defined as one which is exercisable in favor of the holder, the holder's estate, the holder's creditors, or creditors of the holder's estate. I.R.C. §§ 2041(b)(1) and 2514(c). By implication, any other power is a special or limited power. If A, the life income beneficiary of a trust created by her parent, has a power to appoint the trust property at her death "to any person other than A, A's estate, A's creditors, or creditors of A's estate," her power is a non-taxable special power of appointment. The statute expressly provides that "[a] power to consume, invade, or appropriate property for the benefit of the holder which is limited by an ascertainable standard relating to the health, education, support, or maintenance of the [holder] shall not be deemed a general power of appointment." I.R.C. §§ 2041(b)(1)(A) and 2514(c)(1). Thus, in the above example, A may also be given a power to withdraw trust principal for her own health, education, support, or maintenance without incurring any estate or gift tax liability. The statute also provides a separate exception for joint powers exercisable in conjunction with the creator of the power or an "adverse party." I.R.C. §§ 2041(b)(1)(C) and 2514(c)(3).

Broadly speaking, the holder of a general power is treated for estate and gift tax purposes as the constructive owner of the appointive assets. Thus, if a decedent held a general power at death, the property subject to the power is includible in the gross estate, whether or not the power was exercised by the decedent. I.R.C. § 2041(a)(2). A parallel provision applies for gift tax purposes, with the result that the holder of a general power who exercises or releases the power in favor of another person during life is treated as making a gift of the property subject to the power. I.R.C. § 2514(b). By way of contrast, the exercise or release of a special power of appointment ordinarily has no estate or gift tax consequences.

Suppose that A, the life income beneficiary of a trust created by her parent, holds a general power to appoint the trust principal to any person (including herself) during life. If she holds the power until death, the trust property will be includible in her gross estate under § 2041. The estate tax result is no different if A exercises or releases the general power during life in a manner that leaves her with a taxable "string" of the type described in §§ 2036–2038. Thus, if after the exercise or release A continues to receive the trust income until her death, the trust property will be included in her gross estate under § 2041. The consequences are much the same as if A had made a lifetime transfer of her own property subject to a retained life estate. If A wishes to disclaim the power altogether, she can do so (and thereby avoid the gift or estate tax consequences of holding the power) if she acts promptly and complies with the requirements of I.R.C. § 2518, the federal disclaimer statute.

In general, when a general power lapses by its terms during the holder's life (for example, when the holder reaches a specified age, or at the end of a specified period of time), the lapse is treated as a release of the power, which may result in estate or gift tax liability. However, the statute expressly allows a tax-free lapse in any calendar year to the extent that the property subject to the lapsed power does not exceed the greater of $5,000 or 5% of the value of the property subject to the power. I.R.C. §§ 2041(b)(2) and 2514(e). This "5-or-5" exemption makes it possible to set up a trust in which the income beneficiary holds a non-cumulative power to withdraw the greater of $5,000 or 5% of the trust property in any year without any adverse gift or estate tax consequences (except in the year of death) to the holder of the power.

As a practical matter, general powers of appointment tend to be used in a few situations where they serve specific tax objectives (for example, to generate a present interest for purposes of the annual exclusion, or to qualify a transfer for the marital deduction). In most cases, a broadly drafted special power offers nearly as much flexibility as a general power without subjecting the holder to estate or gift tax liability.

§ 13.14 THE MARITAL DEDUCTION

The estate tax allows a marital deduction for property passing from a decedent to his or her surviving spouse. I.R.C. § 2056. A parallel provision in the gift tax allows a marital deduction for lifetime gifts made by one spouse to the other. I.R.C. § 2523. The marital deduction is unlimited in amount, with the result that spouses can make unlimited tax-free transfers between themselves during life or at death. Moreover, the marital deduction makes it possible for a married couple to avoid paying any estate tax at the death of the first spouse, although any property left to the surviving spouse will eventually be subject to gift or estate tax along with the spouse's other property.

To qualify for the marital deduction, a transfer to a spouse must be made in qualifying form. There is usually no difficulty when one spouse transfers his or her entire interest in property to the other spouse. However, if the transferor carves up beneficial ownership of property into successive interests and gives, say, a life estate to the spouse with remainder to another beneficiary, the transfer may be disqualified under the so-called "terminable interest rule." Technically, that rule denies the marital deduction if the following three conditions are satisfied at the time of the transfer: (1) the transferee spouse's interest may terminate or fail upon the occurrence (or non-occurrence) of some event or condition; (2) an interest in the same property passes from the transferor spouse to another beneficiary; and (3) the other beneficiary's interest may become possessory after the termination of the transferee spouse's interest. I.R.C. §§ 2056(b)(1) and 2523(b). For example, suppose that A dies survived by his wife B, and leaves property in trust to pay income to B for life, with remainder at B's death to the couple's issue then living. B's life income interest satisfies the first condition because it will terminate when B dies, and the remainder interest satisfies the second and third conditions because it gives the couple's surviving issue the right to receive the underlying property at B's death. Under the terminable interest rule, such a bequest, without more, does not qualify for the marital deduction. As a result, the full value of the property, including B's income interest, is taxable at

A's death. The same result would hold in the case of a bequest to the surviving spouse "for ten years," or "until remarriage." By way of contrast, if a decedent leaves property in an "estate trust" to make discretionary distributions to a surviving spouse during life, with any corpus and accumulated income remaining at death to be paid to the spouse's estate, the terminable interest rule does not apply and the entire transfer qualifies for the marital deduction.

The terminable interest rule reflects the notion that the marital deduction should be available only if the surviving spouse will ultimately become the beneficial owner of the property passing from the decedent. Thus, the marital deduction does not permanently exempt property from gift or estate tax, but merely defers the tax until the property leaves the hands of the surviving spouse. (Because the surviving spouse might consume the property or make tax-free gifts during life, there is no assurance that a gift or estate tax will actually be imposed on a subsequent disposition of the property.)

In some cases the terminable interest rule may produce a harsh result. For example, in Jackson v. United States, 376 U.S. 503 (1964), the Supreme Court held that amounts paid to a decedent's surviving spouse as a statutory support allowance pursuant to a probate court order were not deductible because, at the time of the decedent's death, the allowance was potentially subject to termination upon the spouse's subsequent death or remarriage, even though these contingencies did not in fact occur. In addition, if a married couple enters into a binding will contract, the marital deduction may be unavailable at the first spouse's death for property that passes to the surviving spouse subject to restrictions on disposition or to rights of other beneficiaries.

The terminable interest rule is subject to several important exceptions. Suppose that A leaves property by will "to my wife B, but if she fails to survive me by 30 days, to my issue then living." This bequest would ordinarily violate the terminable interest rule because it is not certain, as of the moment of A's death, whether B will survive for 30 days. However, a special statutory exception allows a decedent to impose a survival requirement of up to six months on a bequest to a surviving spouse without jeopardizing the marital deduction—provided, of course, that the spouse actually survives for the required period. I.R.C. § 2056(b)(3). Thus, assuming that B survives A for at least 30 days and becomes entitled to the property, the transfer is deductible.

A separate exception to the terminable interest rule applies where a decedent gives a surviving spouse a life estate in property coupled with a general power of appointment exercisable by the spouse "alone and in all events" in favor of the spouse or the spouse's estate. I.R.C. § 2056(b)(5). Such a disposition is commonly made in trust, but a legal life estate coupled with the requisite power of appointment also suffices. To satisfy the requirement that the spouse be "entitled for life to all the income," care must be taken to avoid giving the trustee any discretion to accumulate income; indeed, any limitation on the spouse's right to income may jeopardize the deduction. Moreover, the requirement of a general power exercisable by the spouse "alone and in all events" means that the spouse must have exclusive and unfettered control over the ultimate disposition of the property. The combination of a life estate and a general power of appointment gives the spouse rights approximately equivalent to those of a full owner, and ensures that the marital deduction allowed to the decedent will eventually be matched by a corresponding inclusion in the surviving spouse's gift or estate tax base. A parallel provision is found in the gift tax. I.R.C. § 2523(e).

Another exception to the terminable interest rule allows a decedent to obtain a marital deduction for the value of "qualified terminable interest property" (QTIP) in which the surviving spouse has a simple life estate but no power to dispose of the underlying property. I.R.C. § 2056(b)(7). To obtain the marital deduction, the decedent's executor must elect QTIP treatment. If the election is made, the spouse who actually receives only a life estate—a quintessential terminable interest—is nonetheless treated as the constructive owner of the entire property for gift and estate tax purposes. As a result, the full value of the underlying property qualifies for the marital deduction in the decedent's estate, and—in accordance with the general premise of the marital deduction—the value of the same property is eventually subject to estate tax at the spouse's death, or to gift tax if the spouse disposes of the income interest before death. I.R.C. §§ 2044 and 2519. A parallel provision appears in the gift tax. I.R.C. § 2523(f). QTIP trusts have become extremely popular with planners and property owners, both because they lodge control over the ultimate disposition of the property with the decedent (rather than the surviving spouse) and because they permit the decedent's executor to elect whether to claim the marital deduction in whole or in part based on circumstances existing at the decedent's death. (From the perspective of the surviving spouse, these same features may make the QTIP trust less attractive than absolute ownership or a traditional marital trust that gives the spouse a life income interest and a general power of appointment.)

Using the unlimited marital deduction, a married couple can easily avoid incurring any estate tax at the death of the first spouse simply by arranging for all of the decedent's property to pass to the surviving spouse, but careful planning may be necessary to avoid wasting the decedent's unified credit. In general, if both spouses are to make full use of their respective unified credits, it makes sense to ensure that each spouse will leave a taxable estate at least equal to the exemption amount. To achieve the desired result, two conditions must be met. First, each spouse should own property at least equal to the exemption amount. If one spouse is very wealthy and the other has negligible assets, the couple may rearrange their affairs, using inter vivos gifts (sheltered from gift tax by the marital deduction) to bring the poorer spouse's estate up to the exemption amount. Even if both spouses have large estates, however, there is a second condition which must be met, namely, each spouse must leave a taxable estate, after deductions, at least equal to the exemption amount. If one spouse dies and all of his or her property passes to the surviving spouse in a form that qualifies for the marital deduction, there may be no taxable estate and the decedent's unified credit may be lost. To prevent this from happening, it may be desirable to provide in the decedent's will for a non-deductible "credit shelter" bequest, either directly to beneficiaries other than the surviving spouse or in trust for the benefit of the surviving spouse and other family members. If the marital share is nevertheless overfunded as a result of property passing outside the will (for example, by a marital joint tenancy with survivorship rights or as life insurance proceeds), it may be possible to bring the decedent's taxable estate up to the desired amount if the surviving spouse makes a qualified disclaimer.

In drafting a will or trust, it is common practice to define the size of the marital bequest by means of a formula, which may be phrased either in terms of an amount of property (a "pecuniary" formula) or a fractional share of the estate (a "fractional share" formula). This allows the drafter to specify the size of the marital bequest in terms of the desired tax result, despite the inevitable uncertainties concerning the size and composition of the estate at the time of the testator's death. For example, a pecuniary formula might read as follows:

> If my spouse survives me, I give to my spouse an amount equal to the minimum marital

> deduction necessary to eliminate (or reduce as far as possible) the federal estate tax on my estate, after taking into account all other property passing to my spouse under this will or outside this will that is includible in my federal gross estate and that qualifies for the federal marital deduction, and after taking into account the federal unified credit.

Another variation involves the establishment of a credit shelter bequest to use up any available unified credit, followed by a gift of the residuary estate to the surviving spouse. In choosing between various types of formula clauses, and in drafting particular clauses, the lawyer should consider not only the federal estate and income tax consequences but also the implications for estate and trust administration under state law.

§ 13.15 PORTABILITY OF THE UNIFIED CREDIT

Generally speaking, the unified credit is not transferable; if a decedent dies without using all of his or her unified credit, the amount of the unused credit cannot be passed on to any other person. Nevertheless, a special provision enacted in 2010 allows limited "portability" of the unified credit from a decedent to a surviving spouse. I.R.C. § 2010(c)(4) and (c)(5). Under this provision, the surviving spouse may increase his or her own unified credit by the amount of the decedent's unused credit, if the decedent's executor so elects. (As a technical matter, the surviving spouse's unified credit is equal to the tax that would be imposed on his or her "applicable exclusion amount," which consists of his or her "basic exclusion amount" of $15 million (indexed for inflation) plus the "deceased spousal unused exclusion amount.") Consequently, the decedent's unused credit need not be wasted but instead can be applied by the surviving spouse to shelter additional transfers from gift or estate tax. Because the portability election can be made only on a timely filed estate tax return, the executor may find it advantageous to file a return, even if the estate is of sufficiently modest size that a return would not otherwise be required. The portability provision offers considerable flexibility in tax planning for married couples and reduces the need for each spouse to make full use of his or her unified credit.

One effect of portability may be to encourage wills and trust instruments that leave most or all of a married couple's property at the first spouse's death directly to the surviving spouse. Nevertheless, even though it is no longer necessary to establish a "credit shelter trust" to make full use of the decedent's unified credit, many married couples may continue to find this type of trust attractive for other reasons. For example, because a credit shelter trust is not subject to estate tax at the surviving spouse's death, such a trust may be used to hold property that is expected to appreciate substantially in value (albeit at the cost of foregoing a stepped-up income tax basis at the surviving spouse's death). Furthermore, a credit shelter trust may serve important planning goals entirely apart from tax savings, such as allowing the decedent to control the ultimate disposition of his or her property and protecting the trust property from creditors of the surviving spouse.

§ 13.16 THE CHARITABLE DEDUCTION

Both the estate tax and the gift tax allow a deduction for transfers made to qualifying charitable organizations or for charitable purposes. In general, a transfer is treated as charitable if it is made to the United States or a political subdivision thereof for public purposes, or to a corporation, trust or foundation organized and operated exclusively for religious, charitable, scientific, literary, or educational purposes. I.R.C. §§ 2055(a) and 2522(a). If the organization or purpose for which a charitable contribution is made satisfies the statutory criteria, there is no limit on the amount that may be given. It bears emphasis that an organization that is "charitable" for purposes of state law is not necessarily charitable for purposes of federal tax law, and a lawyer advising a client who intends to make a charitable contribution should verify the charitable status of the recipient for federal tax purposes.

Outright gifts to a charitable organization seldom give rise to serious problems. The deduction may be jeopardized, however, if property is transferred for mixed charitable and noncharitable purposes. Longstanding regulations generally require that the charitable interest must be "presently ascertainable" and that any contingency that might defeat it must be "so remote as to be negligible." Reg. § 20.2055–2(a) and (b). Moreover, under a set of statutory rules enacted in 1969, if a transfer creates both charitable and noncharitable interests in the same property, no charitable deduction is allowed at all unless the transfer is in qualifying form. I.R.C. §§ 2055(e)(2) and 2522(c)(2).

In the case of a charitable remainder interest following a noncharitable interest, a qualifying transfer commonly takes one of three forms: (1) a trust that provides for annual payments of a fixed amount to a noncharitable beneficiary, followed by an irrevocable charitable remainder (a "charitable remainder annuity trust"); (2) a trust that provides for annual payments of a fixed percentage of the current value of the trust property (determined annually) to a noncharitable beneficiary, followed by an irrevocable charitable remainder (a "charitable remainder unitrust"); or (3) a "pooled income fund," administered by a public charity, which accepts contributions from multiple donors and distributes the net income annually to the donors or their designated beneficiaries during their respective lifetimes. I.R.C. §§ 642(c)(5) and 664(d). A qualifying interest may also take the form of a "charitable lead" trust in which the charitable interest consists of an annuity or unitrust interest, followed by a remainder in noncharitable beneficiaries. In addition, the statute allows a deduction for a charitable remainder interest following a life estate in a personal residence or farm, and for an undivided portion of the transferor's entire interest in the underlying property. I.R.C. § 170(f)(3)(B).

The statutory rules concerning split-interest transfers are intended to guard against valuation abuses and to ensure that the charitable beneficiaries will receive the full value of any interest for which a deduction is allowed. To assist in planning and drafting such transfers, the Internal Revenue Service publishes standard forms of trust instruments that comply with the detailed requirements of the statute and regulations.

§ 13.17 THE GENERATION-SKIPPING TRANSFER TAX

The third and final component of the federal wealth transfer tax system is the generation-skipping transfer (GST) tax, which appears in Chapter 13 of the Internal Revenue Code (I.R.C. §§ 2601 et seq.). The GST tax operates as a supplement to the estate and gift taxes, with its own separate exemption and rate structure and its own specialized terminology. In general, the GST tax is aimed at transfers which shift beneficial enjoyment of property to beneficiaries who are at least two generations younger than the transferor without attracting a gift or estate tax at the level of the intervening ("skipped") generation. The basic premise is that persons with substantial means should not be able to avoid transfer taxes by creating long-term trusts which spread beneficial enjoyment over several generations or by transferring property directly to remote generations. In other words, the GST tax is intended to ensure that transfer taxes are imposed as property passes from one generation to the next.

There are three types of "generation-skipping transfers" subject to GST tax. The first is a "direct skip." For example, suppose that A, who has a living child B, makes a gift or bequest to B's child C. The transfer constitutes a direct skip because it puts property into the hands of a "skip person" (that is, a person at least two generations younger than the transferor). I.R.C. § 2612(c)(1). In effect, the GST tax stands in for the gift or estate tax that would have been imposed if the property had passed through B's hands on its way to C. (Similarly, if A transfers property to B, and B makes a qualified disclaimer which causes the property to pass to C, the transfer avoids gift tax in B's hands but constitutes a direct skip subject to GST tax.) By way of contrast, if B is actually dead at the time of A's transfer, a special rule reassigns C to B's generation for GST tax purposes, with the result that C is no longer treated as a skip person and the transfer is not a direct skip. I.R.C. § 2651(e).

The other two types of generation-skipping transfers arise in connection with property held in trust. Suppose that A creates an irrevocable discretionary trust for the benefit of A's child B and B's issue, with any remaining property to be distributed at B's death to B's issue then living. Although the creation of the trust gives rise to a gift or estate tax, no generation-skipping transfer occurs until it becomes clear that property will become distributable from the trust to one or more of B's issue. If the trustee makes a distribution of income or principal from the trust to any of B's issue during B's lifetime, the distribution constitutes a "taxable distribution" for GST tax purposes. I.R.C. § 2612(b). B's death will constitute a "taxable termination" which gives rise to a GST tax on any property remaining in the trust at that time. I.R.C. § 2612(a). If the trust continues after B's death, there may be additional taxable distributions or taxable terminations as successive generations of beneficiaries become entitled to receive distributions from the trust.

Each individual transferor is entitled to a GST exemption of $15 million (indexed for inflation). I.R.C. § 2631. Although the GST exemption is equal to the estate and gift tax exemption in amount, it operates in a completely different manner. Unlike the unified credit under the estate and gift taxes, the GST exemption does not apply automatically to transfers in chronological order. Instead, the GST exemption can be freely allocated to property transferred during life or at death. An allocation of GST exemption to a particular transfer of property directly affects the rate of GST tax applicable to generation-skipping transfers involving the property. For example, if A makes a gift of $1 million to her grandchild C (a direct skip) and allocates $1 million of GST exemption to the gift, the rate of GST tax on the direct skip is zero. If A creates a generation-skipping trust of $1 million for the benefit of her child B and B's issue, and allocates $1 million of GST exemption to the trust property, the rate of GST tax on all subsequent taxable distributions and taxable transfers occurring with respect to the trust will be zero. If a generation-skipping transfer occurs and no GST exemption is allocated to the property involved, the GST tax is imposed at a flat rate of 40%, which is the same as the maximum estate tax rate. I.R.C. § 2641.

§ 13.18 PLANNING CONSIDERATIONS AND THE GST TAX

In planning any disposition of property to beneficiaries two or more generations below the transferor ("skip persons"), it is important to consider how to make the most effective use of the transferor's GST exemption. An allocation of GST exemption can be made to property that is transferred outright to individual skip persons, directly and immediately reducing the rate of GST tax on the transfer, but the tax savings tend to be greater if the allocation is made instead to property that is held in trust for multiple generations of beneficiaries. This is because an allocation of GST exemption generally has the effect of sheltering all or a fractional portion of the trust property from GST tax for the duration of the trust; as the trust property appreciates over time, the value of the exempt portion increases correspondingly. Moreover, the initial allocation remains effective until the property ends up in the hands of a new transferor, no matter how many taxable distributions or taxable terminations occur in the meantime as beneficial enjoyment shifts from one generation to the next. Indeed, a major incentive for creating a perpetual "dynasty" trust (in jurisdictions where such trusts are permitted) is the possibility of complete and permanent avoidance of GST tax on the trust property.

A special problem arises in allocating the GST exemption to property held in a marital deduction trust. Suppose that A dies survived by his spouse B and leaves property in trust to pay income to B for life with remainder to the couple's grandchildren. A's executor makes a QTIP election with respect to the trust. Although A is the original transferor of the trust for GST tax purposes, it ordinarily makes no sense to allocate his GST exemption to the trust property. The reason is that B will become a new transferor when the trust property is included in her gross estate at her death, making it necessary to use her own GST exemption to shelter the trust from GST tax. (Note that the GST tax does not allow a decedent to pass on any unused portion of his or her GST exemption to a surviving spouse; there is no counterpart to the "portability" of a decedent's unused unified credit.) To provide greater flexibility, I.R.C. § 2652(a)(3) allows A's executor to elect to ignore the QTIP election in applying the GST tax to the trust. The effect of such a "reverse QTIP" election is that, solely for GST tax purposes, A (not B) will be treated as the transferor of the trust property with respect to taxable terminations or distributions occurring at or after B's death. This allows A to make an effective allocation of his own GST exemption to the QTIP trust property and leaves B free to allocate her GST exemption to other property.

Some transfers automatically escape the GST tax without using any of the transferor's GST exemption. For example, if the transferor makes an outright gift to an individual skip person, and the gift qualifies for the gift tax annual exclusion, it is ordinarily exempt from GST tax pursuant to the special rule for "nontaxable gifts" in I.R.C. § 2642(c). (However, the special rule does not apply to a gift in trust unless the trust is effectively limited to a single beneficiary.) Furthermore, payments of tuition or medical expenses that qualify for the gift tax exclusion of I.R.C. § 2503(e) are also exempt from GST tax. As a result, a transferor can make substantial lifetime gifts to skip persons without incurring any gift tax or GST tax liability.

For a transferor who has exhausted any available exemptions and exclusions, there is still another way to sidestep the GST tax, namely, by arranging for the transferred property to be subject to gift or estate tax in the hands of a beneficiary who is only one generation younger than the transferor. Recall that the GST tax serves essentially as a backstop to the gift and estate taxes; it applies only where a transfer puts property in the hands of a beneficiary at least two generations younger than the transferor without incurring a gift or estate tax at the level of the intervening generation. Thus, to the extent that property is subject to gift or estate tax in the hands of a beneficiary who is only one generation younger than the transferor, there will be no generation-skipping transfer. In the case of a trust, for example, this can be accomplished by providing for distributions to such a beneficiary or by giving the beneficiary a general power of appointment.

A large number of trusts in existence today were established before the current GST tax was enacted in 1986. By the terms of the enacting legislation, trusts that were already "irrevocable" on the relevant effective date are permanently exempt from GST tax, even if they give rise to generation-skipping transfers occurring after the effective date. Reg. § 26.2601–1. A significant amount of planning is devoted to maximizing the duration and value of grandfathered trusts while preserving their exempt status.

§ 13.19 INCOME TAXATION OF TRUSTS AND ESTATES

In general, a trust is recognized as a separate taxable entity for federal income tax purposes, and the rules governing the computation of taxable income are, with some important exceptions, the same for trusts as for individual taxpayers. (The same is true for decedents' estates, which resemble trusts in important respects.) The most significant income tax problems involve the question of who should be taxed on the income from property held in trust. Usually there are three obvious candidates: the grantor, the beneficiaries, or the trust itself. Although the applicable provisions of the statute and regulations can be quite complex, any lawyer involved in drafting wills and trusts should be familiar with a few basic concepts.

Ordinarily, where the trust is irrevocable and the grantor has severed virtually all strings over the trust property, the trust is treated as a separate taxpayer and its income, deductions, and other taxable items either stay with the trust or "pass through" to the beneficiaries under I.R.C. §§ 641–663. However, if the grantor retains significant interests or powers with respect to the trust, the grantor may be treated as the substantial owner of all or a portion of the trust and taxed on the trust's income pursuant to the "grantor trust" provisions of I.R.C. §§ 671–677. Moreover, if a person (other than the grantor) has a power to withdraw income or corpus from the trust, that person may be treated as a substantial owner under I.R.C. § 678.

In the case of an ordinary trust (that is, one which is not treated as substantially owned by the grantor or another person), the trust's income is generally allocated between the trust and the beneficiaries based on the amounts distributed to beneficiaries in the current taxable year. This is accomplished by allowing a deduction to the trust for such distributions and then including an equivalent amount in the gross income of the recipients. I.R.C. §§ 651, 652, 661, and 662. In this sense, the trust may be viewed for income tax purposes as a "conduit" to the extent of its current distributions; the trust itself incurs tax only on amounts retained in the trust. An important limitation on the conduit principle is the tax concept of "distributable net income" (DNI), which establishes a ceiling on the amount of distributions to be deducted by the trust (and included by the beneficiaries). Roughly speaking, DNI corresponds to a modified version of the trust's taxable income. Items entering into DNI are "carried out" first to beneficiaries who receive mandatory distributions of current trust income, and then to beneficiaries who receive other distributions of income or corpus; any distributions in excess of DNI are treated as tax-free distributions of corpus. Except in limited circumstances, capital gains do not enter into DNI and therefore are taxed to the trust rather than to the beneficiaries.

To the extent that a trust does not distribute all of its income currently, the conduit principle does not apply and the trust itself is taxable on its accumulated income. As a practical matter, there is no other way to ensure payment of the tax on income accumulated in the current year, since the beneficiaries who will ultimately receive it may well be unborn or unascertainable. Under current law, when the trust eventually distributes the accumulated income in a subsequent year, the beneficiaries ordinarily are not liable for any additional tax.

At one time trusts offered significant income shifting advantages. Taxpayers sought to spread income among several different taxable entities in order to take advantage of each trust's low rate brackets and separate exemption. In recent years, however, as income tax rates generally have fallen and brackets have become more compressed, the tax incentives for creating multiple trusts have all but disappeared. Moreover, under a special anti-abuse rule, multiple trusts that have "substantially the same" grantors and primary beneficiaries and have tax avoidance as "a principal purpose" may be aggregated and treated as a single trust for income tax purposes. I.R.C. § 643(f).

INDEX

References are to Section Numbers
